"[Kimmel's] writing is intelligent and entertaining.... his knowledge of SF movies is encyclopedic.... This is the guy you want sitting next to you when Channel 45 has a weekend 'sci-fi' movie marathon.... For anyone who likes SF movies, this volume is worth the price of admission." —Don Sakers, in *Analog Science Fiction and Fact*

"Kimmel's a terrific guide to classic though underappreciated works such as *Things to Come*, and is especially sharp on 1950s sf movies, David Cronenberg, and the art (or lack of same) of movie remakes.... his brief essays are addictively readable and yes, a lot more fun than watching *Revenge of the Sith*." —Elizabeth Hand, in *The Magazine of Fantasy & Science Fiction*

"...one is left wanting more, which is a testament to Kimmel's writing abilities.... Even when you find yourself not agreeing with Kimmel—his take on *E.T.* is just plain wrong damn it!—the book remains worthwhile and thought-provoking.... *Jar Jar Binks Must Die* is worth a purchase." —Sci-Fi Movie Page

"A spirited explanation of the role of science fiction films in our culture. Any serious fan of the cinema must read this book." —Michael A. Burstein, John W. Campbell Award-winning author

"Kimmel displays expertise on the subject along with a lively sense of humor —scarcely a page is turned that doesn't yield a few good laughs.... Readers who already take science fiction seriously will enjoy the book's panoptic breadth and its frank jubilation in its subject matter.... [Kimmel] makes it his business to guide his readers to science fiction films that are worthy of our attention as social commentary, whiz-bang spectacle, or works of entertainment that carry an extra edge.... the best advice to take with you on your foray into *Jar Jar Binks Must Die* is this: keep your Netflix wish list at the ready. You're going to revisit movies you hadn't thought about in years and be irresistibly tantalized by films you've never seen, and maybe never even heard of." —Kilian Melloy, in *Edge Boston*

"...the leading film voice in fandom today... Dan's look at all the SF Films of the previous century-plus is powerful and serious and smart and even sassy at points.... His look at *Metropolis* and *Things to Come* are both brilliant.... I thought it was the best written look at *Destination Moon* I've ever read.... I could spend a day heaping praise on the essay 'Our Batman'.... So many great pieces in here that I should just say this is the best book of essays about film of any nature that I've read in ages.... the best pieces of writing on SF Film you'll ever see!" —Chris Garcia, in *The Drink Tank*

"...deserves the reader's attention.... insightful... Dan has it right. In a time when boomers and the generations to follow have refused to make a choice between the dreams of their childhood and the realities of the adult world, not only are science fiction films deserving of critical discussion, they provide an ideal laboratory for the examination of our struggle to make sense of our lives." —Ernest Lilley, in *The New York Review of Science Fiction*

By the same author

I'll Have What She's Having:
Behind the Scenes of the Great Romantic Comedies

The Dream Team:
The Rise and Fall of DreamWorks—
Lessons from the New Hollywood

The Fourth Network:
How FOX Broke the Rules and Reinvented Television

Love Stories:
Hollywood's Most Romantic Movies
(co-authored with Nat Segaloff)

Jar Jar Binks Must Die

...and other Observations about Science Fiction Movies

by Daniel M. Kimmel

To Dick + Rita,
Keep watching the
skies!

Editor: Ian Randal Strock

Fantastic Books
1380 East 17 Street, Suite 2233
Brooklyn, New York 11230
www.FantasticBooks.biz

ISBN 10: 1-61720-350-5
ISBN 13: 978-1-61720-350-3

First Edition, Version 1.1

Dedicated with affection and gratitude to four friends who
were there when I needed them most:
Betty Smithline
Dr. Davin Wolok
Michael Devney
and, always, Sido Surkis

Table of Contents

INTRODUCTION
Science Fiction: The Forbidden Genre

If there's a common theme to the essays in this book, which were written over a ten year period, it is this: science fiction films are worth discussing. Better yet, science fiction films are *as worthy as any other kind of film* for serious discussion. One would think that would not only be non-controversial but so transparently obvious that it wasn't even worth mentioning. Alas, such is not the case.

Imagine a world where an Oliver Stone could say in an interview, "*Platoon* isn't a Vietnam War movie. It's really about people." Or perhaps Clint Eastwood explaining that *Unforgiven* isn't a western at all, but simply uses the trappings of the genre to explore relationships. Or perhaps Meryl Streep insisting that *It's Complicated* isn't like those other romantic comedies and, in fact, isn't a romantic comedy at all—it's about a woman's issues in remodeling her kitchen. You probably can't imagine such things. These excuses are so transparently absurd and so in opposition to the films themselves that if such "explanations" had been seriously offered you would think these folks were deranged.

Yet writers, directors, and actors who come from outside the genre to create works of science fiction often deny that it is, in fact, science fiction that they have created. They'll even insist that their books and films aren't actually science fiction at all. Unlike what you might expect from this apparently unspeakable and unworthy genre, *their* works are about people. The most notorious—and laughable—example of this was when Margaret Atwood, author of such novels as *The Handmaid's Tale*, argued that her dystopian and speculative books couldn't possibly be science fiction. SF, as she defined it, was about "talking squids in space." In these pages you'll find numerous examples of critics, film historians and others insisting that movies like *Frankenstein*, *The Time Traveler's Wife*, and even *Metropolis* aren't "really" science fiction. One could just laugh off these people as ignorant or prejudiced, for many of them are, but it's such a widely held belief that you come to realize that some of these filmmakers and stars and authors are doing this in self-defense. In effect what they're saying is, "Please don't put me and my work in the science fiction ghetto. We want to be taken seriously." Even writers friendly to the genre and who obviously liked writing in it, such as the late Kurt Vonnegut, Jr., knew that one could be treated as a serious author or as a science fiction writer, but not both.

At the risk of setting up the proverbial straw men, let's consider some of the arguments as to why SF movies are deemed unworthy of serious critical consideration:

* "They're childish. Most of it is geared to the mentality of 12 year old boys."

While, as a well known quote attributed to SF fan Peter Graham has it, "the golden age of science fiction is 12," it is nonsensical to argue that all or even most science fiction is intended for non-adults. Part of the problem is that while there are early examples of science fiction in both literature and film, it wasn't firmly established as a film genre until the 1950s. So while we can point with pride to Georges Méliès and his A *Voyage to the Moon* and Fritz Lang's *Metropolis* as two landmark films that bookend the silent era and William Cameron Menzies' *Things to Come* as a fascinating film that had the participation of H.G. Wells himself, Hollywood's pre-World War II overtly SF offerings were the musical curio *Just Imagine* and the Flash Gordon and Buck Rogers movie serials. Prior to *Destination Moon* in 1950, which started Hollywood's first SF boom, American science fiction films *were* largely for kids. When something was serious and unambiguously SF, such as *Frankenstein* or *The Invisible Man*, it got classified as part of Universal's "monster movie" cycle. Science fiction would get the blame, but never the credit.

* "Science fiction writing isn't literature. It started out in those lurid pulp magazines."

Even putting aside author Brian Aldiss's claim for Mary Shelley's *Frankenstein* as the first true SF novel, only two authors of science fiction were admitted to the modern literary canon before the guardians of cultural standards barred the door: Jules Verne and H.G. Wells. Two later entries, George Orwell's *1984* and Aldous Huxley's *Brave New World*, were obviously important works which could not be denied and thus could not bear the taint of the "science fiction" label, and so would be treated as satires or dark warnings about the present day world. In contrast, nothing written for cheap magazines printed on even cheaper paper would be considered worthy of attention. Well, unless it was written by Dashiell Hammett or Raymond Chandler or any of the other hard-boiled authors who laid the groundwork for not only literary crime fiction (modernizing a genre arguably invented by Edgar Allan Poe), but also providing the stories for the complex cinematic genre of *film noir*. A dividing line here was that most SF wasn't marketed in book form until the 1950s. James M. Cain's *Double Indemnity* had come out in hardcover long before Billy Wilder did his great film adaptation of it. By contrast, an outstanding film like *The Day the Earth Stood Still* was based on a short story ("Farewell to the Master" by Harry Bates) that had appeared in the pulp magazine *Astounding* a decade before. It might or might not have been known by fans, but virtually no one else would have been familiar with it. Without a literary underpinning as a genre, it was hard to get SF films thought of as part of a tradition.

* "Most science fiction films are junk, often little more than special effects shows interrupted by bad writing and amateurish acting."

According to what is usually referred to as Sturgeon's Law, after the SF author Theodore Sturgeon, there's nothing untoward or unusual in noting that 90% of science fiction is, in his words, "crud." As he then went on to say, "90% of *everything* is crud." A case in point would be a genre that no one would seriously dispute is important, having been much studied and written about, and that is the western. When John Ford made *Stagecoach* in 1939, his first western since the silent era, none of the major studios wanted to touch it. Westerns were kiddie fare, he was told. They're churned out for Saturday matinées by Poverty Row studios like Republic and Monogram. Although in the years to come there would be numerous great westerns like *Red River*, *High Noon*, and *Shane*, there would also be lots and lots of, well, crud. Occasionally even the good stuff would be dismissed as crud if it didn't have the right pedigree. It took later critics and historians to rediscover, for example, that the westerns made by Budd Boetticher starring Randolph Scott were, in fact, spare dramas that rewarded careful viewing. Science fiction movies have had few such champions who could point out that movies like *Forbidden Planet*, *Them!* and *Invasion of the Body Snatchers*, for example, were as worthy of such attention as any intelligent but low budget western or *film noir*.

* "Serious filmmakers make serious movies, not science fiction, and when they do it's a break from their 'real' films."

Among the great directors who have one or more science fiction films on their resume are Fritz Lang, James Whale, Robert Wise, Don Siegel, Stanley Kubrick, Richard Fleischer, Woody Allen, Steven Spielberg, Philip Kaufman, Peter Weir, Danny Boyle, David Cronenberg, James Cameron, and Ridley Scott. Howard Hawks, a master of genres, never directed a science fiction film, but did produce *The Thing from Another World*, and is thought to have had a hand in guiding director Christian Nyby, a protégé of his. What usually happens when important directors make such films is that they are dismissed as larks or mere "entertainments." Their careers will rest on their other films. What if it turns out that the SF offering turns out to be an outstanding achievement? Ah, then it turns out that the film "isn't really science fiction" after all. Instead, like the Orwell and Huxley novels, such movies are reclassified as "satires" or "horror movies" or "dystopias" or "romances." Sometimes we're told the movies are grounded in real world speculation about the future as opposed to those talking squids in space stories.

This argument is essentially summed up as "if it's good, it can't be science fiction." The flip side also proves convenient: "if it's bad, it *must* be science fiction." The only film that seems to have escaped this trap is *2001: A Space Odyssey*, arguably one of Stanley Kubrick's *three* SF offerings, the other two being *Dr. Strangelove* with its Doomsday Machine and *A Clockwork Orange* with its futuristic dystopia and mind control. In the case of *2001* it was just too hard to file off the serial numbers. Not only did it have a crazed computer and a space ship, not only was Kubrick's collaborator renown SF author Arthur C. Clarke, but Kubrick himself had posited his effort as an attempt to do "the proverbial good science fiction movie." The result was such a towering masterpiece that Kubrick was granted Hollywood's equivalent of the philosopher's stone wherein it was allowed that he had transmuted this leaden genre into cinematic gold.

If all these arguments could be shot down without much effort, it's obvious that Hollywood was not much interested in trying to alter the debate. Instead, they surrendered without a shot being fired. SF films might occasionally get Oscar nominations but the only ones they could win were for special effects, makeup, and the like. You have to go back to Frederic March winning Best Actor for the 1932 *Dr. Jekyll and Mr. Hyde* to find an exception and since that was based on the novel by Robert Louis Stevenson (i.e., "literature") it couldn't possibly be science fiction. Director Steven Spielberg won his Oscar for *Schindler's List*, one of his "serious" films dealing with the quite serious subject of the Holocaust. With the exception of *Minority Report* his SF offerings are all variations on a child's adventure story (although sometimes a very twisted and misguided adventure, as with *A.I.*) while his "serious" films about adult concerns are strictly non-genre, or at least not this particular genre.

In the early 1950s there were a number of SF films that attracted general audiences like *Destination Moon*, *The Day the Earth Stood Still*, and *Forbidden Planet*, but by the end of the decade it seemed SF was a genre for movies like *I Was a Teenage Caveman* and *The Attack of the 50 Foot Woman*. It was something teenagers could ignore at the drive-in while they were making out. When the genre came roaring back twenty years later with *Star Wars* and *Close Encounters of the Third Kind*, Hollywood once again proceeded to learn the wrong lessons. Aided and abetted by the filmmakers themselves, the studios saw SF films as potential blockbusters, heavily reliant on special effects. A movie like Ridley Scott's *Alien* might not be for youngsters, but reviewers found it a "monster movie" where we could be scared while admiring the impressive creatures designed by artist H.R. Giger. Certainly critics like Pauline Kael were not writing book length treatises on the significance of the modern SF film. (Roger Ebert, an admitted SF fan, may have been a lonely voice on the subject.)

Today the science fiction label is still one to to be avoided. Indeed it was a noted film historian who was one of the people responsible for the *Metropolis* restoration who insisted that viewing the complete film proves how "thin" the "SF trappings" of the movie are, even though this is a movie with a robot that almost destroys a city. Such dismissal completely misunderstands the function of genre in film, and how great storytellers can address timely or profound issues by *using* what the genre offers, not ignoring it. A movie like *Invasion of the Body Snatchers* is a devastating statement about mindless conformity coming during the complacent '50s and its paranoid witch hunts over "subversives." When one of the pod people makes the case for becoming part of the collective mind, it's a compelling critique of how painful the human condition can be what with dysfunctional families and flawed marriages. Movies as different as *The Twonky* and *Colossus: The Forbin Project* could tap into our fears of living in a technological age where we don't know how the equipment we rely on works nor how much control it may have over our lives. *Blade Runner* was a complex meditation on finding meaning in our lives with no guarantee that our desire for such meaning will be granted, while *The Fly*—for all its gore and goo—was one of the most intense romantic dramas of the '80s showing how often people sabotage their own relationships.

In this book I examine some classic, and not so classic, SF films. Sometimes it's to elaborate on some of the issues the films present, sometimes it's just to have fun with a bit of pop culture. It is not intended to make the case that SF is better than other genres. I enjoy many other genres and have taught courses on several of them. Indeed, my book before this was on romantic comedies. However, I've always wanted to do a book on science fiction films, because I think that the genre gets a double whammy. It's not taken seriously by film people as discussed above, and it's often not taken seriously by those who do take science fiction seriously because it's "media SF."

For those who dismiss SF out of hand, I argue that as with the western, the romantic comedy, or the mystery, science fiction has a rich history and its classics are as worthy of study as that of any other genre. The films work as genre pieces, building on what came before while also reflecting and commenting upon the times in which they were made. A movie like *District 9* reveals as much about South Africa, for example, as Clint Eastwood's sports movie/hagiography of Nelson Mandela, *Invictus*.

As for those who embrace SF but turn up their noses at its media iterations, I note that film and print each have their strengths, and the best on screen—

movies like *The Day the Earth Stood Still*, *2001*, and *Gattaca*—can more then hold their own as exemplars of the genre. It's a truism that the literature is often far ahead of where the movies and TV shows are in terms of real science, extrapolation of the future and some of the other issues discussed, scientific or not. Movies have to appeal to much larger audiences than books do in order to be financially successful, yet as will be noted in the pages to come, there's some serious discussions to be had on the best the genre has to offer.

Where science fiction, both print and media, is unique is in having to explain itself. Unless a film is part of a series, like *Star Trek*, a person entering the world of an SF film needs to get his or her bearings. Noted author Isaac Asimov made the case in an essay many years ago where he noted that someone watching a genre film like a western or a prison movie or a historical romance doesn't necessarily require a lot of explanation. We know a great deal about the conventions of the genre even if they're not necessarily connected with reality. You know what a saloon is like or a courtroom or a royal ball even if you've never encountered them in real life because you've seen (and read about) them in so many other stories. However in SF the writer has to set out the ground rules. In *Destination Moon* the characters—and the viewers—get a crash course in rocket science from none other than Woody Woodpecker. In *Gattaca* the details of a society that favors designer gene babies, and which discriminates against those born naturally, needs to be spelled out or the story will make no sense. This information can be cleverly salted throughout the film, or presented in a clever—or awkward—"info dump," but it means that even if you've seen artificially created humans in movies before, you need to find out what the story is behind the replicants of *Blade Runner* before becoming fully immersed in this particular world. That learning curve puts the critic and film scholar on the same level of everyone else in the audience. For some, that's mere exposition, and it detracts from the "people" the movie ought to be about, meaning that science fiction becomes a lesser genre by definition. For those who know how to play by the rules, such as Christopher Nolan in his masterful *Inception*, it means the whole complex world created for the movie is not at all difficult to follow... so long as you didn't go out to the concession stand for five minutes and miss a crucial bit of dialogue. Knowing how to convey this information without being heavy-handed about it is simply the challenge of those who would work in this genre, just as someone making a war movie had better get acquainted with the weapons that were used in that particular war.

In the end, these essays are meant to make you think, to agree or disagree, and even, occasionally, to amuse. Most important, though, they should make you want to see the films. In my more than a quarter century as a film critic, I have found the words with which Donald Spoto ended his informative *The Art of Alfred Hitchcock* to be the guidepost I have used in my own writing about film, "If the reader is impelled to see again the films of Alfred Hitchcock, I shall have considered my work successful."

If after reading these essays you find yourself wanting to rewatch an old favorite or become acquainted with a film you have yet to see, then I will have done my job.

ACKNOWLEDGEMENTS

While the author of any book has to accept ultimate responsibility for what appears between its covers, many people deserve gratitude for their influence on the process that led to the essays in this book. First and foremost is Garen Daly, executive director of the Boston 24 Hour Science Fiction Movie Marathon which, on President's Day Weekend 2011, held its 36th annual event. Started in 1976 at the long gone Orson Welles Cinema in Cambridge, it has moved from theater to theater and seems to have found a welcome home at the Somerville Theater in Somerville, Massachusetts. Since my first "'thon" in 1979 I have only missed two of them. Although newcomers find a warm embrace and quickly become part of the community, there are a number of us veterans who see each other once a year, catching up with each other's lives between films. I first saw many of the films discussed herein at the marathon or wrote about them after a fresh viewing. Attendees come from as far away as Seattle and Dublin. Why? As the program from the 1983 marathon put it, noting that many in the audience would have already seen the previous summer's *Blade Runner* which had had a less than spectacular debut: "See it with the right audience this time."

Most of the essays here originally were written for other publications, and I've been fortunate to work with some savvy editors over the years. Pride of place has to go to Ian Randal Strock, head of Fantastic Books, who—when offered this project—noted that of course he was interested as he had bought several of the essays here in the first place when they appeared in the since defunct *Artemis Magazine*. Ian is a writer as well as an editor and publisher, and it's a pleasure to be working with him again.

A good number of the pieces herein were written for another defunct publication, the *Internet Review of Science Fiction*. As I didn't want to take away work from a friend and colleague who was then reviewing current films for them, I hit on the idea of writing about classic SF movies, and was pleased to have created a forum to spotlight (and occasionally chastise) the films of the past. Blunt Jackson, Stacy Janssen, and many others made it a wonderful home for those of us who take science fiction seriously, and it is missed.

Two other publications have provided similar spaces amidst their fiction, and I have enjoyed working with editors Cheryl Morgan at *Clarkesworld* and Hildy Silverman at *Space and Time* magazine, and look forward to continuing those associations. The essay on several decades of "Batman" movies was written for the

SmartPop series from BenBella Books, and if you're not familiar with their books on various pop culture phenomena from *Buffy the Vampire Slayer* to *24* and many others, you should check them out. My editor there is Leah Wilson and I've told her she is one of the toughest editors I've ever worked with and I'd write for her again in a heartbeat. My latest for her, not included here, is in *A Taste of True Blood*, where she let me write at length on the 90-second opening credits sequence.

I also have to give a tip of the hat to Rob Newton, colleague, friend, and now editor. When a 25-year newspaper gig dried up given the horrendous changes in the newspaper world, I barely had time to catch my breath before I was reviewing for his *NorthShoreMovies.net*. Some of the reviews I've done for him provided portions of my "2009" essay in this volume.

Also having an impact on my approach to these films are the science fiction conventions I have attended, having come to them only as a adult. Indeed, I attended my first World Science Fiction Convention, Noreascon 3, in 1989 as a journalist in Boston. I have recounted many times since my twofold reaction to seeing thousands of fans under one roof: a.) these people are crazy and b.) where do I sign up? I have attended, and been on panels, at many Worldcons and NASFiCs (the North American Science Fiction Convention, held when the WorldCon is overseas) since 1998, and have been a regular at two Boston conventions, Arisia and Boskone, as well as New York's Lunacon, since the '90s. Whether it was discussions on panels or in hallways or at parties, having to present coherent thoughts on SF films, as well as either being inspired by or having to answer the views of others, has greatly informed my thinking on them.

On a personal level, I have to thank Alison Picard, my agent, who has brought four of my five published books to fruition. Indeed, it was her unsuccessful attempts with an earlier SF film book proposal that led to the eventual publication of my first solo book, *The Fourth Network*, which went on to win the Cable Center Book Award. So it's taken a while, but I finally have my SF film book.

This project came together for me during a particularly bumpy time in my personal life. It is dedicated to four friends who were especially supportive, but there were numerous family members, friends, colleagues, and fellow fans who, in ways big and small, helped me move forward one step at a time. They are too numerous to mention individually here, but they continue to have my undying love and respect.

Finally, I have to mention my daughter Amanda or, as she prefers these days, Manda. I *have* to mention her. Really. Since she's been old enough to read she has eagerly picked up each of my new books to see where her name appears, whether in the dedication or the acknowledgments. I won't further embarrass her in case any of her friends are reading this (she is a teenager, after all), but she is an unending source of inspiration, and being her father is my proudest accomplishment. I hope to have many more opportunities to mention her in the years ahead.

Part I. Mandatory Viewing

There are some films you just *have* to see if you have any pretense to being well-versed in the field. How could someone claim to be an Alfred Hitchcock fan without seeing *Psycho* or a lover of movie musicals without having seen *Singin' in the Rain*? In this section some of the films I write about are ones I think are some of the greatest achievements in science fiction. It's okay if you haven't seen them all. They were all new to me once, too. However, it's fair to ask: what are you waiting for?

DAYS OF FUTURES PASSED

The release of the restored 1927 *Metropolis* is the cinematic event of the year. Fritz Lang's visionary film was the first science fiction epic. It proved tremendously influential, despite the fact that for more than 80 years it was available only in incomplete form. Shortly after its premiere in Berlin it was cut, first by its German studio Ufa and then by American distributor Paramount Pictures. What had originally run at nearly three hours, including intermission, arrived in the United States at closer to 90 minutes.

That is the version that had been in circulation for years, until people began to notice that prints varied in different countries, and began to try to put it back together. A notable attempt was made by music producer Giorgio Moroder in 1984, who restored some of the subplots, using contemporary pop music for the film's score. Additional footage subsequently turned up in various film archives. By 2002, what was billed as the most complete restoration we'd ever see was released. It was still missing approximately 25 minutes, but it was the best that could be done. Incredibly, the story didn't end there.

In 2008, in Argentina, a damaged 16 millimeter print was discovered that was virtually the entire original cut of the movie. Work began on putting together the most complete *Metropolis* possible. The new version of *Metropolis* bowed in Berlin in early 2010, 83 years after its original debut. It's been playing in select US cities throughout the year and will subsequently be out on DVD. Now that we can finally see this masterpiece as its director intended, it is proof, according to one of the film historians instrumental in the restoration, that *Metropolis* isn't a science fiction movie after all.

Say what? Here's Martin Koerber, interviewed by the *New York Times*: "It's no longer a science-fiction film... The balance of the story has been given back. It's now a film that encompasses many genres, an epic about conflicts that are ages old. The science-fiction disguise is now very, very thin."

Now this is the man who helped restore *Metropolis*, so clearly he's no *dumbkopf*. However, as someone who has written about and taught SF films, I can say that Herr Koerber clearly doesn't have a clue, particularly with regard to genre. It is his attempt to "rescue" this classic film from the horrible fate of being labeled a science fiction film that is "very, very thin."

His argument seems to be that the dystopian society, the mad scientist Rotwang, and the robot he transforms into the evil Maria, are simply SF trappings which Lang lightly donned to tell his more profound story. That story is about how the head (representing capitalism) and the hand (representing labor) must be mediated by the heart (represented by the film's empathetic hero Freder, who becomes the go-between between the exploited workers and his exploiting father). Wow, sure glad we didn't let that science fiction stuff get in the way of that message, which even Lang thought was the weakest aspect of the movie.

Koerber would apparently argue that *Love Story* isn't a romance, but instead a critique of class rivalry. No doubt *The Searchers* isn't really a western and *The Maltese Falcon* isn't really a detective story. No, wait, all of *those* genres are on the approved list. We can admire *The Searchers* as a western *and* as a story about "conflicts that are ages old." Only science fiction carries such a stigma that it must be scrubbed off any movie deemed a classic, with Stanley Kubrick's *2001: A Space Odyssey* being the only exception to the rule. Sorry, Herr Koerber, but that *hund* won't hunt.

Metropolis opens on a future city supposedly inspired by Lang's first views of Manhattan. It is a world of towering skyscrapers, massive highways, and graceful dirigibles. Joh Frederson rules this world so that the privileged elite, like his son Freder, can live lives of ease. Joh may have to attend to business, but Freder can devote himself to athletics and a sybaritic lifestyle. (It's notable that the women we meet above ground are there for the pleasure of the men.) Meanwhile down below, the workers lead lives of drudgery, without even the pleasure of pride in their work. These laborers are little more than parts of the machines they service. In one of the most celebrated sequences Freder, exploring this underground world, sees the big machine as a fiery idol consuming the workers fed to it. These dystopian views are such a part and parcel of science fiction that it's incredible to see *Metropolis* denied its strong claim as SF. Herr Koerber is like those English professors who insist that Orwell's *1984* and Huxley's *Brave New World* aren't science fiction either since these are really works of "literature."

The fact that *Metropolis* is first, and foremost, SF does not rest on the dystopian aspect alone. Freder has been lured to the underground by the appearance of Maria, a teacher and social activist who brings her young charges "upstairs" to see how the other half lives. Freder is strangely attracted to Maria and follows her, discovering the hellish existence of the workers supporting his idyllic lifestyle.

Leaning of this, his father—whose spy network is newly elaborated upon in the restoration—meets with Rotwang, the proverbial mad scientist, to plot a way to discredit Maria. Joh and Rotwang have their own tangled history. They were both in love with the same woman, who subsequently married Joh, and then died giving birth to Freder. Rotwang has never forgotten this, and looks at his new mission not only as an opportunity to carry out Joh's orders, but to get his revenge as well. He has built a robot, the first great robot of SF film, which, in an elaborate special effects sequence, is transformed into an evil version of Maria. She will not only discredit the do-gooder, she will lead the workers in a revolt that will bring down Metropolis.

Perhaps Herr Koerber would point out that *Metropolis* isn't about the robot at all, but about the human desires and pains of the other characters. And it would be our job to note that that is correct. That's precisely what makes it science fiction. It's the use of the scientific extrapolation to tell us something about ourselves. *Metropolis* is no more about evil robots than *2001* is about faulty computer programming. It uses these tropes the same way a western might use a shootout at high noon. Lang and his collaborator on the script (and then wife) Thea von Harbou utilize such science fiction staples as the dystopia, the deranged scientist, and the robot passing for human in order to tell their story. This is not a movie that is great in spite of its science fiction trappings. It is great *because* of the brilliant way those trappings are conceived and used to examine the human conflicts set forth here.

It's truly amazing that one has to defend *Metropolis* as a science fiction movie. What Herr Koerber has revealed is not an insight into *Metropolis*, but into the narrow-minded ignorance—for that's what it is—among film academics and historians. Having taught courses on the western, romantic comedy, *film noir*, and the gangster film, as well as on science fiction and horror movies, I am well aware of how genre functions. It provides plots, characters, settings, themes, and motifs which can be adapted for other purposes. Science fiction is no better or worse than any other genre at performing this task. Fritz Lang was well aware of the uses of genre as well, having made a number of classic films that were crime thrillers, spy movies, westerns, war stories, and *film noir*. *Metropolis* isn't even his only foray into science fiction. Two years later he would do *Woman in the Moon*, a movie about the first trip to the moon that has been credited with inventing the countdown.

So, Herr Koerber, all of us owe you a tremendous debt of gratitude for your role in making sure that this nearly complete *Metropolis* has seen the light of day and been made widely available. However when it comes to whether it is science fiction or not, you need to shut your mouth and open your mind. *Metropolis* is *great* science fiction. And that doesn't require any apology.

FUTURE TENSE

To help promote Arisia, a Boston area convention, some people have launched "Arisia TV." It's a website where they hope to have lots of SF content that will be of interest to fans. As a long-time participant, I was asked to do a series of brief vignettes on SF films on the theme "The Five Essential Science Fiction Movies." In my introduction to the series, I pointed out that such lists are interesting, but are more points for discussion than definitive judgments.

Of course I couldn't resist the challenge, and my choices are a mix of the obvious and the quirky. I limited myself to no more than one film per decade, so that once I picked *Forbidden Planet*, all those other great '50s films were out of the running. Fortunately, it's only an exercise, so that other than comparing notes and, perhaps, seeing films you may have missed, there's really nothing at stake. However, I began to wonder what would have happened if they had made it more difficult, by asking me to name five essential SF films *prior* to 1950. That would be more of a challenge, simply because there are few films to choose from in order to come up with five titles that are enduring classics. No *Buck Rogers* or *Flash Gordon* serials for me.

I'd start with the Georges Méliès's 1902 short "A Trip to the Moon." It's a film that still delights more than a century later, from the chorus line seeing off the rocket to the Man in the Moon getting it right in the eye. Of course the most important of all the silent feature-length SF films—not that there are all that many —is Fritz Lang's 1927 masterpiece *Metropolis*, which gives us robots, underground cities, and the mad scientist Rotwang. Moving into the sound era, the fantasy giant ape movie *King Kong* (1933) may be a stretch as science fiction, but most SF fans have no problem with that, and the original is a film that has to be seen. Of course a slot must be reserved for one of the "Frankenstein" movies with *Bride of Frankenstein* (1935) getting the nod.

So that leaves the fifth film. The general consensus—with which I agree—is that a contender for any all-time greats of SF film list is *Things to Come* (1936). Yet of the five, it's the one that seems to be the least known. Part of the problem may be, as others have noted, the poor quality of most of the prints available (including transfers of public domain prints to VHS tapes and DVDs). However, it may also be due to a certain smugness at its look at the future which is—for most of the film—*our* past. Perhaps we need to view this as alternate history or, if possible, put aside the actual history of the last seventy years and try to imagine how this looked to viewers in 1936.

The story, based on the book by H.G. Wells, takes place in "Everytown," although those insisting on seeing it as London will not be too mistaken. It opens at Christmastime in 1940, just a few years in the future. As most people try to stay in the holiday mood, there are ominous headlines of imminent war. We know that World War II is just around the corner, but in 1936 that wasn't a certainty, just a foreboding. John Cabal (Raymond Massey) believes it's too late to avoid war and, in the next scenes his worst dreams come true, as the enemy bombs start falling.

Future history then veers off from the world we know, as the war continues not for a few years but for a few decades. By the 1960s, Everytown is more rubble than city, and the "government" consists of the Boss (Ralph Richardson), a petty tyrant who promises peace while continuing the fight. The "enemy" is no longer a foreign power, but the people in the rubble of the next community. What's fascinating about the sequence is its pre-atomic view of a post-apocalyptic world. There's a struggle with the outbreak of the mysterious "Wandering Sickness," a plague for which there is no cure but death. Finally it subsides and people can start rebuilding. No one is worrying about radiation, yet they are pessimistic about the restoration of civilization. The Boss wants airplanes, but there's no "petrol" for fuel, and young mechanic Richard Gordon (Derek DeMarney) doesn't think the planes they have will ever work. He bleakly tells his girlfriend that humanity will never return to the skies. This is even more frightening than the "Wandering Sickness." It's the notion that society can be so badly damaged by war that we will actually regress to more primitive conditions, unable to repair the damage.

Of course that's the signal for the arrival of a plane, flown by a much older John Cabal, representative of Wings Over the World. Cabal's arguments with the Boss are fascinating, in no small part because we know we're supposed to be on Cabal's side. He represents peace, progress, and technology, but he also represents authoritarian rule, however benign it might be. When the Boss insists on local sovereignty, he's told in no uncertain terms that that will no longer be permitted. Everytown will be brought into this new world order on the terms the airmen dictate, no negotiation. Ultimately, Everytown is gassed from above in order to incapacitate the residents. The gas is supposed to simply temporarily knock out the people but, conveniently, the Boss dies in the attack.

The story jumps forward once more, now to 2036. Cabal's great-grandson Oswald (also Massey) is now a leader of an Eden-like Everytown. Director William Cameron Menzies devotes several shots to how it was constructed and transformed. Civilization has not only come back; it has greatly advanced. For viewers in 1936, this glimpse of a world a hundred years hence must have been truly amazing. Yet all is not well. There is grumbling about plans to send a rocket to the moon. The sculptor Theotocopulos (Cedric Hardwicke) goes on worldwide television to rouse the populace against the "space gun" arguing, "What good is all this progress?"

This last part focuses on whether the mob or the scientists will prevail, with the film's conclusion going to Oswald, who would sound almost cold-blooded if we didn't consider him the story's hero. He allows that people will die as mankind moves into space, but what is really important is progress and the advancement of knowledge. When his colleague asks when we get to rest and enjoy ourselves, Oswald sardonically notes that rest—the permanent rest of death—comes to all soon enough. In the meantime humanity must always look for new goals: the moon, the planets, the stars. That's the choice, he insists. "All the universe, or nothingness," he says. "Which shall it be?"

This is intelligent SF filmmaking that focuses on ideas as much—if not more—than the special effects. Of course bad movies have been made from H.G. Wells's books, but Wells himself is credited with the screenplay adaptation here. The film was produced by Alexander Korda, and some of the top names in the British film industry were part of the production team. It's not without its flaws, from the 19th Century feel of some of the speeches (Wells was in his 60s when he wrote the screenplay) to the jumps in the plot. Apparently the original premiere length of the film was in the vicinity of two hours, though most current prints are in the 90-minute range. However, what some might see as confusion might be more properly seen as complexity. We may agree with the viewpoint of John Cabal and, later, his great-grandson Oswald, and see their opponents as blowhards and buffoons. Yet the arguments they make do raise questions, and the criticism they receive is not without reason.

Things to Come is not some musty relic relying on its past reputation, but an important part of the pantheon of SF cinema. As with any classic or overly literary novel, it may take some time to get in sync with the story, but it is worth the effort. Serious fans should sit down to a showing of *Things to Come* with the same attention with which they consider the issues of *2001*, *Blade Runner*, or *Gattaca*. This isn't cheese. This is filet mignon.

SCIENCE FICTION OR NOT?

For those of us who take science fiction seriously—and you obviously do, or you wouldn't be reading this—it's frustrating that the very people who ought to be promoting the best in our field are often standing with the Philistines and making fun of it. It's intellectual laziness, to be sure, since if science fiction can be dismissed out of hand, one doesn't have to go through the bother of actually learning anything about it.

Several years ago, I mentioned to a film critic colleague (still working but thankfully no longer in my city) that I would be attending the local 24-hour science fiction movie marathon held annually in the Boston area. She gave me a disdainful look and asked what movies they would be showing. I noted that the event ran the gamut from recent films to schlock to the classics.

She seemed surprised at the last word. Classics? What "classics" could this degenerate genre have produced? Oh, you know, I replied, *Metropolis* or *Frankenstein*. Now she was even more amazed. *Frankenstein*? How could I possibly consider *Frankenstein* to be a science fiction movie?

It was my turned to be surprised. How could it be a science fiction movie? How could it *not* be? A scientist experiments with bringing dead tissue to life. What else could it be?

Ah, she replied, it's a *monster* movie.

See, that's how it works. Science fiction is garbage. If something is good it can't be science fiction, and therefore must be something else.

Of course the 1931 *Frankenstein* is part of the cycle of classic Universal horror films. Some entries, like *Dracula* and *The Wolfman*, are clearly pure horror films, with their tales of vampires and lycanthropy. Others are just as clearly science fiction. *The Invisible Man*, for example, was based on H.G. Wells's famous novel. As for *Frankenstein*, no less an authority than science fiction writer Brian Aldiss—in his SF history *Billion Year Spree* (later updated to *Trillion Year Spree*)—cites Mary Shelley's novel as the very start of modern science fiction.

Over the years, Shelley's novel has served as the basis for countless movies. The earliest one is from 1910 and can be seen online. While no masterpiece, it remains a fascinating curio. Since then, the story of a man attempting to master the power of creating life has become a cinematic mainstay. Indeed, the Internet Movie Database lists over one hundred titles with the name "Frankenstein" in them, from credited adaptations to cartoons to films using the name as a marketing tool. Even allowing for the usual confusion between Dr. Frankenstein the scientist and his creation, sometimes referred to as Frankenstein but more properly as the Monster, Shelley's novel has spawned a cinematic classification all its own. Frankenstein has "met" everyone from Dracula to Abbott and Costello to Alvin and the Chipmunks. He's returned, he's been reborn, he's created woman, he's been a teenager. He's taken revenge, he must be destroyed, he's fought aliens in Puerto Rico, and had his daughter meet Jesse James. Over the years, the Monster has been played by Robert DeNiro, Glenn Strange, Lon Cheney, Jr., John Schuck, Christopher Lee, Bo Svenson, David Warner, and even Peter Boyle, in Mel Brooks's affectionate and hilarious spoof *Young Frankenstein*.

With all these choices, though, there's a surprising consensus as to what the best film is, and who should be playing the monster. The actor, of course, is William Henry Pratt, better known to generations of horror fans as Boris Karloff. A gentle, soft-spoken Englishman, he was a veteran actor when, at age 44, he got his big breakthrough as the Monster in James Whale's 1931 *Frankenstein*. To add to the mystery, he isn't even listed in the credits, with the Monster billed as being played by "?". The movie was a hit, and it made his career. Although he would still play some non-horror roles, he became an icon of the genre. Yet he appeared as the Monster only twice more. It is in his second outing, the 1935 *Bride of Frankenstein*, that we get the most romantic, surreal, horrifying, and poignant rendering of this story of a mad scientist playing with life.

After a prologue featuring Elsa Lanchester as Mary Shelley, where she reveals that she has written a sequel to her story, the film picks up where the first one left off. Baron Viktor Frankenstein (Colin Clive) is near death after the fiery climax which supposedly destroyed the Monster. However the Monster is alive and as out of control as ever, claiming as his first victims the parents of the little girl he accidentally drowned in the first movie. While the now-recuperating Baron and his bride Elizabeth (Valerie Hobson, replacing the original film's Mae Clark) hope the nightmare is over, it's really just beginning. Almost at once, the maddest of mad scientists, Dr. Pretorious (Ernest Thesiger), arrives to goad him into reviving his experiments.

The theme of the story is that classic of old science fiction: there are some things Man is not meant to know. Frankenstein and Pretorious try to create a new life, a female creature who can mate with the monster. Pretorious imagines a future world where "gods and monsters" will co-exist, but it's clear that *he* is the real monster here. At film's end, when the Monster brings about the apocalyptic destruction of Frankenstein's laboratory, he sends the Baron and his wife away, but holds Pretorious back to die in the rubble with him and the "Bride" who has rejected him.

Our understanding of the Monster as a sympathetic creature derives a great deal from this film. It's not so much that the Monster is evil but that he is amoral. He is born into a lumbering, powerful body without having grown into it. Likewise, his understanding of the world is much like that of a child. He needs. He wants. He gets upset. He has to learn, but under the obsessive Frankenstein and the vice-ridden Pretorious (who uses the Monster to kidnap Elizabeth as a means of controlling the Baron), his moral education is lacking. In a pivotal scene, the Monster—fleeing the always fearful and enraged townspeople—comes across a cottage in the woods inhabited by an old blind man (O.P. Heggie). Unable to see the Monster for what it is, the old man treats him as a mute and troubled stranger in need of kindness. It is here the Monster begins to learn to speak and to show enjoyment of music and food. This idyll comes to an end when huntsmen arrive, forcing the Monster to flee, but during this brief respite, the Monster becomes a figure not of horror but of pity. If only he could have been treated with such kindness and support all along, he might not have acted like the wild animal he has become.

At this point, more so than earlier or in the first film, we perceive the Monster as a sentient being. He becomes sympathetic because he is redeemable, which makes what follows all the more tragic. The two scientists complete their experiment and bring their new creature to life (played by Elsa Lanchester in her famous lightning-streak hairdo). This time they are using an "innocent" brain created by Pretorious, which will have none of the criminal past of the "used" criminal's brain installed in the Monster. Her awakening is a breathtaking moment. She sees the Baron and Pretorious, and takes in her surroundings. Everything is new to her. Then she sees the Monster, who reaches out to her with affection. At last he will have the companionship of someone just like himself. And what does she do? She screams and recoils in horror. It is this rejection that sets the Monster on his climactic rampage.

Why does she react this way? I'm indebted to a student in a class where I showed the film, for asking how she could possibly know the Monster was frightening when her brain was supposedly a blank. The film offers no answer. I suggested that perhaps it meant that every brain is hardwired with certain archetypal images, as pioneering psychiatrist Carl Jung argued. For the story, what is important is that she *does* react that way, and that the Monster is rejected even by his own kind. (Karloff would don the extensive makeup just one more time after this, for *The Son of Frankenstein* with Basil Rathbone and Bela Lugosi, making for a horror funfest if not quite a great film.)

In answer to my former colleague, *The Bride of Frankenstein* isn't merely a "monster movie." It is a film that deals with profound issues: the meaning of life, the ethics of experimentation, the limits of knowledge, and what within us is inborn versus what is learned. Fortunately, we have a name for stories that deal with such issues.

We call them "science fiction."

SLEEP NO MORE

As this is being written [2005], plans are being made for *The Invasion*, scheduled to star Nicole Kidman. It will be the *fourth* movie version of Jack Finney's novel, *Invasion of the Body Snatchers*.

The original and, arguably best, version is Don Siegel's 1956 film. The '50s were a golden age for SF features, and a touchstone for fans of the good, the bad, and the ugly. However, while several films of the era have been remade—including *The Thing*, *Invaders from Mars*, *The Blob* and, more recently, *War of the Worlds*—the obsession with *Body Snatchers* puts it into a category by itself. What is the appeal of this story, and why does it keep coming back to haunt us?

The common reading of the original film is that it is a thinly disguised critique of the Red Scare, or what historian David Caute has called "the Great Fear." Senator Joe McCarthy claimed there were Communists in the State Department, the House Un-American Activities Committee investigated Hollywood, people in all walks of life had to sign loyalty oaths. To be sure, our fear of the Soviet Union wasn't a completely irrational fear. The USSR had swallowed up Eastern Europe behind the "Iron Curtain," and they began testing their own atomic bombs. We were in a Cold War. It was a nervous time, and there was plenty of suspicion to go around.

So along comes *Invasion of the Body Snatchers*, where Dr. Miles Bennell (Kevin McCarthy; no relation to the senator) returns from a trip to the sleepy California town of Santa Mira. He's glad to be home, and to meet up with his old friend Becky Driscoll (Dana Wynter), since both are recently divorced and a bit lonely. However, something odd is going on. There's been an outbreak of a strange delusion, with people claiming that family members aren't themselves.

As Miles investigates, he uncovers the truth. Strange pods from outer space have landed in Santa Mira, bringing a deadly threat. When left near a human, the pod forms an exact physical duplicate of the person. When that duplicate is complete, it absorbs all of the human's memories, killing the real person in the process. The "pod person" then takes his or her place. The pods are soulless and emotionless but, as with all good '50s' invaders, they are relentless. Slowly, the pods take over Santa Mira, until only Miles and Becky are left. Miles objects to a world without love, but as his psychiatrist colleague Danny Kaufman (Larry Gates) points out, both Miles and Becky have been in love before—with their ex-spouses—and it didn't last. Danny proceeds to spell out the new world order: "Love. Desire. Ambition. Faith. Without them life's so simple, believe me."

The film was originally meant to end with Miles alone, after Becky succumbs. He's screaming on the highway—as truckloads of pods are being shipped to other American communities—"You're next! You're next! You're next!" And, of course, no one believes him.

When the producers saw the finished film, they were panic stricken—not at Miles' fate, but at the downbeat end of their movie. This was more than a decade before George Romero shocked everyone with the nihilistic finale of *Night of the Living Dead* (1968), where the good guys didn't make it. Siegel, who would go on to a distinguished career that included several films with Clint Eastwood (including *Dirty Harry*) and John Wayne's final performance (*The Shootist*), did not yet have the clout to insist that the film remain as he had shot it. Instead, screenwriter Daniel Mainwaring persuaded him that they could save the film by "fixing" it themselves. They brought back McCarthy and shot the framing device in which Miles is brought to a hospital and relates the story in flashback, ending with him finally being believed. The authorities now know to destroy the pods.

For many people, the film's political message is easy to read. Miles is the well-meaning but complacent American, not paying attention to the threat of the pods (read: Commies) until it directly affects him. Then he discovers that this alien regime wants to transform America into a regimented society where everyone will think and act alike. Those who deviate will be captured and held until they become pod people, too. It's not an unfair interpretation of the film, and certainly fit the mood of the country at the time.

Many SF films of the '50s played on audience's fear of World War III, and not just the movies with giant atomic insects or mutants. In *Destination Moon* (1950), American industrialists are skeptical about financing a private venture to send men to the moon, until they are warned that if America doesn't conquer space, another nation might do so, and put missiles up there aimed at us. The checkbooks quickly open. The following year Klaatu (Michael Rennie) warned humanity about the dangers of nuclear war in *The Day the Earth Stood Still*. In one of the most curious films of the era, *The 27th Day* (1957), aliens select five humans, and give them pellets capable of destroying the world. One of the humans is from the Soviet Union.

So for many viewers and critics, the time of *Invasion of the Body Snatchers* and its story of fighting a menace seeking to crush the will of the individual for a collective purpose fit right into the template of the Red Scare. However, it's a mistake to limit the film to political allegory. In interviews, director Don Siegel felt that the movie wasn't warning about Communists or—as some have asserted—the Red-baiting witch hunters. As he told film critic Stuart Kaminsky, he was warning about turning into pod people:

> Well, I think there's a very strong case for being a pod. These pods, who get rid of pain, ill health, and mental disturbance are, in a sense, doing good. It happens to leave you with a very dull world, but that, by the way, my dear friend, is the world that most of us live in. It's the same as people who welcome going into the army or prison. There's regimentation, a lack of having to make up your mind, face decisions.

Instead of being a film with a political agenda, it seems Siegel was warning us about people of whatever persuasion who are all too willing to let others do their thinking for them. It didn't matter whether it was Joseph McCarthy or Josef Stalin. If you unthinkingly accepted whatever you were told and acted accordingly, you were a pod person. The film is a condemnation of thoughtless conformity of every type. It was fear as real as the Red Scare, which found its expression in the Beat movement and in non-fiction like *The Organization Man* and *The Hidden Persuaders*. Perhaps it's no surprise that a mainstream Hollywood feature released that same year focused on a man questioning a life lived according to the expectations others have for him—*The Man in the Gray Flannel Suit*.

Twenty-two years later, Miles was still running down the public streets trying to warn people, but now it was just Kevin McCarthy doing a cameo in the 1978 remake directed by Philip Kaufman. Some critics lamented the lack of a political subtext for this new version, but as memories of Watergate and Vietnam faded into the malaise of the Me Decade, it was just such narcissism that was the new danger. It's worth noting that the character who was an authoritative psychiatrist in the original turns into the author and self-help guru played by Leonard Nimoy in the new film. It was an era of est and Silva Mind Control and other such fads. People had discovered new ways to become pods and let others do their thinking for them.

Although the action has moved from the small town to the big city of San Francisco, there's one important difference: audiences were not put off by downer endings any more. In the more than two decades since the original, Americans had seen the assassination of one president and the resignation of another. We had experienced a long and unpopular war where, if we didn't quite lose, we couldn't really say we had won, either. Cities had exploded in riots in the '60s, Martin Luther King and Bobby Kennedy had been murdered, protesting college students were gunned down at Kent State. We still liked our happy endings but we were no longer surprised when we didn't get them. Movies from *Bonnie and Clyde* to *Carrie* dared to violate the Hollywood formula.

So now, when the rechristened Matthew Bennell (Donald Sutherland) and Elizabeth Driscoll (Brooke Adams) flee for their lives at the end, we had no certainty that they would make it. Fans of the original knew Elizabeth was doomed, and weren't disappointed. It was the film's final moments that caught us unawares. Nancy (Veronica Cartwright), wife of Matthew's friend Jack (Jeff Goldblum), has somehow not been taken over by the pods. Trying to pass as one, she's startled to see Matthew. She's not alone! She speaks to him—and the pod-Matthew lets out a blood-curdling shriek, announcing to his fellow pods that he's found yet another unconverted human. This was even more horrifying that the original ending for the '56 film, and it packed a wallop. There was no last-minute rescue. The government could not save the day. It was hopeless. We weren't so sure of ourselves any more, nor could we be certain that those pods wouldn't prevail.

By 1993, director Abel Ferrara was ready to tackle the story in what was released as *Body Snatchers*. The action was moved to an army base, and the protagonist was no longer a wise adult professional, but a teenage girl (Gabrielle Anwar) who moves to the base with her father and stepmother. The soldiers and officers start succumbing to the pods, but as Don Siegel might have asked, how could anyone tell? Already living a regimented life in uniform, with a strict chain of command, many of them are already pods *before* they're taken over. The film might have explored whether the military really wants *unthinking* conformity, or it could have focused on a teenage girl at odds with her family discovering that they really are different from her. It could not successfully do both.

Films like *Invasion of the Body Snatchers* are, on one level, about the fear that you will lose the ability to trust the people whose stability and reliability are a matter of personal faith. It's losing one's friends and neighbors, family members and colleagues. In *Invaders from Mars* (1953) the Martians take over humans through surgical implantation. The young boy sees nearly everyone he's supposed to trust taken over: his father, his mother, the police. In *I Married a Monster from Outer Space* (1958) a new bride can't understand why her husband has changed so much since the wedding, not realizing he's been taken over by aliens. In real life we may not fear creatures from outer space, but sometimes someone close surprises us by suddenly acting in ways we don't expect of them. Is this merely a side we haven't seen, or is it a sign that something is seriously wrong?

So now we anticipate yet a fourth film version of Jack Finney's tale. Reportedly, the focus will be on a psychiatrist (to be played by Nicole Kidman) trying to protect her young son from something strange that's happening around them. It's coming at a time when we take off our shoes at the airport to be X-rayed, out of fear that the person next to us in line might have hidden an explosive in them. We are so divided as a country that we talk of "red states" and "blue states," and people listen only to those opinion leaders who will reinforce their views. President George W. Bush is a divisive figure whose supporters claim is a great leader and whose detractors claim is one of the worst presidents in our nation's history. If the pods were to come today, how would we know? Whichever side you're on, don't your political opponents *already* seem like pod people, letting their favored politicians and media figures tell them what to believe?

The time seems right—indeed, overripe—for a new *Invasion of the Body Snatchers*. If the makers of *The Invasion* can think for themselves, they just might have something.

(POSTSCRIPT: *The Invasion* was directed by German filmmaker Oliver Hirschbiegel. From what's left of his work in the finished film, it was to be a story of paranoia and betrayal set in Washington, D.C., with the pods replaced by a blue goo that is transmitted from those who have changed to those not yet infected, making it a powerful metaphor for sexually transmitted diseases. Unfortunately, the pod people at the studio got cold feet, and they brought in the Wachowski Brothers to write additional scenes, which were directed by James McTeigue. It's easy to spot where the film changes. A moody thriller suddenly turns into an action movie with a big chase scene and an utterly absurd happy ending. Alas. The pods won again.)

REAL ALIENS DON'T ASK DIRECTIONS

When the aliens arrive, the movies tell us, we really only have one thing to find out: we need to determine if they are friendly or not. If they are friendly, they will try to guide us toward peace (*The Day the Earth Stood Still*), ask for our help (*Starman*, *E.T.*), or simply want to be friends (*Close Encounters of the Third Kind*). It might be the start of an exciting new chapter in our history.

Of course, if they're not friendly, then we're in real trouble. They might try to kill us (*War of the Worlds*), use us as incubators (*Alien*), hunt us for sport (*Predator*), drink our blood (*The Thing*), take over our bodies (*Invasion of the Body Snatchers*), or even steal Earth's women (*I Married a Monster from Outer Space*, *Mars Needs Women*). The key thing to remember when the spaceships arrive is that it's always about *us*.

That Earth-centric view shouldn't be surprising. After all, movies are made for Earth audiences; there isn't much of a market—so far as we can yet tell—anywhere else. It's the reason that Godzilla always attacks Tokyo in his Japanese movies, but when Hollywood did their misbegotten 1998 version he attacked New York. You try to play to your audience. It's just good business sense.

That's what makes the 1953 *It Came from Outer Space* so interesting. The humans are utterly irrelevant to the visiting aliens, and only get caught up in the plot out of necessity. Set in the small town of Sand Rock, Arizona, it begins when writer John Putnam (Richard Carlson) and his girlfriend Ellen Fields (Barbara Rush) see what seems to be a meteorite crash in the desert. Putnam is a bit of an oddball—a freelance writer who specializes in articles about science—so when he becomes convinced it was a spaceship, the townspeople are skeptical. Nonetheless, odd things are definitely happening, with a weird creature appearing and disappearing along the road. Then people start acting strangely. The big revelation comes early, when we see two telephone linemen (Joe Sawyer, Russell Johnson) taken over by the aliens. The real people remain alive (although Putnam mistakenly believes them dead), but are held hostage by the aliens, while their doubles move about the town.

The movie consists of much running around trying to get to the bottom of this mystery. There's even a scene where Putnam beats up the sheriff to prevent him from taking action against the aliens, and then steals a police car. Apparently, freelance writers were given free rein to indulge their eccentricities back in the 1950s. It's only when we discover the aliens' fiendish plot that we learn what makes this film truly distinctive.

It seems they're using Earth as the space lane equivalent of a soft shoulder. They need to do some repairs on their spaceship. They have no interest in enslaving us or in curing all our diseases. They really don't even want to meet us. They just want to get the work done and be on their way. The reason they've taken over the few humans they've borrowed is that they have to be able to move about and get supplies without attracting attention. Indeed, when Putnam demands that they reveal themselves, they refuse, saying that humans would not be able accept their appearance. When he makes his cooperation contingent on their doing so, we see that the aliens are correct. They are as horrible looking—one big eye, tentacles, wild hair—as could be expected in an early '50s, black and white science fiction movie, even one in 3D. His curiosity satisfied, Putnam manages to protect the aliens from the armed posse that has come to get them, succeeds in getting the human hostages freed, and then lets the aliens get back into space, allowing them to go to wherever it was they were heading in the first place.

Directed by Jack Arnold and based on a story by Ray Bradbury, this was clearly intended to be a scary film, impressing us with the mysterious unknowns that await us in space. What makes this distinctive is that it challenges the coding that usually helps us distinguish aliens in the movies. Good aliens are human, or at least humanoid, speak English, and make it clear they mean us no harm. Some are so warm and cuddly they might easily be mistaken for a child's favorite stuffed doll, as in the famous scene in *E.T.* where the extra-terrestrial hides in plain sight in a pile of plush animals.

Bad aliens fall into one of two categories. The obvious bad guys have one eye or multiple eyes, tentacles, make no attempt to communicate with us, and quickly respond to peace overtures with death and destruction. From *The Thing* to *Independence Day*, anything that is markedly different from the human norm is evil and to be killed on sight. Those who don't realize this suffer the consequences.

Not to so obvious are the aliens who are shape shifters (as in the 1981 remake of *The Thing*) or who can possess humans (*The Puppet Masters*, *Invaders from Mars* and the multiple versions of *Invasion of the Body Snatchers*). What's clear about these aliens is that while they may outwardly look like us, they can't get away with it. Children and other close family members may grow suspicious, and dogs and cats will howl and hiss as if the alien is a vampire, which he may well be. One giveaway is that these aliens have no emotions or human feeling at all, so that they all sound like former vice president Dick Cheney assuring people that torture is no big deal.

It's the job of the real humans in these movies to decide whether to be afraid of the aliens or not. Make the wrong choice (*War of the Worlds*) and you can be zapped. Make the right choice and the musical aliens will dance you aboard their spaceship (*Close Encounters of the Third Kind*).

It Came from Outer Space is the exception in that it sends out mixed signals. They take over several humans, which makes it truly eerie, as when Putnam confronts the two linemen and, from a shadowy doorway, they warn him off, threatening death if he continues his pursuit. When we see the aliens for real they are indeed hideous. Yet they aren't evil, merely cautious. They turn out to be right in their desire to avoid humanity as much as possible. When Putnam explains to the sheriff how much we fear things that are different from us, he points to a spider on the ground. The sheriff's response is to step on it.

Yet more than a half a century later, those scary aliens aren't quite that frightening any more. What impresses now is just how mundane they are. They're not interested in our culture, our wars, our availability as food, our women, or our water. They don't even want to be friends. Earth is the equivalent of a gas station in a strange town off the highway. The idea is to get up and running as quickly as possible, and get out of here.

It's not surprising to find Ray Bradbury's name on the film, for this is a science fiction writer's concept, not a Hollywood one. When Hollywood wants to deal with an alien invasion they do *Independence Day* or *Mars Attacks!* The idea of adapting Robert Silverberg's *The Alien Years* would make no sense to them. It's an epic novel where the aliens who take over the Earth treat humanity with about as much regard as a farmer worrying about animals getting at his crops, something to be controlled, not engaged. Nor is this a film seen as satire, along the lines of Kurt Vonnegut's *Sirens of Titans*, where all of human history turns out to be a by-product of the need for one alien race to convey greetings to another. When seen in contrast to all the other alien invasion films, *It Came from Outer Space* turns out to be the exception to the rule and a stirring rebuke to egocentric Earthlings.

Maybe it's not all about us, after all.

KEEPING WATCH

Let's take a moment to laugh at the mundanes. Not the people who simply don't "get" science fiction and don't want to, but the ones who think they know all they need to about the genre: teenage boys at conventions wearing "Spock ears," stories about robots and ray guns instead of people, and—most importantly —escapism for people who can't face reality. Of course, even Leonard Nimoy hadn't worn Spock ears in over a decade, until returning to the screen one last time in 2009's *Star Trek*, and defining SF as "robots and rays guns" puts you somewhere in the era of Buck Rogers serials.

It's the last, though, that really grates. Even some of the people who make quality SF films and TV shows—or mainstream authors dabbling in the genre—are quick to put down the field even as they play in it. It's a condescension that you rarely see from those making westerns or mysteries or love stories. David Langford's multi-award winning newsletter *Ansible* runs a regular section entitled "As Others See Us" where he chronicles these snarky put-downs. In a recent issue he culls these gems about, of all things, the new *Battlestar Galactica*:

> "It's sci-fi, yes, but there are no aliens; there are androids, but they look just like us and are fervently religious; and both the best fighter pilot and the president are women. In other words, the conventions of sci-fi are borrowed only to be subverted..." (*Radio Times*, 7-13 Jan)

> Katee Sackhoff, who plays Starbuck in the series, seems to agree: "I'll meet people who haven't watched the show purely because it's on Sci Fi. I'm like, you've gotta be kidding me. It's not really science fiction. [...] they've turned it into a drama first and a science-fiction series second." (*Seattle Post-Intelligencer*, 19 Jan).

> (Both from *Ansible*, February 2006.)

It takes an astute critic—or, at least, an honest one—to recognize that science fiction is as legitimate as any other genre, and certainly more so than, say, the umpteenth horny teenage comedy obsessed with bodily functions. Academics, journalists, and critics should not make any apologies for considering SF as something worthy of study and analysis. In fact, the argument should not be limited to serious recent SF films, like *Gattaca* (1998) or *Serenity* (2005), as if this is a modern development, but should also take in the classics from the past, including the genre's Golden Age of the 1950s. Yes, there's plenty of prime cheese from the era that gave us such gems as *Catwomen of the Moon* (1953), but there are many great films as well.

Take two of the acknowledged classics that came out in 1951, *The Day the Earth Stood Still* and *The Thing*. For some, this might sound like a "Creature Double Feature" for a rainy Saturday afternoon, but in fact these are two serious movies that upon closer inspection are engaged in a debate over complex issues. Can we rely on our political and military leaders to always act in our best interests, or should we turn to our scientists for wisdom? Should the individual conform to what society deems is best for us, or should we stand up for what we believe is right, even when everyone is telling us we're wrong? Are there some things man is not meant to know, or is the pursuit of knowledge our highest calling?

These are questions with no easy or pat answers, and at a time when people tried not to attract attention, lest they be deemed subversive or worse, it was science fiction movies that grappled with them head on. Both *The Day the Earth Stood Still* and *The Thing* deal with humans encountering their first alien. *Day* shows the arrival of Klaatu (Michael Rennie), who lands his flying saucer in Washington and appears with his robot Gort. He comes in peace with a warning for humanity that if they think they can develop nuclear weapons and take them into space, they will find a galactic force out there ready to destroy the planet. On the other hand, if they are willing to let Gort-like robots police the planet and wipe out war and violence, Earth will be welcomed into the larger community of the stars.

The Thing, on the other hand, shows a remote scientific outpost at the North Pole which has discovered an alien who is best described as an intelligent vegetable. When the carrot man (James Arness) thaws out, he kills whatever he encounters. Cuttings obtained by one of the scientists grow and thrive when fed human blood. Here is a creature who, arguably, is the scout for a larger force ready to use Earth as a giant home and garden store, with us as the plant food.

Should we welcome these strangers or fear them? These aliens make clear that these competing films have two very different agendas. In *Day*, we are invited to share Klaatu's viewpoint and his frustration in not even being able to obtain a meeting to address all of Earth's leaders. He's offered an appointment with the president of the United States, but he is insistent that it must be all world leaders. Invitations are extended, but foreign leaders insist that the meetings must take place in their own countries. Meanwhile the military keeps Klaatu locked up at a hospital after he's shot by a nervous soldier who mistook an educational device for a weapon. The authorities are fearful and narrow minded, ignoring the evidence right in front of them, as when doctors express bafflement that the elderly Klaatu (by Earth standards) has the body and vigor of a man half his age. They have this discussion while sharing a smoke.

Klaatu escapes, assumes a human identity, and finds that all Earthlings are not as paranoid as their leaders. A mother and son (Patricia Neal, Billy Gray) befriend him, as does Dr. Barnhardt (Sam Jaffe), an Einstein-like scientist whose reaction to meeting his first space alien is to announce that he has a thousand questions to ask him. *Day*'s overt message is a warning about nuclear war, wrapped in a Christ-parable: Klaatu becomes "Mr. Carpenter," he's later killed and resurrected. As Peter Biskind points out in his book on the films of the '50s, *Seeing is Believing*, "*The Day the Earth Stood Still*'s respect for intellect makes heroes of professors and aliens..." Those who go against authority figures and the mainstream consensus are the ones worth heeding.

Now compare that with *The Thing*. The alien is thawed out at the remote North Pole site and goes on a rampage. The brilliant Dr. Cornthwaite (Robert Carrington) argues that learning from the alien is more important than life itself, and even takes blood from the medical supplies to feed cuttings from the invader. It is the patriotically named Captain Patrick Hendry (Kenneth Tobey) who successfully argues that strict military discipline must apply, and that they have to destroy the alien. Cornthwaite is isolated and nearly dies trying to communicate with the monster. At film's end, his willingness to risk his life earns the respect of the other scientists, but it is Hendry's decision to destroy the invader that is deemed the correct one. We're told to "keep watching the skies," which might apply to Soviet invaders as well as vegetable men from outer space.

The attitude toward authority, particularly that of the government and the military, is quite different. *Day* shows them unable to appreciate the message from space or the opportunity Klaatu's arrival represents, while *Thing* shows caution and lack of curiosity to be the only sensible reaction. Biskind, in *Seeing is Believing*, argues that this debate was taking place across numerous films in the '50s, and he doesn't condescend to the SF films that were very much part of that discussion.

What may be peculiar to SF films in particular is the question of whether there are some things "Man is not meant to know," a debate as old as the Bible and as recent as the Bush administration. *Day*'s Klaatu obviously represents an advanced civilization, with interstellar flight and robots only the most obvious technological improvements. To avoid charges of blasphemy, his revival from death is carefully delineated as finite since only the "Almighty Spirit" has the power of life and death. Even so, *Day* endorses the notion that humans—and other sentient beings—should take their explorations as far as they are able. It's notable that while Earth's political leaders squabble, Dr. Barnhardt has no trouble rounding up the planet's leading scientists and philosophers to meet with Klaatu.

Meanwhile *The Thing*'s Dr. Cornthwaite has clearly gone too far. He gives no thought to what will happen if the little alien cuttings he's been growing start to turn into an army seeking human blood. He talks about dying for knowledge, and while he is willing to risk his own life, he is also all too ready to risk the lives of others, without a second thought or even stopping to ask their permission. Cornthwaite's curiosity is seen as intellectualism run amok, and it is the sensible scientists who join with the military in destroying the alien. Here, deferring to authority and majority opinion prevails, and the free thinking scientist nearly dooms us all.

One would think science fiction would be the genre that unequivocally endorsed exploration and experimentation, but for every *Destination Moon* or *Close Encounters of the Third Kind* there's a *Frankenstein* or *Forbidden Planet* or *The Fly* that tells us that some knowledge is beyond the ability of mere mortals to handle. The current pseudo-debate over evolution can be better understood when we see that there is a long line of argument, even within science fiction, for putting limits on man's knowledge. Claiming to know the origins of life, to this way of thinking, is encroaching on God's territory. Like the myth of Icarus, these cautionary tales warn that too much knowledge can be a dangerous thing, and in 1951—only years after Hiroshima and Nagasaki—was that really an outrageous view to have? Are the Krell of *Forbidden Planet*, who lost their advanced civilization overnight when they unleashed the power of their minds over matter, all that alien to us? Films like *Day* and *Thing* allowed this debate to be played out in our popular culture, even as most people were unable or unwilling to tackle them directly.

The best SF films, like the best SF literature, seek to provoke thought. People who are only noticing the robots and ray guns haven't really been paying attention at all.

DON'T CALL ME SHIRLEY

When I show my students *Forbidden Planet*, one of the first things I tell them is to remember that the fact that it stars Leslie Nielsen doesn't mean it's a comedy. The actor today best known for his numerous spoofs like *Airplane* and *The Naked Gun* was once considered a serious mainstream player. In *Forbidden Planet*, he is the hero of the story who saves the day and wins the girl—without a hint of irony in sight.

The more one learns about the movie, the more it becomes clear that this, more than any other film, is the crown jewel of the "Golden Age of SF movies." There are other films that endure from the 1950s, such as *The Day the Earth Stood Still* and *Invasion of the Body Snatchers*. There are others that are historic landmarks, like *Destination Moon* and *War of the Worlds*. However, *Forbidden Planet* is on the short list—along with later films like *2001: A Space Odyssey*, *Star Wars*, and *Blade Runner*—that can be said to have been the pinnacle of SF movies for their era. More importantly, it is a film that has had tremendous influence on what came after.

Start with the fact that this was an MGM production at a time when that studio was still considered the most prestigious of the Hollywood majors. Although not considered an A-list film by the executives, just the fact that it was being made at MGM meant that the movie's production values would be a cut above anything else out there. Walter Pidgeon, who played Morbius, was not the star attraction he had been in the 1940s (in movies like *How Green Was My Valley* and *Mrs. Miniver*), but he had matured into a leading character actor, having just appeared in *Executive Suite* in 1954. Putting Pidgeon in the movie was a signal that this was no schlock production, but a film worthy of serious attention.

Having a "name" actor in the cast freed the filmmakers to cast young up-and-comers for the rest of the film. Morbius's innocently sexy daughter was played by Anne Francis, who would become TV detective *Honey West* in the '60s and continue to work in TV in the decades to come. Warren Stevens, cast as the doctor, continues to work steadily, mostly on the small screen. Jack Kelly, who played Jerry, would enter the TV pantheon as Bart Maverick, a role he would reprise several times in a long career before his death in 1992. However, besides Leslie Nielsen, for many viewers of a certain age, the most recognizable face in the cast is probably Earl Holliman, playing the comical cook. He later found his niche as Angie Dickinson's partner in the '70s TV hit *Police Woman*.

To showcase this cast, MGM gave the movie the sort of polish that could only be dreamed about by other SF filmmakers of the era. As is well known, the writers looked to Shakespeare's *The Tempest* for their inspiration. The similarities may seem superficial, but they're there. Instead of shipwrecked sailors landing on an island run by the wizard Prospero and his daughter Miranda, a United Planets cruiser makes a landing on Altair IV, where a colony of Earth settlers has gone missing. All that's left is Professor Morbius and his daughter Altaira. Instead of the magical sprite Ariel from Shakespeare, we get Robby the Robot, living proof of the late Arthur C. Clarke's axiom that any sufficiently advanced technology is indistinguishable from magic. The misshapen beast Caliban becomes the film's "monster from the Id" that nearly destroys them all.

Having adapted the structure and some of the characters from Shakespeare to their own purposes, the writers developed their own story of the lost civilization of the Krell and how Morbius's growing mastery of their technology unleashed his own inner demons, killing off the other colonists as the Krell once self-destructed. This is a prime SF trope: there are some things that Man—or Krell—are not meant to know. Yet *Forbidden Planet* is clearly in love with technology as well, taking every opportunity to show off not only the alien tech, but also what humanity has achieved on its own. This is a universe of interstellar space travel, where United Planets can be seen as a peaceful force that is the precursor to *Star Trek*'s Federation. When Morbius gives Captain Adams and Doc Ostrow a tour of the Krell facility, everything is meant to impress us with its power and vastness. Robby, whose technology, we're told is "child's play," can produce parts for the space cruiser as well as sixty gallons of bourbon for the cook, simply by collecting and combining available molecules. So should there be limits on knowledge, as Morbius argues when he tells Adams he will dole out information from the Krell archives as he deems humanity is ready for it, or should we be racing into a fantastic and amazing future, as nearly every frame of the film seems to suggest?

Although the crew's ray guns seem like a cheesy special effect now, much of what we see is still impressive. Robby, complete with circuits that prevent him from harming humans, is one of the screen's great robots. The Krell sets and the space cruiser also continue to amaze. (One of SF film's great mysteries is what the Krell must have looked like given the equipment we see and, especially, those odd triangular doorways.) Credit goes to veteran MGM art director Cedric Gibbons and his crew for constructing a set to act as the surface of the planet, rather than simply going on location to the desert and hoping some exotic props and lens filters would do the trick. That included a 350' x 40' cyclorama surrounding the spaceship, creating the illusion that one could see for miles around it.

Special effects being what they were at the time, MGM decided to farm out some of the most difficult work to another studio. Animator Joshua Meador was brought over from Walt Disney Pictures to animate some of the effects, most notably the shots where the Id Monster is caught in the force field. Most of the visual effects, like the disintegration of the tiger that attacks Altaira, or the sparks when Robby is short-circuiting, included Meador's animation. Also brought in were Louis and Bebe Barron, who created the eerie electronic score used in the film. In order to avoid any conflicts with the Musicians Union, the landmark compositions were billed as "electronic tonalities" rather than "music." Nonetheless, no other '50s film comes close to making an SF film's music as an integral a part of the movie experience.

If it was simply that MGM put more money and effort into an SF film than other studios did at the time, it might not have been enough. For the studio, after all, this was still only a B movie. It's the fact that all this effort resulted in a film that rewards careful viewing that makes it still worth seeing more than fifty years later. Just two years before, Universal had attempted to make an expensive SF film, resulting in the lavish but vapid *This Island Earth*. In *Forbidden Planet* we not only get the ongoing debate on the limit of knowledge, but an equally interesting—if unspoken—discussion of human sexuality. Why is Morbius so jealous of the men attracted to his daughter? Note that when we see the miniature of Altaira—as she appears in his own thoughts, Morbius explains—it is in a most revealing outfit. We also note that after she makes clear that she welcomes the men's attention, even if she doesn't fully understand it, the tiger that was previously a tame pet to her turns into a wild beast. *Forbidden Planet* is among the few '50s SF films that can be said to have a rich subtext. Indeed, it quickly becomes obvious that the Krell technology isn't the only thing being repressed on Altair IV.

Forbidden Planet would point the way for future media SF in a number of ways. From Robby the Robot's numerous appearances in subsequent movies and TV shows to the special effects, from *Star Trek* to *Star Wars*, this is a film that continues to influence the genre. It's a film that showed more than fifty years ago that a science fiction movie could succeed with wit and intelligence, indeed, even with Leslie Nielsen playing it straight.

RED ALERT

As you get older—pay attention, kids, this will happen to you someday—you discover that the things you assumed everyone knew are no longer true. It's a wake up call letting you know that time has marched on and the things you thought of as "current events" have now slipped into "history." It can become a problem when you're looking at an old movie or novel where understanding "topical references" suddenly requires footnotes.

It happened to me when I was watching *The Russians Are Coming, The Russians Are Coming* (1966) with my daughter, then in second grade. It's a comedy about a Russian sub that gets stuck off of Martha's Vineyard, and the crew's desperate attempts to get away before they are discovered. My daughter asked what to her seemed a perfectly obvious question: "Why are the Americans and Russians scared of each other?"

She knew Russians, of course. Her baby sitter was Russian. So why were the Russians afraid of being found, and why did the Americans get so hysterical when they learned there were Russians on the island? It wasn't easy compressing nearly half a century of history into a simple explanation. I told her that this happened a long time ago, when America and Russia were afraid they were going to have a war. Fortunately, it didn't happen. Satisfied, she went back to the movie.

However, it got me thinking. There are a lot of Cold War-era films that will make as much sense to younger audiences as Shakespeare's histories. *Fail Safe. Seven Days in May. The 27th Day. The Bedford Incident.* Are these films doomed to be forgotten or, worse, treated as "nostalgia," or can they transcend the concerns of their time and still speak to modern audiences? Of particular interest are two classic SF films that I've used in college courses, *Dr. Strangelove, or, How I Learned to Stop Worrying and Love the Bomb* (1964) and *Colossus: The Forbin Project* (1970).

In *Dr. Strangelove*, General Jack D. Ripper (Sterling Hayden) gives the Strategic Air Command orders to attack the Soviet Union under a protocol that assumes that Washington and the civilian leadership have been destroyed. Of course, this hasn't happened, and President Merkin Muffley (Peter Sellers) is appalled that such a plan even exists. He's chagrined when he's reminded that he approved it himself after a rival politician claimed "our nuclear deterrent lacked credibility." When the president insists that there were supposed to be safeguards to make sure a lunatic like Ripper couldn't launch a nuclear war on his own initiative, General

Buck Turgidson (George C. Scott) insists that they needn't throw out the whole program because of one slip up.

This is black comedy about bureaucracy out of control. Director Stanley Kubrick would dabble in satire again, but he would never go for laughs the way he does here. It helps to have Peter Sellers in three roles—not only as the Adlai Stevenson-like president, but as Lionel Mandrake, a British officer temporarily assigned to work with Ripper, and as ex-Nazi scientist Dr. Strangelove himself. Kubrick moves effortlessly back and forth between three locations: Burpelson Air Force Base, which Ripper has cut off from the outside world; one of the attacking war planes, led by Major "King" Kong (Slim Pickens, in a role originally intended for Sellers, who couldn't master the Texas accent); and the top secret War Room at the Pentagon. Everyone is working at cross purposes. Ripper is intent that there be no turning back, leading to American troops firing upon each other when the president orders that communications be re-established with Burpelson. The president invites Soviet ambassador DeSadeski (Peter Bull) into the War Room to demonstrate to the Russians that this is a horrible accident and not an attempt to start World War III. Meanwhile Kong and his crew (including a young James Earl Jones in his first film role) "show initiative" by doing whatever it takes to complete their mission, not knowing that it will set off the Doomsday Device that will end life on Earth as we know it.

Quite apart from the Cold War trappings, this is a film in which irony abounds. Indeed, someone looking for an illustration of irony need look no farther than the scene where the president breaks up a scuffle between DeSadeski and Turgidson (who found the ambassador taking photos with a hidden camera) with the immortal words, "Gentlemen, you can't fight in here—this is the War Room!" There's also DeSadeski's explanation of why the Russians built the Doomsday Device, which will enshroud the planet in a radioactive cloud should their country come under attack. Tired of the arms race, and with a population demanding consumer goods, the Soviet leadership saw this as a comparatively cheap way out. The deciding factor, though, was learning that the US was developing the same technology. When the president claims to have no knowledge of any such research, DeSadeski's reply is withering: "Our source was the *New York Times*."

Dr. Strangelove is also filled with unexpected sexual humor, starting with the names of the characters. Most are easy to decode, all suggesting potency, fertility or, in Ripper's case, sexual violence, but those looking for a challenge should try to explain the derivation of the president's name to a roomful of college students. (A Google search should do it if you need assistance.) These join with a variety of visual and verbal gags linking nuclear madness to sex. The opening scene is of a bomber refueling in mid-air. While the two planes are linked in seeming coital bliss, the soundtrack provides a lush arrangement of the romantic standard, "Try a Little Tenderness." Later, when Col. "Bat" Guano (Keenan Wynn) finds Mandrake in an office with Ripper's body, he decides that Mandrake is a "deviated prevert" who has killed Ripper to cover up his "preversions." And, of course, at the end, there's Strangelove's explanation of how they could survive a nuclear winter hiding in mineshafts, with ten women for every man. When asked if that will mean the end of traditional monogamy—for men, at any rate—Strangelove chortles, "Regrettably, yes."

Ripper's motivation may be the biggest joke of all. He's trying to protect "our precious bodily fluids" from contamination, a theory he developed when he noticed his "loss of essence" after experiencing "the physical act of love." What it sounds like is that Ripper is either ignorant of the male arousal cycle or, even more appropriately, he's impotent. By starting World War III, he's firing off his missiles by other means.

These sex jokes are not just schoolboy humor inserted into the political satire. In mixing life and sex with death, Kubrick shows just how confused these characters are in sublimating their sex drives into nuclear annihilation. In one of the film's best gags, Major Kong goes through the crew's survival kits, which include nylons, lipstick, chewing gum, tranquilizers, sleeping pills, pep pills, one hundred dollars in gold, and one government-issue prophylactic. "Shoot, a feller could have a pretty good weekend in Vegas with all that stuff," says Kong. (Actually, he says "Dallas" but the line was rerecorded after the assassination of President John Kennedy.)

Dr. Strangelove remains a potent brew for modern audiences, which should have no trouble relating to self-serving officials, wars built on lies, and the fact that plain reason and logic seem to have no effect against those hell-bent on death and destruction. The enemy in *Dr. Strangelove* only seems to be the Russians. As with other Kubrick films, our real problem is ourselves.

In many ways *Colossus: The Forbin Project* came too late to be fully appreciated in its time. *Dr. Strangelove* and *Fail-Safe* had taken us through doomsday scenarios with no hope of escape years earlier. Then Kubrick's collaboration with Arthur C. Clarke, the landmark *2001: A Space Odyssey* (1968), changed the face of SF films. After HAL 9000, a mad computer was old news. It would be some time until *Colossus* could stand as an important film in its own right.

Dr. Charles Forbin (Eric Braeden) has completed a massive scientific undertaking. All of America's nuclear weapons and defenses are now under the control of Colossus, the most advanced computer ever created. The theory is that war has now been taken out of human hands. If you attack us, Colossus will retaliate without fail. We needn't worry about any General Rippers; the human element has been removed.

What happens next is as predictable as it is inspired: Colossus discovers there's a Russian supercomputer called Guardian performing the analogous task for the Soviet Union, and demands a link between the two. Every time the humans attempt to thwart Colossus, they fail, since it has the ability to rain nuclear death anywhere on the globe, including within the US. Much of the film is given over to attempts to outwit Colossus: by cutting off the link between the computers, by replacing the nuclear warheads with dummies, by coordinating action with the Russians. All are futile. What's worse, after each attempt, Colossus takes steps to make sure that such actions cannot be repeated. In one of the most chilling scenes, Forbin's Russian counterpart is executed on Colossus's orders under the threat that missiles will be launched if his colleagues do not comply.

The film raises some fascinating questions. Isn't Colossus simply carrying out its programming? It has been set up to prevent war, and it ruthlessly does so, taking any and all necessary actions to fulfill its task. As General Turgidson said about the bomber crew that wouldn't give up, Colossus is showing initiative. It's easy to misread the film as simply another story about a man-made creation gone out of control. Dr. Forbin even recommends that *Frankenstein* be required reading for all scientists. Yet is Colossus really out of control? Indeed, even Forbin denies that the computer is actually capable of independent thought. Unlike HAL 9000, which killed off most of the *Discovery*'s human crew in the belief it was saving the mission, Colossus is merely doing what it was programmed to do: prevent war, and protect itself against those who would attempt to keep it from fulfilling its task.

Once Colossus realizes that Forbin is the one behind these various attempts, it orders round-the-clock surveillance on its creator. In order to escape such scrutiny, Forbin has Colossus research its own data files on human sexuality, explaining that he needs privacy for this purpose and then bringing in a female co-worker as his supposed lover. During these rare moments of privacy, they are able to exchange information and escape detection.

What's ultimately frightening about *Colossus* is that it offers no way out. *Dr. Strangelove* ironically presents us the end of the world, complete with Vera Lynn singing "We'll Meet Again." *Colossus* offers us the end of human freedom as we know it. Forbin's final defiant speech about never giving in isn't very reassuring. As Colossus promises humanity peace and prosperity, perhaps the most disturbing thing is how many people would be willing to make the trade off.

Both *Dr. Strangelove* and *Colossus* contain messages that transcend their Cold War-era roots. While fashions and technology change, it's clear that some things stay the same. We're still pretty good at creating our own problems all by ourselves.

2001: A SPACE ODYSSEY IN 2001

When it was first released in 1968, *2001: A Space Odyssey* immediately garnered several claims to fame:

1. The special visual effects of spaceflight were "state of the art" even though that expression itself had not yet come into vogue. Not until *Star Wars* was released nine years later would the standard set by *2001* be surpassed.

2. It was a "head trip." The voyage by David Bowman (Keir Dullea) through the monolith in the final portion of the film became one of the key cinematic drug experiences of the era.

3. It was "incomprehensible." What *happened* to Bowman once he arrived in that sterile hotel room? What *was* the "Star Child?" How come the movie didn't tie up everything neatly in a bow? It's not surprising that the Oscar for best original screenplay went not to Stanley Kubrick and Arthur C. Clarke for *2001*, but to Mel Brooks, for his classic comedy *The Producers*.

More than a quarter of a century later, *2001* is considered a landmark in cinematic SF, and one of the few achievements in the field hailed as an artistic triumph (instead of merely a commercial success) by mainstream critics. Yet today's SF film audiences—trained by *Star Wars* and MTV to expect constant action and predigested story lines—may wonder why their elders make such a fuss over an old sci-fi film. The effects, while still impressive, are regularly equaled or surpassed each week on television, even on shows as pedestrian as *Star Trek: Voyager*. The "head trip" is passé in the era of "Just Say No." And the story may now seem less accessible than ever.

The problem is that the film requires the viewer to be an active observer rather than a passive couch potato. Director Stanley Kubrick lays it all out for the audience, but they've got to grasp it. He refuses to hand it to them.

Take the dialogue. For more than a half an hour into this 139 minute movie, there isn't any. The entire "Dawn of Man" sequence consists of grunts and howls, as the apemen scratching out a meager existence are transformed into the first tool users by the mysterious monolith. When the story shifts to the future—in a startling jump cut that equates a tossed bone with a space shuttle as merely different kinds of instruments—it's still a silent movie. We notice Strauss's "Blue Danube" soaring on the soundtrack, but Dr. Heywood Floyd (William Sylvester) is fast asleep on his way to the orbiting space station.

When conversation finally begins, we wait a long time for somebody to say anything of substance. Indeed, with one notable exception, the conversations of this film are *completely* small talk. We hear discussions of birthdays, conferences, sandwiches, and office morale. When the story jumps from the moon to the *Discovery* mission to Jupiter, astronauts Poole (Gary Lockwood) and Bowman engage in conversations consisting of little more than soundbites for the BBC or technojargon as they decide what to do with the HAL 9000 computer. By paying close attention, you can gather the details of the story, but because the conversation is so banal, the result is that we are kept at arm's length from the people on screen. Instead of identifying with the putative heroes of the story, we look at them with the same detached objectivity that the monoliths—or whoever is controlling them—regard humanity.

The one exception to this is, of course, HAL (voiced by Douglas Rain). The artificial intelligence is, ironically, the most "human" character in the film. It is noted that he speaks "with pride" of his work and his record of infallibility. When Bowman lobotomizes him, it is the most emotional scene in the entire film. Compare his "death" with the death of Poole or the scientists in hibernation. We don't see Poole asphyxiate; we see an anonymous and almost comic figure in a spacesuit. We never even meet the rest of the crew. Their deaths are depicted by a series of medical readouts as HAL turns off their life supports.

Yet when HAL pleads for his life, and then reverts to the "childishness" of his early programming, we are meant to sympathize with his plight. His breakdown, after all, was caused by *human* error: He was programmed with the truth about the *Discovery*'s mission, which was then to be kept from Bowman and Poole. HAL was meant to both serve and conceal, and the contradiction became too much.

While the adventure with HAL provides a good deal of the drama, it also provides a contrast with humanity's own adventure. Professor Richard Gollin of the University of Rochester has pointed out that *2001* is really a battle between Arthur C. Clarke's optimism and Stanley Kubrick's pessimism. Clarke may occasionally despair at humanity's ability to muck things up, but one comes away from his fiction feeling that intelligent and rational people, especially scientists, are the cure for what ails us. His sunny view of technology takes over in his sequel novels *2010*, *2061*, and *3001*, where he was no longer beholden to Kubrick's collaboration on the script. (See, also, Clarke's *Lost Worlds of 2001*, where he outlines some of the story ideas that were discarded along the way. Rather than featureless monoliths, Clarke's early intervenors are humanoid creatures who take a benevolent and almost sympathetic view of humanity's potential.)

Kubrick, on the other hand, believed that man's best-laid plans are merely foolish attempts to impose order on chaos. From the racetrack heist in *The Killing* to the American military in *Full Metal Jacket* to the sexual machinations of *Eyes*

Wide Shut, chaos wins every time. In his SF films, it isn't the technology that screws up so much as it is man's use and misuse of it. Think of the Doomsday device in *Dr. Strangelove* (1964) or the Ludovico mind control technique in *A Clockwork Orange* (1971): the machines do what they're supposed to do, but because the characters in the film rely on these tools to impose order for them, they inevitably fail.

In *2001* this scenario plays itself out with HAL, showing that Man the Toolwielder has taken this stage as far as it can go. People coming to the film from Clarke's fiction (especially the short story "The Sentinel") naturally assume that the discovery of the buried monolith on the moon is proof that mankind has matured and is ready for the next stage. Certainly, the ability to travel to the moon and discover a buried artifact is a long way from clubbing a rival with a bone. However *2001* suggests that we may not have traveled all that far after all.

Like the apes, the humans of *2001* are still engaged in tribal rivalries. (As with the collapse of Pan Am and the breakup of Bell Telephone, Kubrick and Clarke didn't predict the downfall of the Soviet Union either.) These 21ˢᵗ century humans still engage in hierarchical behavior with followers doing as they are told regardless of the harm it may cause. The cover story for the lunar discovery is the outbreak of a mysterious plague at the Clavius moon base. This is undoubtedly causing a panic among the families of those working at the base. Everyone, however, dutifully follows orders, even though it might have meant the death of a Russian crew that needed to make an emergency landing there and was denied permission.

We also get hints that several thousand years of evolution and civilization has still left us as beings primarily concerned with creature comforts, like good food and a warm bed. Nowhere in the film is there a hint that anyone is focusing on questions larger than those of power and advantage. Given that context, the climactic "light show" takes on a potentially subversive meaning. While it can be enjoyed as '60s kitsch (*MAD* magazine lampooned the film by having the monolith tell Bowman he had just crashed through the multi-story Jupiter Museum of Modern Art), rarely does anyone ask what affect the light show has had on *Bowman*.

When we see him at the end of the sequence, he appears shell-shocked. We might consider that he has been deprogrammed. Thousands of years of the assumptions and predispositions of a toolwielder have been stripped away, preparing him for the next step: his transformation into the "Star Child." The one real action we see him take here is as an old man eating dinner, a scene that ends with him clumsily knocking over and shattering a glass. Physical tools aren't going to be that important anymore.

As the first monolith arrives when the apes are asleep—and their guard is down—so does the final monolith arrive when Bowman is near death. Only then is he prepared to accept whatever it is that the monolith or its operator is offering humanity to nudge us to the undefined next stage.

As with most great science fiction, *2001* is more concerned with the present day than the future. The year 2001 was nearly forty years away when Kubrick and Clarke began their collaboration in the mid-'60s. Time moves on but, like *1984*, the questions of *2001* transcend the calendar. Depending on your age, you've witnessed major technological marvels becoming commonplace in your lifetime: radio, television, jet planes, personal computers, fax machines, home video, microwave ovens, cell phones, laptops, iPods.... Yet as we assimilated these new tools, did we change, or did we become more nearly the same? Does speedy travel make us consider that we all share a single planet, or does it ensure that every place looks like every place else, with generic hamburger franchises and cinema multiplexes? Has the speed of communication affected the quality of our communications, or we are just saying the same stupid things a lot faster?

2001 is really more a comment on the human odyssey than a "Space Odyssey," since it demands that we ask where we have been and where we are going. The ambiguity of the ending becomes clear when you note that, like the rest of us, Kubrick and Clarke don't have a clue as to where humanity is going to end up. Rather than pretend that they do know, they leave us with the Star Child contemplating the Earth, as we in the audience are left to contemplate it.

NERDS IN LOVE

A number of years ago, a student in one of my film classes did his term paper comparing the 1958 version of *The Fly* with David Cronenberg's 1986 remake. His argument was that the earlier version was better because it didn't have a lot of icky special effects, and the story focused on the scientist whose experiment had gone horribly wrong instead of the romantic triangle at the heart of the remake. He defined his standards well, applied them to the films, and drew the obvious conclusion. I gave him an A. I also felt he was completely wrong.

Film criticism is opinion, not received wisdom, and so the fact that he disagreed with me was less important than the fact that he presented his thesis well. However, I did note on his paper that I *did* disagree with him, and that the '58 film was little more than a lurid potboiler, while the remake was one of the best films of the 1980s. Note, I didn't say one of the best science fiction films. I think it is one of the best of the genre, but I think it goes beyond that. I think the film is one of the best films of the decade, without qualification.

When I teach the film, the first thing I have to do is warn the students to take Chris Walas's Oscar-winning special effects in stride. Yes, they're icky and gooey, but they're not there just for the shock effect. When Seth Brundle (Jeff Goldblum) completes his transformation into what he calls "Brundlefly," the character is played by a puppet. Yet at that point, we are so invested in the character that we sense Goldblum's presence even though there's no reason to believe he was even on the set when those final scenes were shot.

Ordinarily, my discussion of the film focuses on the romantic triangle between Seth, Veronica Quaife (Geena Davis), and Stathis Borens (John Getz). Stathis is the editor of the science magazine Veronica had worked for, and also her ex-lover. He is a creep in many ways, showing up at her apartment to take a shower because he still has a key. Yet in a film in which all three of the leads are broken people, it's hard to say that he is worse than the other two. When Veronica discovers she is pregnant by Seth, it is Stathis who is by her side as she seeks to abort what is almost certainly a horrible mutant. (That's director Cronenberg as the OB/GYN, by the way, fulfilling the punchline of Martin Scorsese's surprised reaction upon meeting the director of *The Brood* and *Scanners*: "You look like a Beverly Hills gynecologist.")

That romantic triangle is there, and it is the answer to those who moronically deny something is science fiction because "it's about people." There's no question that *The Fly* is a science fiction/horror story, and yet it is undeniably about people as well. Essentially, it is a chamber piece, as these three characters try to work out their fates in the horrific situation they find themselves.

For the purposes of this essay, however, I'd like to come at the film from a slightly different angle. This is a movie about us: the nerds, the geeks, the ones who preferred science or English class in high school to football or planning for the senior prom. It's a romantic tragedy about the problems smart people face, rather than focusing on winning the big game or becoming prom queen.

As Seth, Jeff Goldblum is the science nerd turned into romantic hero. His problem is not that he's the former nerd, but that he lacks the experience to handle being the hero. Veronica meets him at a party for cutting edge scientists, and he promises her that if she comes back to his place she'll see something really amazing. It sounds like a line, and she says as much, but he's serious. He's been working on something that will truly change the world if he can work the bugs out, so to speak: transporting matter through space by breaking it down at one end and reconstituting it at the other. He operates alone, farming out pieces of the project for others to work out, but remaining the only one who knows the end goal. (In that sense, he also serves as a surrogate for the film's director.) Seth is eager to share his accomplishment with someone, and Veronica—a stunning and articulate science journalist—is the answer to his prayers. He's not ready to go public, though, and panics when he realizes she's ready to write him up immediately. They negotiate a deal where she will sit on the story while being given exclusive access to his working out the one great flaw he has yet to solve: transporting flesh as opposed to inanimate objects.

Seth is the nerd's nerd. He can rhapsodize about the "romance of the flesh," but he has reduced his wardrobe to numerous sets of the exact same clothes so that he never has to worry about what to wear. When Veronica becomes genuinely interested, not only in his work but in him, he is stunned. One can imagine that his romantic life has been nil, waiting in vain for the time when he will meet the woman who will finally appreciate him on his own terms, and here she is. That ought to lead to a happy and satisfying ending in which Seth finally comes into his own. That is not to be. Seth can't quite believe his good fortune, or the fact that Veronica really cares for him. When she goes off to deal with Stathis, who is threatening to run a story about Seth in spite of her agreement to wait, Seth completely misreads the situation. She says she's going to "scrape off" the remains of her past, as if Stathis is something she stepped in, but Seth becomes jealous, convinced that she is seeing her old lover because she still has feelings for him.

This is what is at the core of *The Fly*. Seth conducts the experiment that leads to his being "spliced" to a fly out of a sense of revenge. Veronica has gone off, and he doesn't get that she's not betraying him but is, in fact, acting out of a sense of loyalty to him. His interpersonal skills are so underdeveloped that he can only respond with jealousy. He simply can't accept that this beautiful, brainy woman likes *him*. As a result, he does the wrong thing, leading to all that horrific goo and gore.

On the old *Mary Tyler Moore Show* (this was in the '70s, for you youngsters) there was an episode in which a couple of Mary's friends commiserate about how horrible high school was for them. One of them notes that only two people are happy in high school: the captain of the football team and the head of the cheerleading squad. Everyone else, for whatever reason, feels they have fallen short. While Mary reluctantly admits she was head of the cheerleading squad, the joke works because it applies to all the rest of us. Wherever we were in high school, we felt inadequate, and our nervous fumblings and unrequited loves were a big part of it.

Seth Brundle resonates for us because he *is* us. When that great love comes along later in life, there's still that adolescent inside telling us we're not quite worthy, and that he/she will soon wake up and realize that a terrible mistake has been made. That's Seth's dilemma. When Veronica heads off to settle her score with Stathis, Seth leaps to the conclusion that she is somehow being unfaithful to him, leading him to take the stupid risk that transforms him into "Brundlefly." That's what makes it science fiction, and that's what makes it scary.

Yet all that goo doesn't gainsay the real human emotions that are driving the film. At times, nearly all of us feel like we're frauds who are only a step away from being exposed as the inadequate dweebs we suspect we really are. That's why the Cronenberg remake of *The Fly* is so powerful. Where the 1958 version has all sorts of scientific inconsistencies and exists mostly for it's now-dated shock value, the remake affects us not because of its gore, but because it cuts too close to the bone. Deep down we're afraid that the loves of our lives are just in it for themselves and are ready to head for the exit when something better comes along.

It may not be rational, but it's human. Ironically, for Seth Brundle, the price for learning this is that he loses his own humanity in the process.

WE COME IN PIECES: THE ALIEN AS METAPHOR

When, in a movie or TV show, the aliens arrive on Earth, or we meet them somewhere out in space, one thing is certain: whatever they're supposed to represent, it's *not* life on other worlds. Each genre has certain stock characters and situations which, in the hands of a master storyteller, can be used to turn a story into a work of art, or at least great entertainment. They can also be used to discuss things in a kind of code where facing it head on might be too heavy or controversial. For example the western *High Noon* is often seen as a parable about the Hollywood blacklist, with the Gary Cooper character systematically abandoned by all his friends and neighbors. In 1952, the blacklist was a topic filmmakers were unable to tackle directly.

Inevitably, stories where humans encounter beings from other worlds are really about us, not them. Often it's about the ways we deal with people we view as "other." If, at times, viewers become caught up in the lives of the alien characters, it's because they, too, are being used to tell us something about the human condition. Once we know what kind of human in alien guise we're dealing with, the point of the story becomes clear. Let's take a look at five different metaphoric aliens.

The alien as healer: He comes to Earth with a message of peace, assumes the guise of a Carpenter, is persecuted, killed by the authorities, and is then brought back to life with a warning that we must change our ways. That's the narrative of the Christian Bible, of course, but it's also the plot of the 1951 version of *The Day the Earth Stood Still*. Here the alien Klaatu (Michael Rennie) looks and speaks like us and wants to help us avoid destruction by getting us to give up our warlike ways. Although the film is obviously a product of the Cold War, the antagonists here are not the merely the Russians, but any political and military authority. Klaatu's message turns out to be best appreciated by scientists and other intellectuals, along with a widowed mom and her young son. In addition to the overt and deliberate borrowings from Christian theology, Klaatu is delivering the equally subversive message to question authority. Humanity will advance when it places its trust in wise people instead of powerful ones. Equally important, we must trust ourselves.

The aliens in both *Close Encounters of the Third Kind* and *E.T.* don't have that kind of agenda (*E.T.*, of course, just wanted to find his way home) but they also bring a message of healing. The characters most open to the message of the aliens in *Close Encounters* are those who haven't lost their childlike sense of wonder, while it is actual children who befriend and rescue E.T. In the latter film, it is the authorities—including the scientific ones—who risk the alien's life. Since we in the audience are asked to cheer for the aliens and the humans who befriend them, the message of peace and love and being open to new and wondrous things is key. It's grown ups who have forgotten how to see the world with a child's eyes who need help.

Even in the marvelous spoof *Galaxy Quest*, the silly but lovable aliens who put all their hopes in the cast of a canceled TV show end up helping the jaded actors realize their true potential. The pompous star (Tim Allen) who played at heroism must now truly act heroically while the bit player (Sam Rockwell) gets the opportunity to become a lead. Even the actor embittered by his career as a TV alien (Alan Rickman) learns to embrace what was great about his character.

In all these films, the kind-hearted, benevolent aliens serve as the means for both the viewer and the on-screen characters to realize what is best about humanity.

The alien as evil empire: There's no question that many aliens in Cold War era movies and TV shows were stand-ins for the Soviet Union. It's not surprising that those who attacked us in the 1950s films *War of the Worlds* and *Invaders from Mars* came from the Red Planet. If *The Blob* wasn't Red, it was certainly pink, and its goal was to overtake and consume everyone around it, almost like a Communist front group. These aliens were all after land and power, as even Marvin the Martian demonstrates in the classic Warner Bros. cartoon "Duck Dodgers in the 24th and a Half Century." Dodgers has already claimed Planet X for the Earth when the *Martian Maggot* spaceship makes a belated landing. Marvin tries to steal the planet, the only known source of the "shaving cream atom," for Mars.

The 1950s and 1960s gave us many examples of aliens as metaphorical Cold War rivals. In the original *The Thing*, the alien may have been a carrot monster from space, but here the military authority was shown to be correct in engaging in a shoot first, ask questions later policy. The brilliant scientist who wants to try to communicate with it endangers everyone. Even in carrot form, the movie makes clear, Communists can't be reasoned with. They must be defeated with brute force. When, at film's end, we're told to "Keep watching the skies," audiences knew it wasn't only for UFOs. It was also for those Soviet weapons which would signify the start of World War III. Similarly, the sneaky aliens of *Invaders from Mars* set up a base where they can plant devices that transform humans into willing slaves. Those parents, teachers, police officers, and military officials under Martian control become stand-ins for Communist fifth columnists.

The Klingons in the original *Star Trek* TV series served much the same purpose. Where the peaceful Federation (read: the West) wants only to explore the galaxy, the Klingons are out there stirring up trouble for their own nefarious ends. Such was the power of the metaphor that when the real Russians complained about the absence of a Russian crew member on the Enterprise—an egregious oversight given the successes of the Soviet space program—the character of Chekhov (Walter Koenig) was added. Yes, he was part of the Federation, but he would also brag about various Russian accomplishments, often rewriting history in the process. If the "real" Russian was now one of the good guys, the alien Klingons represented what we really feared about them.

The alien as corrupter: Sometime aliens represent our own worst excesses, not an external threat. One of the most famous alien invasions on television occurred in *The Twilight Zone* episode entitled "To Serve Man." The benevolent visitors cure our diseases, end famine and war, and even offer to take Earthlings to the paradise of their home world. The humans become complacent, happy to take all these gifts as their due without asking the price. The memorable price is that the alien book that gives the episode its title turns out to be a cookbook.

More recently, the revival of the series *V* has brought similarly benevolent aliens with ulterior motives. When the aliens offer their free advanced medical treatments to humans, was it a swipe at President Barack Obama's health care proposals or was it a critique of how we weren't taking care of our own? Whatever side of the issue you came down on, *V* had the answer: be suspicious.

The original *Alien* would seem to have a simple message: if you encounter an alien designed by H.R. Giger, go screaming in the opposite direction. However, in watching the film closely, it is clear that it is personal and corporate greed that sets the story in motion. The crew of the *Nostromo* see the opportunity for bonuses in retrieving the alien egg, while their corporate masters see their employees as expendable if they can manage to bring back alien technology or lifeforms. The profit motive proves to be a death sentence for nearly all concerned.

Two of the sequel *Star Trek* series—*Next Generation* and *Deep Space 9*—offer many alien races and metaphors, but in this context, the arrival of the Ferengi offered not only comic relief but a chance to show capitalism run amok. Their "Rules of Acquisition" spell out a philosophy that would not have been out of place on Wall Street in the last few decades, with adages like, "Once you have their money, you never give it back," and "Anything worth doing is worth doing for money." In the guise of aliens, these characters suggested that we are our own worst enemy.

The alien as victim: Sometimes the alien stands in not for our exploiters, but for our victims. The "Prawns" of the South African *District 9* were an obvious substitute for the native black Africans who had been subjected to apartheid. Often we'll see in a story set in the future that humanity has moved beyond racism and now projects their xenophobia and prejudice onto alien species. This was the driving force of the plot of *Avatar*, with the Na'vi substituting for American Indians, Australian aborigines, or whatever native population subjugated by western colonialism you prefer. Where mainstream critics compared it to *Dances with Wolves* and the animated *Pocahontas*, science fiction fans might have noticed the similarities to Ursula K. Le Guin's short story "The Word for World is Forest," which pitted militaristic humans against the native population on another planet. Instead of asking us to be open to other ways of thinking and living, as in the "alien as messiah" films, these are harsh warnings about the damage powerful civilizations do to the powerless.

Sometimes the victimized aliens are closer to home. Both the movie and TV series *Alien Nation* used the Newcomers as a marker for prejudice in our everyday lives. Although it was set up as a buddy cop story, *Alien Nation* was really about integrating the Newcomers into the American way of life. The human cop in both versions had to overcome negative attitudes toward the aliens and, in the series, eventually started dating one of them. This led to a hilarious scene where he's introducing her to one of his favorite aspects of Earth culture—the Three Stooges—and she looks at him admonishingly and says, "If you only knew what 'Nyuk, nyuk, nyuk' meant in our language." It was a low-key example of the theme of *Alien Nation*: each subculture in our society has things to offer, as well as providing a unique perspective on the mainstream world.

The alien as unknowable: Why do the unseen aliens in *Independence Day* attack Earth? Why do the pods in *Invasion of the Body Snatchers* want to replace humanity? What is the agenda of the superior beings who created the monoliths of *2001*? Why couldn't the super-intelligent Krell realize what unleashing the power of the mind could mean in *Forbidden Planet*?

In each case, the answer is, "We don't know." We like to have things explained and to see that things make sense. When confronted with the unknown, there's usually someone who wants to make it known, whether it means conquering a disease or climbing Mount Everest or heading into space. Yet there is much we don't know and can't know, and these aliens stand in for our fears and frustrations in such situations.

In movies like the original *War of the Worlds* and *Independence Day* there are people who want to welcome the space visitors to Earth; they must have so much to teach us, this could be the start of a beautiful friendship. Instead, the humans get blasted. One of the hardest things for people to understand is that not everyone sees the world as we do. It's why westerners who prize freedom of the press and Muslims outraged by editorial cartoons mocking their Prophet can't communicate with each other. The views are so divergent they might as well be from different planets. Aliens who don't appreciate humanity's diplomatic overtures are truly alien to us.

On the personal level, the truth is that we can never really know another person fully. Think of friends and family members who turn out to have interests —legitimate or clandestine—that are surprising when they come to light. Nowhere is this clearer than in a marriage where two people make continuing discoveries about the other, or evolve and change in unexpected ways. This often plays out in movies like *Invasion of the Body Snatchers*, where characters are taken over by aliens, making their loved ones feel that their family members or neighbors are not the "real" ones but not being able to explain why. In *I Married a Monster from Outer Space*, the aliens take over the bodies of men in a town, and one newlywed bride can't understand why her husband is acting so differently. Has there ever been a clearer metaphor for marriage? "You're not the person I married," is a claim that only needs the excuse of alien mind control in the movies.

Yet another level of the unknowable is for those who lives are informed by religion. To a western monotheist, the mind of God is beyond human understanding. Even when there's direct evidence of God's intentions, as in a Biblical text, mere mortals can't agree on what it really means. A film like *2001* approaches this ambiguity by keeping its aliens off-camera, instead letting them intervene through the mysterious monoliths. One monolith has a hand in evolution, when it turns primitive apes into tool users. Another is buried on the moon, ready to send a signal when humanity sufficiently advanced to have bases there. Yet another one is some sort of interstellar gate off of Jupiter, taking Dave Bowman (Keir Dullea) to be transformed into—possibly—the next evolutionary step. Whomever or whatever is behind the monoliths seems benign and even helpful, but we can't be sure. The rival ape killed by a crack to his skull certainly wouldn't have felt that way.

Finally, there is much we still don't know. Scientists and others keep pushing back the borders of human knowledge, but there are always others who will argue that we go too far. There are some things man is not meant to know or is not yet prepared to handle. If the arguments against stem cell research and cloning seem familiar, it's because they're the same arguments used by Morbius (Walter Pidgeon) in *Forbidden Planet*. Those long-dead and unseen Krell are a warning to us to turn back from the path of forbidden knowledge before it's too late. If they couldn't control the power of the mind, what chance do we puny humans have?

What's clear is that, whether friend or foe or beyond our ability to understand, the aliens in our popular movies and TV shows tell us little about whether life exists on other planets, but they speak volumes as to the nature of life back home on the planet Earth.

...BUT SOMEBODY'S GOT TO DO IT

We know all about space exploration from classic movies and TV shows. Except for the initial pioneers, everyone will be flying in pristine, high-tech spaceships with everything available at a touch of a button. There'll be a robot, of course, which will eagerly cater to your every whim. And what will happen when you touch down on the moon or Mars? There are various scenarios: ancient civilizations with beautiful women eager to be rescued by the Earthmen; alien artifacts ready to transport us to some transcendent stage; hideous monsters that must be destroyed or, at least, evaded.

Few films seem ready to address harsh reality. Both *Alien* (1979) and *Outland* (1981) broke the mold in at least one important way. They each presented life in space as just another dirty job. Reflecting the cynicism and malaise of the era, the films declined to romanticize life in space, and didn't assume their characters were gods, royalty, or larger-than-life heroes. Instead, whatever the films' other problems, they both raised some serious questions about what day-to-day life in space might actually be like.

In their setups, the films betray their non-science fictional roots. *Alien* presents us with the "commercial towing vehicle" *Nostromo*, which is carrying a refinery processing twenty million tons of ore, and is now returning to Earth from deep space. It has a crew of seven. *Outland* introduces us to a mining town on Io, the third moon of Jupiter, where they are digging out titanium ore. It has a crew of 2,144.

Does the *Nostromo* seem a bit understaffed? Do you wonder how the Io settlement feeds and supports all those people? It helps to know what films the directors are actually (re)making. After *Alien*, Ridley Scott would go on to do the SF landmark *Blade Runner* (1981) as well as the special-effects laden *Gladiator* (2000). Here he is essentially telling a haunted house story. Some like to compare the film to the low-budget chiller *It! The Terror from Beyond Space* (1958), but its roots go back much farther, to movies like *The Cat and the Canary* (1927) and *The Old Dark House* (1932). That's why the *Nostromo* only needs a few characters. The model is a group of people trapped in a remote space with no chance of escape, and then getting picked off by fiends, ghouls, ghosts, or, in Scott's version, a metamorphosing alien that bleeds acid.

Peter Hyams is essentially an action/thriller director. His forays into science fiction—including *Capricorn One* (1978) and *2010* (1984)—have been somewhat problematic, and *Outland* would not be an exception. His most successful SF film is arguably *Timecop* (1994), where he could play up the action aspect. In *Outland*— for which he also wrote the script—Hyams was consciously doing an American western in space, specifically the 1952 classic *High Noon*, in which Gary Cooper as a marshal is systematically abandoned by the townspeople when he has to face the bad guys for a showdown. Indeed, the film was called "*High Moon*" by many. So the same sort of operation that seems on auto-pilot in *Alien* requires a couple of thousand people in *Outland* because it's supposed to be the space counterpart to the frontier town.

Both films were criticized for failure to be "true SF" (whatever that might mean), although *Alien* was generally treated much more respectfully because of the surreal and original designs for the alien created by H.R. Giger. We hadn't seen anything like the monster of *Alien* before, and when it burst out of Kane's (John Hurt) chest after we thought he had been rescued from the "face hugger," audiences screamed. Tellingly, it would be James Cameron's adrenaline-driven sequel, *Aliens* (1986) that would eclipse the original and is considered the standout of the series.

Outland gets no respect. Indeed, after reading Harlan Ellison's savaging of it in the 1984 book *Omni's Screen Flights/Screen Fantasies*, edited by Danny Peary, one is hard-pressed to take the film seriously at all. Ellison picks it apart for its scientific inaccuracies, plot holes, and for attempting to take a western plot (that was, as he notes, being used as a metaphor for the McCarthy Era blacklisting of suspected Communists) and put it into a rough and tumble mining community in space. Where one could see why the meek settlers might be scared to help the marshal in *High Noon*, says Ellison, why would the roughnecks working a mine back off from helping someone going after the people who are poisoning them?

Given all that, it's significant that both films still make some very interesting— and serious—points about what life in space might actually be like. The first thing that strikes the viewer in both films is that the characters are unlike the space-faring characters that would have been best known to audiences of the time. Un-like Luke Skywalker and the rest of the *Star Wars* gang, they're not interested in saving the galactic empire or other issues larger than themselves. As for *Star Trek*, the first movie wouldn't be out until a few months after *Alien*, but the original TV series was thriving in rerun heaven. Yet other than in the secret agenda of the company in *Alien*, no one here is interested in boldly going to seek out new civilizations. People just want to do their time, make their money, and get home.

Alien begins with the crew of the *Nostromo* being woken out of hibernation. Their conversation indicates what's really on their minds. "Before we dock, I think we ought to discuss the bonus situation," says Parker (Yaphet Kotto). Parker and Brett (Harry Dean Stanton) work in maintenance, and aren't eligible for a full share of profits, in contrast to the rest of the crew. When the alien artifact is discovered, their initial reaction is to ask whether this accomplishment means they will finally get a full share.

The miners of *Outland* are single men—only top administrators get to bring their families—and we're told they work hard and play hard. Mark Shepard (Peter Boyle), the corrupt company manager, is there to maximize profits for the company and advance his own career. He tells Marshal O'Niel (Sean Connery), "There's a guy like me on every mining operation all over the system. My hookers are clean. Some of 'em are good looking. My booze isn't watered. My workers are happy. When the workers are happy, they dig more ore, they get paid more bonus money... It works. That's enough."

Their living conditions are not the best. We see rows of stacked bunks with only minimal privacy. Compact apartments are for the upper echelons—and the brothels. At least the workers in *Outland* get to relax when they're not killing themselves because of the drugs being pushed by the company that causes them to labor until their brains are fried. On the *Nostromo*, the only sense of rest outside the hibernation units seems to be in the communal dining area, where we're repeatedly told how bad the food is. Parker lingers over breakfast asking Dallas (Tom Skerritt), "Can I finish the coffee? It's the only good thing on this ship." Later, just before his chest explodes, Kane remarks, "The first thing I'm going to do when I get back is get some decent food."

The fact that the "town" in *Outland* allows for some recreation doesn't make it all that much more preferable. At the start of the film, Marshal O'Niel's wife and son take the shuttle out, tired of the mean life his one-year tour of duty offers them. We're told his young son has never even seen Earth.

If the conditions are rough and the motivations are less than noble, who *are* these people who make the journey into space for a living? In *Alien* we learn little of the characters' backgrounds. One can assume, although it is not stated, that they have few ties on Earth. The characters have traveled out of the solar system, and spend much of the time in hibernation. It will be many years before they return to their home planet. There's no indication of any shipboard romance. A love scene between Dallas and Ripley (Sigourney Weaver, in her first film) was scripted but never shot.

On Io, we learn that space mining doesn't attract the highest caliber of employee, even in the top positions. Crusty Dr. Lazarus (Frances Sternhagen) denigrates herself, "Company doctors are like ship's doctors: one shuttle flight ahead of a malpractice suit." Marshal O'Niel may be in charge of the law enforcement unit, but it's not a prestigious job, and we're told his career appears to have hit a dead end. As his second-in-command (James B. Sikking) puts it, "Nobody's here for their health. And they're certainly not here for the scenery."

So, quite apart from their surface stories of deadly aliens and showdowns in space, both films suggest that those who support space exploration and colonization have their work cut out for them. Actual people are going to have to be motivated to live under harsh conditions that may take years to improve, and they're not likely to be the white-robed philosophers of Things to Come (1936). More likely they will be the clock punchers of Alien and the people with nothing left to lose of Outland.

Both films touch on the issue of robotics as one possible solution, but both with dark results. In Alien, science officer Ash (Ian Holm) has been added to the crew at the last minute, but turns out to be not only an android, but also a company spy with an agenda. In order to bring the alien back for study, the human crew is "expendable." In Outland, miners grumble about automated units taking over their jobs. It was supposed to be a "temporary experiment," complains one, "They're still there."

That idea would be taken to an extreme with Blade Runner. Although set entirely on Earth, we learn that the robots (called "replicants") are doing much of the dangerous work in space—and some of the not-so-dangerous work as well. There must be some humans out there, or why build "pleasure models?" Perhaps the clearest sign of the task facing future recruiters are those ubiquitous electronic billboards in Blade Runner promising a wonderful new life in the off-world colonies. As with everything else in the future society the film depicts, we don't trust the happy, upbeat message about the exciting adventure ahead.

There will eventually be inhabited colonies on the moon and elsewhere, or at least many of us would like to believe that it is inevitable. However, these movies suggest that the road from barren wasteland to settled suburban community will be anything but smooth, even if such issues as energy, food, water, and oxygen are resolved. Those who think otherwise might contemplate the labor/management problems presented in Alien and Outland, and think about how they might be resolved without the benefit of Hollywood special effects.

BLUE GENES

It's rare that my interests as a fan and that of being a professional film critic so neatly overlap as they did when I got to interview writer/director Andrew Niccol upon the release of his underrated SF comedy *S1m0ne* (2002). Two years before, I had moderated a panel at the World Science Fiction Convention in Chicago on "The Best Science Fiction Films of the Decade." After a thorough discussion, three of the four of us named Niccol's previous film, *Gattaca* as the best single film of the 1990s. He was touched, if surprised, to hear himself listed as an SF filmmaker, in spite of having written *The Truman Show* and written and directed *Gattaca* and *S1m0ne*.

Gattaca was not a hit when it came out in 1997. It got mixed reviews and quickly vanished. Even the marriage that came out of the film—between stars Ethan Hawke and Uma Thurman—didn't last. Yet this is a film that looks better and more prescient with each passing year, and constitutes Exhibit A in any debate over why contemporary media SF can't be as full of ideas as written science fiction.

Part of the problem was that, at the time it was released, a story about people whose whole lives are determined by their genetic inheritance—with no regard to who or what they actually are—seemed far-fetched to most viewers, if they even understood what it meant. The movie came out several years before the completion of the Human Genome Project, and so the subject matter of the film seemed alien to many filmgoers. More recently, in showing it to college students, there was no such confusion, as DNA is now the stuff of prime time television melodramas.

Gattaca is the story of Vincent (Hawke), whose tragedy is that he's born the way nearly all of us were... the product of his parents having intercourse. In the near-future society he inhabits, this makes him an oddity. Prospective parents now design their babies, eliminating illnesses and defects, but also selecting hair and eye color, body type, and other features. A few even get some extra help, as we discover when we see a pianist with a few extra digits on his hands.

In one of the most quietly chilling scenes in contemporary SF film, the infant Vincent is taken by a nurse, some blood is drawn and tested, and almost instantly, his entire life is written for him. He is less than perfect, and therefore, most options are closed to him. Schools don't want him for fear he might get sick or injured, and his dream of becoming a scientist and space explorer is simply out of the question. He lives on the margins of society and remains largely invisible to them. He is an "invalid" in a society whose "valid" members are those who have been genetically screened before birth.

Niccol's brilliant idea for the film is to take what used to be a story of "passing" as another race (see, e.g., *Pinky*) and figure out how Vincent can "pass" as a member of the genetic elite. Such stories were inevitably an exposure of the false values of those elites that make such tactics even necessary, and it strikes close to home for the viewer who realizes that in this society, every one of us would be on the outside as well. It doesn't matter how healthy or fit or intelligent you are, if you carry the wrong marker in your genes, the discussion is over.

Vincent hires a shady fixer (Tony Shahloub) who, for a fee, will transform him. He has surgery to lengthen his legs, gets contact lenses to overcome his faulty eyesight, and—key to the whole subterfuge—meets Eugene (Jude Law), a perfect specimen who, unfortunately, is now paralyzed from the hips down. Nature may have won out over nurture in *Gattaca*, but real life experience still has a role to play. Vincent, now calling himself Jerome, gets a job at the Gattaca research facility where he will get his chance to go into space. In order for him to pass the numerous physical and medical tests he is required to take on an almost daily basis, Eugene will provide him with the human detritus "Jerome" needs to demonstrate proper DNA: hair, flaked-off skin, urine, blood.

This is where Niccol's world becomes especially rich in invention. This is not merely a society where the state is obsessed with DNA. Everyone is. A romantic couple might demonstrate their feelings by offering up samples, like a strand of hair, that the other can get tested to assess pedigree. Indeed, it needn't be voluntary. At a testing center, we see a woman having her mouth swabbed to collect some residue from having kissed her boyfriend. She can check him out without his knowing.

Meanwhile, Vincent daily risks exposure as a "de-gene-erate," someone trying to gain status through the use of someone else's DNA. He meticulously keeps his own desk and work station clean not because he's a futuristic Felix Unger, but because he knows that one strand of his own hair can give the whole game away. Vincent has no choice but to buy into the values of the culture that will allow him his dream of space travel. He has to deny who he really is, a terrible indictment of how a member of a minority must suppress himself to fit in.

What of that majority culture? Eugene is a bitter, broken "superman," who should have everything on a platter and instead finds cruel reality has trumped his designer genes. Most of the people who work with "Jerome" have to willfully ignore the evidence that indicates he's not who he says he is: when his ID photo pops up on screen after one test, it is Eugene's picture, not his. Yet no one sees anything but the sparkling example of genetic perfection they believe him to be.

Most interesting is Irene (Uma Thurman), a colleague of "Jerome" who becomes romantically involved with him as well. She has the right genes, but because a genetic marker indicates the possibility she might develop a heart murmur, she is limited in her choices. Unlike Vincent, she accepts the limitations society puts on her, and incorporates them into her self-image. It is not until, inevitably, she finds out the truth that she discovers she has been limited not by her genes, but by her attitude.

The plot turns on a murder at the Gattaca facility, so cops are all over the place, and Vincent risks discovery at any moment. One of his real hairs is found, and since he is there as "Jerome" and there is no record of Vincent—except, ironically, as a janitor who once worked there—he becomes the prime suspect. The only thing he has going for him is that no one really sees him. They see who he is successfully pretending to be. Niccol makes sure we don't get too smug about this by pulling off a few tricks of perception himself. When two detectives arrive to take charge of the case (Alan Arkin, Loren Dean), we automatically assume that the older cop is the senior one, and are pulled up short when it is the younger one giving the orders. We see what we expect to see, Niccol seems to be saying, until we can not avoid the truth any longer.

Indeed, while no one—including Niccol—seems to think the society of *Gattaca* will come to pass in this form, we are already seeing aspects of it in our lives. The ever-expanding testing in schools and workplaces for the "war on drugs" is supposedly for our own good, opening us up to all sorts of further intrusions. Insurance companies and employers who want to exclude (or charge higher premiums) for illnesses you may not have, but carry a genetic marker for, provide yet another sign of what might be called the "Gattaca" culture popping up in the real world.

The ad line for the film in its original release was "There is no gene for the human spirit," and that's what the film is really getting at: we're more than our DNA. The fate of the various characters turns on their choices, not their genes. Vincent's secret becomes known to a few characters, including one unexpected moment at the end of the film—not to be given away here—which reminds us that people are a combination of what they are born with and what they do with it. Vincent can no more transform himself into "Jerome" and eradicate who he really is than society can force Vincent into the discard heap they label "invalids."

In an essay, my friend and colleague MaryAnn Johanson bemoaned the dearth of serious SF films coming out of Hollywood in recent years. While her point is well taken, I'm not quite as willing as she to write off Hollywood all together. *Gattaca* may prove to be the exception to the rule, but it deserves a place of honor in any pantheon of the great SF films.

2009: A MIRACLE YEAR?

For film historians, 1939 was an incredible year at the movies. It was the year of *Gone with the Wind* and *The Wizard of Oz*. It was the year of *Intermezzo* and *Mr. Smith Goes to Washington* and *Gunga Din* and *Ninotchka*. So many directors and stars did their best work in 1939. In many ways, it's the high watermark for the classic Hollywood studio system. Many reasons are given for why it happened, from the studios having overcome the effects of both the Depression and the transition to sound, to this being the eve of World War II.

For science fiction movie fans, the Golden Age is the1950s, the era of *Destination Moon* and *The Day the Earth Stood Still* and *The Thing* and *Forbidden Planet* and *Invasion of the Body Snatchers*. In the aftermath of the war and the dawn of the atomic age and the space age, as well as the onslaught of the baby boom generation, there was a new audience for movies about outer space and science and the unknown. Sure, there was plenty of trash, but the great films of the era remain great more than half a century later.

Such eras are only obvious in retrospect. Those of us lived through the 1970s may have noticed that there were a lot of good movies out there, from *The Godfather* to *Taxi Driver* to *Star Wars*, but it took a number of years to appreciate that we had lived through a cinematic renaissance, with the coming of age of a new generation of filmmakers including Francis Ford Coppola, Woody Allen, Martin Scorsese, Brian DePalma, and Steven Spielberg. When you're in the midst of it, it's hard to have the perspective to be able to see if you're witnessing something extraordinary and lasting, or simply enjoying a bunch of good movies that happened to come out at the same time. So take the following with a grain of salt.

It's obviously too soon to know if 2009 was a pivotal year for the science fiction film, but there's no question that we saw an amazing array of quality movies within a twelve-month period. What was impressive were not simply how many good movies there were, but how diverse they were. Looking over the best of the year demonstrated a breadth and depth in the genre that was not typical where, usually, the truly memorable examples are few and far between. What happened in 2009 was that we saw films that advanced the technology and we saw films from new voices and new locations. Even material that seemed familiar was taken in new directions.

Perhaps the biggest surprise of the year was the rebooted *Star Trek*. J.J. Abrams, best known for the TV series *Lost* and *Fringe*, took a beloved, if tired, franchise and breathed new life into it, immediately putting it in a league with *Batman Begins* and *Casino Royale*, movies which reinvented the Batman and James Bond series. The new *Star Trek* was essentially the story of how James Kirk (Chris Pine) joined Starfleet, met Spock (Zachary Quinto), Dr. McCoy (Karl Urban), and the rest of the classic crew, and eventually became captain of the Starship *Enterprise*. There was a villain in there, a rogue Romulan named Nero (Eric Bana), but we needn't worry too much about that. While the action and special effects were more than acceptable, what made this one of the best *Star Trek* films in some time was the reimagining of the characters.

Tackling a project like this had to be daunting. Gene Roddenberry's original television series ended its run 40 years ago, spawning a movie series and several sequel TV shows in the process. There was a lot of history here, with more than a few obsessive fans ready to quibble over any deviation from the "canon." The new film deftly solved that problem by positing that the story was taking place in an "alternate timeline." Viewers were invited to go with the flow. When characters died or did something they're not "supposed" to do, that's because this is a different universe. This was not your father's *Star Trek*. Literally.

The characters were not only recreated, they were reinvented. In many ways they were younger versions of Sulu (John Cho), Chekov (Anton Yelchin), Uhura (Zoe Saldana), and Scotty (Simon Pegg), as well as Kirk, Spock, and McCoy. There were some marvelous performances here as they succeeded in making the characters their own without doing damage to the memory of the original cast. Fans of the original could enjoy all sorts of details that evoked the original show, while newcomers had fun as this feisty crew got to know one another.

Much attention was given to the performances by Pine and Quinto, since Kirk and Spock are the central characters. They nailed it. Pine caught the swagger and bravado of a young William Shatner the way Ewan McGregor was able to channel Alec Guinness when he was playing the younger Obi-wan Kenobi in the *Star Wars* prequels. Quinto's Spock had the most difficult character arc of the story, and the hardest acting challenge. The original Spock, Leonard Nimoy, appeared in several scenes. To Quinto's credit, seeing Nimoy in the role that made him famous did nothing to detract from Quinto's younger version.

The consensus among fans seems to be that the story was weak (what was the problem with the Romulans again?), but it didn't matter because the characterization was so rich and the audacity of the reboot—destroying Vulcan!?—made this so incredible to watch. The inevitable sequels will need stronger plots if they are to survive, but *Star Trek* showed that an SF franchise can be shaken up and still be accepted by the fans, especially if it is done with affection and respect.

# # #

Of course, getting a blockbuster SF film out of Hollywood isn't a big deal. They have their hits and misses, but it *is* what they're good at, especially if there are competent directors and writers involved. Science fiction films from other countries are not quite as common, but not unheard of, as when Mexican director Alfonso Cuarón adapted the British *Children of Men* (2006). However, what were we to make of *District 9*, a wholly original science fiction movie out of South Africa? As it turns out, it was to recognize it as one of the best SF films of the year.

Like *Alien Nation* (1988), it begins with the premise of a large alien population being stranded on Earth. The similarities end there. Their huge spaceship stalled out over the skies of Johannesburg, South Africa. When humans investigated, they found a demoralized and starving population. The aliens—dubbed "prawns" because they look like human-sized shrimp—were brought down to what was supposed to be a temporary refugee camp.

Twenty years later the area, called District 9, has become a crime-ridden shantytown. Some of the film is presented in documentary-fashion, with interviews and news footage. Although a couple of the aliens become important and even sympathetic characters, they remain completely unknown to us. Why they came here and what their goals are (other than survival) are a mystery. Even their clicking speech requires subtitles, although the human characters on screen seem to understand it.

The story focuses on Wikus van der Merwe (a memorable performance by first-time actor Sharlto Copley). Wikus is a cheery corporate bureaucrat who was put in charge of evicting the aliens to an even more remote location because his father-in-law's company had been given the job. He is casually bigoted toward the aliens, not really hating them the way some of the other humans do, but treating them with about the same respect you might give a stranger's bratty child. When he gets exposed to some alien substance, it starts transforming him into one of the prawns. As the humans, including his own father-in-law, seem ready to sacrifice him for their own ends, he is forced to rethink his loyalties.

Director Neill Blomkamp, who co-wrote the film with Teri Tatchell, doesn't make it easy for us. At first, it plays like a thinly disguised parable about apartheid, with the white and black South Africans showing equal ease at suppressing the prawns. (It's telling that we never learn what name the aliens give themselves.) However, as the film shifts its focus to Wikus—with Copley going through a roller coaster of emotional upheavals over the course of the movie—it becomes more complex. Like Wikus, audiences found themselves siding with the aliens, but we couldn't be sure if that was the right choice. As one of the talking heads says at the end, we aren't certain about what's going to happen next. When some of the "prawns" escape, we don't know if it's a happy ending. Are they finally free, or are they coming back with an armada to wreak their vengeance?

What lingers is the casualness with which we are willing to reduce others to sub-human conditions. The fact that they are aliens is almost beside the point. Is it part of the human condition to need someone to look down upon? If so, this wholly unexpected film from South Africa made us realize that science fiction is a more international genre than we may have realized.

District 9 was not only the SF offering that wouldn't have been out of place in the arthouse. *Moon* was another surprise, it being the feature directing debut of Duncan Jones, who was formerly known as rock star David Bowie's son Zowie. This minimalist film was essentially a tour de force for Sam Rockwell, whom genre fans first noticed as the anonymous crew member in *Galaxy Quest*. Rockwell played Sam Bell, who works on a moon base by himself with his only company being a robot named Gerty (voiced by Kevin Spacey). His job is overseeing a lunar mining operation that is crucial to supplying Earth's energy needs. It's almost all automated, but it needs some human oversight, and that's where Sam comes in.

He's near the end of a three-year stint, and the isolation from his wife has been telling. The loneliness of space is not a new idea in science fiction, but it is usually not the subject matter of cinematic SF. When it's been tried, as in Andrei Tarkovsky's *Solaris* or the more recent remake, the result is affected and off-putting. Here the focus wasn't on the meaninglessness of life or how alienation is the human condition, but on what would drive a man to take this job and how it would affect him. Over the course of the story, we learn that things are not quite what they seem, and the focus is less on humanity than on one human struggling to retain his sanity.

Moon was the sort of film that was never going to be a big hit with audiences craving action, and was too wrapped up in its lunar setting to hit the sweet spot of the arthouse crowd. Yet discerning SF fans who found it discovered a remarkable movie that was intelligent, moving, and provocative. It's not surprising that when the Hugo Award nominations came out for the 2010 World Science Fiction Convention, *Moon* joined *Star Trek* and *District 9* among the nominees. (The other nominees were *Avatar*, discussed below, and Pixar's delightful—if not really science fictional—*Up*.)

Not every SF film that came out in 2009 was a masterpiece, but there were a number of very good films which added to the sense the year was special for the genre. As with Audrey Niffenegger's best-selling novel of the same name, the movie version of *The Time Traveler's Wife* was positioned as a mainstream romance rather than as science fiction.

Henry DeTamble (Eric Bana) discovers at an early age that he can travel in time. He has no control over where or when he goes or how long he stays. He can't even bring his clothes with him, which leads to him not only being lost but naked, with no idea of when he will return to his "present." The story makes some attempt to explain this as a genetic defect, but the why and the how aren't really important. As with the best science fiction—indeed, as with the best books and movies—we focused on the characters and the issues in their lives. When Claire Abshire (Rachel McAdams) first encounters Henry in a research library, it's an odd moment. She's known him for years. He's been visiting her since she was a little girl. She already loves him, knowing they are destined to be together. Henry is meeting her for the first time.

The story is rife with these paradoxes—as when one version of Henry disappears at their wedding and another shows up—but it's the love story that moves us. Henry comes and goes, and Claire can only wonder when he will return. As with any couple, they have to make their situation work without ever fully understanding the other person. His time shifting becomes a metaphor for the challenges any couple faces in going through life together. Director Robert Schwentke and writer Bruce Joel Rubin do a nice job of adapting the novel, simplifying and abridging the story but maintaining the spirit of it. Some may object to the changed ending, but what works on the page isn't necessarily what works on screen. Both leave us with an appreciation of the power of love over time.

Zombieland was another hybrid. All zombie films are horror films of a sort, but depending on the details, some cross over in the Venn diagram of SF/fantasy/horror into science fiction as well. Ever since George Romero's *Night of the Living Dead*, the source of the zombification has shifted from magic to pseudoscience. *Zombieland* proved be a delicious send-up of the genre, and the perfect American counterpart to *Shaun of the Dead* (2004). After *Shaun*, one might have thought the ultimate spoof of "living dead" movies had been done. *Shaun* was great fun, but it was a decidedly British take of this SF/horror subgenre. The British can do great zombie films (such as *28 Days Later*), however, there remained plenty of room left for an American take-off.

Jesse Eisenberg played our hangdog narrator, known only by the name of his hometown of Columbus. He's a loner—actually a bit of a loser—who has survived the zombie apocalypse by keeping to himself and following the strict rules he shares with us, such as always wearing your seatbelt and not thinking you've killed the flesh-eating monsters with only one shot. He's headed to Ohio to see if his parents have survived when he runs into Tallahassee (Woody Harrelson), a gun-toting redneck who doesn't simply defend himself against the zombies, but positively enjoys killing them. He's the one who insists on "no names," arguing that the few humans left can't afford to develop emotional attachments. This is proven when they run into two sisters Wichita (Emma Stone) and Little Rock (Abigail Breslin) who cause almost as much trouble as the zombies. Soon the four are linked together on a trip to California, where Little Rock believes a zombie-free enclave exists on the grounds of an amusement park.

What makes this work is a sharp cast—including a hilarious cameo by Bill Murray—and the script by Rhett Reese and Paul Wernick, which turns the end of the world into a joke. One has to go back to *Night of the Comet* (1984) to find a movie that plays the apocalypse for laughs like this. There's no mourning for humanity, no vowing to find a cure or restart civilization. As Columbus tells us, they're living in Zombieland now, and new rules apply.

Less successful, but nonetheless interesting, was *The Invention of Lying*, Ricky Gervais's parable that proved quite inventive before spiraling out of control. Gervais, who co-wrote and co-directed the film with Matthew Robinson, gave us a recognizable world with the notable exception that no one knows how to lie. That doesn't simply mean falsehoods are unthinkable. It means that everyone blurts out the truth, even when discretion would dictate otherwise. When Mark (Gervais) shows up early for his date with the luscious Anna (Jennifer Garner), she volunteers that she had not only been getting ready, but that she had been masturbating. TMI (too much information), as the kids would text.

The early portion of the film examines the ramifications of its premise. When Mark learns how to utter false statements, everyone immediately accepts them at face value. It doesn't matter if he's trying to withdraw more money than he has in his account, telling a woman that if they don't have sex the world will end, or telling his friend that he is black. The fact that he has said it means it must be true.

Obviously, fiction is impossible in this world, so movies consist of experts lecturing people on historical events. Mark is a writer of such films, but since his expertise is in the area of the Black Plague and the 13th century, no one is really interested. When Anna blows him off and his boss (Jeffrey Tambor) fires him, Mark discovers that the ability to say things that are not so gives him a leg up.

This is where the film gets into a potentially controversial area, unless viewers are willing to understand it differently than Gervais may have intended. When his mother (Fionnula Flanagan) is dying, he comforts her by telling her that she's going to a place where she will be reunited with friends and family, and live in a great mansion. When this gets out, the public wants to know more, and Mark ends up creating a story about "The Man In The Sky" who rewards those people who do good and punishes those who do not. It's easy to take this as a criticism of religion, which may be how Gervais intended it. Yet when we hear the ridiculous questions Mark gets asked, we see it's really a critique of those who deny free will. People who refuse to think for themselves are the proper subject of scorn, not simply those who act on faith. It makes us think about all the ways in which expressions other than verifiable facts serve us well: from sparing feelings with "white lies" to the truth of our lives expressed in fiction to the unprovable tenets of religious faith. Honesty is the best policy, but as Gervais's film makes clear, sometimes we need something more than just the facts.

Also little seen but worth tracking down was the animated *Planet 51*. The film opens with a couple necking in a car when an alien spaceship appears. It's a scene right out of the catalog of 1950s SF movies, and sure enough, it turns into *War of the Worlds*. The twist is that this is another planet which is replicating the 1950s by way of *Back to the Future*. Lem (voice of Justin Long) has just gotten a job at the local planetarium and is getting up the nerve to ask out the girl next door (Jessica Biel) when a real spaceship arrives containing a truly horrifying alien: an astronaut from the planet Earth.

Captain Charles Baker (Dwayne Johnson) is the astronaut as celebrity, sent out to explore with no real skills except playing well to the press and public. He is, in a sly reference to *The Right Stuff*, little more than "spam in a can." Now he needs to get back to his orbiting ship, but with everyone in an uproar over the "alien," he has to rely on Lem and his friends to help him out. There's a heavy of course, General Grawl (Gary Oldman), and a crackpot scientist (John Cleese) who wants to examine the astronaut's brain, but you can pretty much guess where the story is going to come out.

What was unexpected is where it came from: Madrid. Ilion Animation may not be well known yet—this is their first theatrical release—but it is a debut that shows great promise the way so many animated also-rans do not. It spoofed the SF classics of the past without making you feel you'd seen it all before.

Of course 2009 provided its share of embarrassments as well. *Astroboy* was an attempt to reboot the classic Japanese *manga/anime* character. *The Road* was a bleak adaptation of Cormac McCarthy's equally bleak post-apocalyptic novel, which unfortunately led nowhere. And *2012* was a great amusement park ride but an utterly ridiculous movie. At the press screening in Boston, someone said before the film started that the dog will survive the end of the world because the dog always survives in Roland Emmerich's movies. At this point we didn't even know if there was a dog in the film, but sure enough there was, and it did survive, in one of the most ludicrous scenes in an already over-the-top film.

And then there was *Avatar*. Although not every one of James Cameron's films has been an artistic success, the simple fact about the King of the World is that he doesn't make boring movies. He's a compelling storyteller, and if he chose to be as prolific as, say, Steven Spielberg, he might have developed a much more varied body of work. Instead, his model seems to be the late Stanley Kubrick, spending years developing each project and always pushing the envelope. Cameron is no Kubrick—he's more from the heart than from the head—but with each movie, he strives to dazzle audiences with something they've never seen before. In movies like *Aliens*, *Terminator 2*, and *Titanic* he bypassed intellect and went right for the lizard brain. Love them or hate them, it was hard not to get caught up in the moment. With *Avatar*, he did it again.

The plot is *Aliens* in reverse. Instead of an evil corporation using humans as fodder against monstrous aliens, this time it's the humans who are the monsters and the gentle Na'vi—the seemingly primitive inhabitants of Pandora—who are facing doom. Jake Sully (Sam Worthington) has been recruited into a special program in which people are able to project themselves into specially grown Na'vi bodies. The humans want certain mineral rights on the planet and need the locals to get out of the way, but Dr. Grace Augustine (Sigourney Weaver) would rather make a peaceful deal than go in guns a-blazing.

It's essentially a battle between the corporate/military side, who treat the natives as a deadly nuisance, and the scientific/humanist side, who argue that the Na'vi may have something to teach us. The fight over Jake's soul—which divides its time between his war-injured human body and his dynamic Na'vi "avatar"—is the core of the film. Naturally, there's a love interest in Neytiri (Zoe Saldana), who is destined to be a tribal shaman, but for now is stuck teaching Jake how to live in his Na'vi form.

While it's easy to get caught up in the story, which culminates in a battle to determine the fate of Pandora, what really makes this a cinematic landmark is its vivid creation of an alien world. Watching it in 3D, the viewer became immersed in the flora and fauna of the world. Using a variety of technologies, including computer graphics and motion capture (for the actors playing Na'vi) the result was breathtaking and beautiful. Where movies like Robert Zemeckis's *Polar Express* and *A Christmas Carol* tried to create human characters and ended up creepily unreal, here the characters are supposed to seem strange and unhuman. Ironically, it makes the Na'vi seem that much more alive.

Just as audiences were wowed by the initial "morphing" effects in *Terminator 2*, the bringing to life of Pandora and the Na'vi is a quantum leap forward in movie special effects. It seemed so real you might have been tempted to book a trip there yourself. Indeed, there were reports of people who watched the film repeatedly and were depressed when they had to "come home."

A fair criticism of *Avatar* was the formulaic script (which had obvious antecedents in stories by Poul Anderson and Ursula K. Le Guin, as well as in western/historical movies as different as *Dances with Wolves* and *Pocahontas*). In the end, it didn't matter. While movies like *Moon*, *District 9*, and *The Time Traveler's Wife* showcased quality SF scripts, movies like *Star Trek* and *Avatar* showed that vivid acting or imaginative visuals could overcome flaws in writing.

Indeed, what the year 2009 showed us was that not only is the science fiction movie alive and well, but that it was so sturdy that filmmakers could take numerous approaches—from romance to animation to comedy to arthouse chamber piece—and come up with a winner. The critics and academics may still be behind the curve, but audiences and filmmakers alike see SF not as an embarrassment, but as a genre that continues to provide tremendous creative freedom.

(NOTE: The surprise winner for best dramatic presentation, long form, at the 68th annual World Science Fiction Convention, held in Melbourne, Australia, was *Moon*.)

PART II. CAMERA OBSCURA

The historic "camera obscura" was a device that could project live images through a small hole into a darkened room, where they were then turned right side up with mirrors. It is one of the precursors to photography and, thus, filmmaking. The movies in this section are ones that may not be deemed classics, or were well known at the time and then possibly forgotten, but that deserve to be seen anew. Not every work has to be a classic. There are times when sitting through five pretty good movies is a lot more satisfying than watching one masterwork and four disasters. There are some pretty good movies here, worth talking about if you've seen them, worth catching up with if you haven't.

SF, MY PARENTS, AND ME

A few years ago I got my mother to read Robert Sawyer's novel *Illegal Alien*. It's a courtroom drama involving a visiting alien charged with murdering a human. She enjoyed it. However, in order to convince her to read it, I had to explain to her that it was like a John Grisham book, only with some space aliens mixed in. A few years earlier, she had turned me on to Ken Grimwood's *Replay*, which I enjoyed. It's about a man who gets to keep reliving his adult life, keeping his memories. The time travel element is never really explained, which has never seemed to bother the many fans of the book.

Thus ends my SF history with my mother. This is very different from, say, the numerous infants and toddlers in tow I see at various cons. My mother never took me to a convention. I didn't attend my first Worldcon until the age of 34, and that was as a reporter.

Other than the two previously mentioned books and taking her to see *2001: A Space Odyssey*, my mother and I have no real SF ties. When I tell her I'm off to the annual 24-hour marathon of SF movies, which has been held at various theaters in the Boston area, she inevitably says something like, "Oh, that's that crazy thing you do. Have fun." I'm sure she doesn't bring it up in conversation the way, say, she might mention when I've been on television. (Just in case my mom should see this: she is a lovely woman, a devoted mother and grandmother, and never once raised an objection to my large library of comic books and, later, SF books.)

Now my father is a slightly different story. If you were to tell him he was a science fiction fan, he would deny it. He certainly doesn't read the stuff, and probably couldn't name any authors beyond Asimov, Bradbury, and Clarke, if even them. Yet in looking at how I came to be a fan in the first place, I'd have to pin it on him.

Certainly he would acknowledge taking me to the movies at an early age. I'm told I saw some monster movies around age 4. Obviously they didn't traumatize me. According to family lore, I was too busy consuming Chiclets to be frightened by what was going on onscreen. As I got older, I not only got to see the usual Disney fare, but such films as *The Seven Faces of Dr. Lao*, *Fantastic Voyage*, *The Wonderful World of the Brothers Grimm* (in Cinerama!), and *Planet of the Apes*. Indeed, I remember going with him to see all five *Apes* movies in one night when the last one of the original series was released.

On TV we watched some of the older SF films, including *Invasion of the Body Snatchers*, *King Kong*, *The War of the Worlds*, and *The Time Machine*, as well as such early '60s television fare as *The Twilight Zone* and *The Outer Limits*. Then, one night in 1966, a new show came on, and we were instantly hooked. It was the original *Star Trek*.

We weren't necessarily watching for the same reasons. I was 11, and was less interested in Captain Kirk's reputation as a babe magnet than with his encounters with the Klingons and Romulans, but it was something we could share together. Years later when, as a media critic, I acquired a couple of tribbles during the promotion of the *Deep Space Nine* sequel to "The Trouble with Tribbles," I made sure to send him one. I didn't have to explain what it was. He knew.

Since I've grown up, he doesn't follow SF as much any more, although he did become a devoted fan of *Next Generation*. (I have standing instructions to notify him if I ever meet Marina Sirtis, who played Counselor Troi. He's ready to travel on a moment's notice.) But *Babylon 5* or *Buffy the Vampire Slayer*? No, not even *The X-Files*.

So how did I become an SF fan without parents carefully paving the way? I don't think it's that odd at all. My parents encouraged me to read, to use my imagination, to explore. They didn't see movies or TV as wastes of time (with the possible exception of when I was going through my "Three Stooges" phase), but simply as another way of storytelling. Becoming an SF fan—both literary and media—was the most natural thing in the world. I liked the books and movies and shows, and they seemed to like me back.

Now that I'm a parent myself, I spend a lot of time wondering how I can introduce my daughter to this world. I've bought SF children's books. Artist and Godzilla authority Bob Eggleton provided the means to introduce her to Japanese monster movies. (If you think your youngster will like monster movies, start with *Godzilla's Revenge*. Ignore the title.)

In 2004, I took her to her first World Science Fiction Convention, and by the next January, she was wowing the crowd at the masquerade at Arisia, a Boston area regional convention. As she gets older, she'll either continue or develop her own interests and go her own way. With any luck she'll do both. Since she's only in third grade, I think I've got some time.

Meanwhile, what I've learned is that parents can only open so many doors. Kids will eventually decide on their own which ones they want to go through. It's not so much about choosing the doors to open for them. It's teaching them how to open the doors for themselves.

(NOTE: This originally appeared in *Emerald City*, a fanzine edited by Cheryl Morgan who would go on to become a professional editor at *Clarkesworld*. My daughter, entering high school at this writing, has yet to flee fandom or SF.)

DESTINATION MOON IN THE 21st CENTURY

The year 2001 was a good year for Robert A. Heinlein, even though he had died twelve years before. Under the wonderfully arcane rules that govern the Hugo Awards given at the annual World Science Fiction Convention, occasionally the organizers are eligible to give out "Retro-Hugos." These honor achievements in science fiction and fantasy that occurred in years prior to the institution of the award. The Millennium Philcon—as 2001's 59th convention was dubbed—engaged in balloting not only for the best works of 2000, but for the best works of 1950 as well. (The first Hugos were not given out until 1953.)

As it turns out, 1950 was a very good year for written fiction (besides Heinlein, the nominees included Isaac Asimov, Cordwainer Smith, C.M. Kornbluth, Damon Knight, Poul Anderson, E.E. "Doc" Smith, and Theodore Sturgeon). The best dramatic presentation category was more problematical, however, as 1950 is generally regarded as the year that the "modern" science fiction film began. Prior to that, there was the rare *Metropolis* (1926) or *Things to Come* (1936), but SF on film was usually relegated to the movie serials. That would change in the 1950s, and the movie that opened up the floodgates—and snagged the award—was George Pal's production of *Destination Moon*, with a script by Heinlein, Rip van Ronkel, and James O'Hanlon.

The other nominees make it clear just how empty the field of media SF was at the time. Even granting the different perspective of picking the best of a year half a century later, there was not a lot to choose from. Clearly the best *movie* on the list was *Harvey*, an acknowledged classic with Jimmy Stewart as Elwood P. Dowd, a genial inebriate whose best friend is an invisible six-foot rabbit. That may have been a bit too whimsical for the Retro-Hugo voters, but it was good for a second place finish. Next was Disney's version of *Cinderella*, a charming film in its own right but hardly among the studio's very best. Fourth was the brilliant—if questionably nominated—Bugs Bunny cartoon "The Rabbit of Seville."

And in last place was the only other major science fiction movie released that year, *Rocketship X-M*. The film is usually given the back of the hand in film histories, since it was a low-budget production rushed into release to beat the higher profile *Destination Moon* into theaters. It got one less vote than "No Award" on the first counting of the ballot, with people ranking their choices. Surprisingly, *Rocketship X-M* is, in many ways, the better film. It has a more talented cast (including Lloyd Bridges, Hugh O'Brien, and Noah Beery, Jr.) and it's a lot more fun. Astronauts are heading to the moon and get thrown off course, ending up on Mars. It's pure hokum—or "space opera," if you prefer—but it still engages and entertains.

The Retro-Hugo voters, though, were not to be denied. Heinlein's *Farmer in the Sky* won for best novel, and his novella, "The Man Who Sold the Moon," won in its category. As far as the fans were concerned, it was a sweep for Heinlein, never mind that he was only one of several people involved in *Destination Moon*. It remains one of the most prestigious SF films in which an acknowledged grand master of science fiction directly participated, and it was the film that paved the way for the SF movie boom of the 1950s, including *The Day the Earth Stood Still* (1951) and *Forbidden Planet* (1956). It may not have been the best film on the list, but there was no question it deserved the honor.

That said, other than as a historical curio, what does *Destination Moon* have to say to 21st century viewers? After all, this was a speculative adventure about man's first landing on the moon, and it was rendered moot by Neil Armstrong, Buzz Aldrin, and Michael Collins back in July of 1969.

Even the look of the film has dated. George Pal is best remembered for his great special effects movies of the era, like *When Worlds Collide* (1951), *War of the Worlds* (1953), and *The Time Machine* (1960), but time has not been kind to *Destination Moon*. The rocketship is the typical cigar-shaped cylinder with fins that is such a beloved SF cliché it was adopted as the shape for the Hugo Awards. The advanced equipment on board looks like it was built with a kit ordered from a 1950 issue of *Popular Mechanics*. Meanwhile, the view of Earth looks suspiciously like something you would see at a Rand McNally store, rather the big blue and white marble the real astronauts would later show us.

The moon set is a bit cheesy, but give them credit for trying. Legendary SF artist Chesley Bonestell was hired as "technical advisor of astronomical art." The backgrounds of the lunar landscapes are breathtaking, but the foregrounds—containing a cracked surface reminiscent of a dried riverbed—look silly. However, it was a deliberate choice by the filmmakers. It allowed the production designers to create a forced perspective that would make the lunar set look much larger than it actually was, adding to the sense of wonder that appreciative audiences greeted the film with in 1950.

The story is cornball, complete with a comical crew member (Dick Wesson) added to the team at the last minute. A streetwise Brooklynite caricature, he gets to deliver lines like, "It won't woik… You're gonna look like a bunch of dummies." A few moments like that, and *Rocketship X-M* starts looking better and better.

What amazes about the film five decades later isn't what they get wrong, but what they may yet get right. The first half hour seems very topical, as a group of scientists, industrialists, and ex-military people wonder if they can't do the job better than the government. *Destination Moon* not only raises the issue, but it allows the debate to dominate the first third of the film, literally up to the moment the rocketship, named Luna, blasts off.

In one scene, industrialist Jim Barnes (John Archer) is meeting retired General Thayer (Tom Powers) for lunch. Thayer wants Barnes to get involved in a privately financed space project. Barnes identifies himself as "just a plain manufacturer, not the Department of Defense," and adds, "Building a rocket satellite is big stuff. I couldn't begin to finance one of those."

Thayer lets him know that they're moving beyond satellites. They're planning a trip to the moon. It's hardly enticing. A scale model of the atomic powered engine they're going to use ran for less than an hour and a half "before it blew up." General Thayer presses his point. Such projects aren't a national priority at the moment, he notes, but eventually they will be, and the government will turn to private industry to do the job for them, "Government always does that when it's in a jam. It has to. This time, I thought we might be ready for the government. Preparedness isn't all military, Jim."

The next scene is even more fascinating today than it was then. Barnes, realizing that a privately funded moon project will require a coalition of businesses, has to make his case. He shows a Woody Woodpecker cartoon that has to be the most entertaining infodump in the history of SF movies. Woody gets to ask all the questions about how rockets work that audiences would be wondering about, and ends up ready to contribute to the project himself. When the lights come up, the serious discussion starts.

"Can you imagine me going before a meeting of my stockholders and reporting I'm putting millions into a trip to the moon," says a businessman with a Texas twang. "Why, son, they'd lynch me."

Another asks the obvious question: "If it's that important a project, why doesn't the government undertake it?"

For today's viewers, that question is as pointed as ever. After all, the American space program that most of us have grown up with is a government project. Other models for space exploration haven't really played a large part in the public debate. Barnes points out that the know-how for this project is all in the private sector, and if they succeed, the government will take it over and foot the bill. He also acknowledges that if they fail, the loss will be theirs. Barnes is appealing to their sense of adventure, their willingness to take calculated business risks, and their pride in American industry. It doesn't seem to be working. What finally makes the case to the businessmen proves to be the same thing that would win the argument in the real American space program a decade later. If we don't get there first, someone else will.

General Thayer doesn't name names, but audiences in 1950 knew exactly who would be our opponent in World War III, and that it would be a war fought with atomic missiles. "There's absolutely no way to stop an attack from outer space," says Thayer. This pronouncement is greeted with stunned silence. The businessmen then agree that they have no choice. They *must* fund this project.

When President John Kennedy vowed to land an American on the moon by the end of the '60s, it wasn't because he had grown up reading *Astounding*. It was because the U.S. was falling behind in the "space race," and only by framing the project as a competition where we dare not lose would the will—and the money—be found to persevere in such an ambitious undertaking.

That's where we find ourselves today. Hardly anyone thought that the manned moon landings of the early '70s would peter out and leave us with a space program content with orbiting laboratories and unmanned probes. The race, however, was over, and with its conclusion went any sense of urgency to pursue bigger and grander efforts in space. That's a lesson for contemporary supporters of space exploration. If there was a fear that China or Iran was ready to launch a credible program to build a permanent base on the moon, it would become a major priority for Americans as well. In the absence of such competition, Earthbound problems will inevitably be considered as having a greater claim on time and resources.

Destination Moon may be overly optimistic in how quickly and effectively such a private operation can work. We're told it will take just a year (in 1950!) if the top scientists and businessmen put their heads together on this. There's opposition, but Barnes brushes it aside with a bit of bravado one is tempted to attribute to Heinlein's libertarian streak: "There's no law against taking off in a spaceship. It's never been done, so they haven't gotten around to prohibiting it." As it is, the *Luna* blasts off just a step ahead of a court order to shut down the whole operation.

Destination Moon deserved its Retro-Hugo because it is the movie that launched the modern age of SF film, because it inspired many of the people who would grow up to work in the actual space program, and because it showed that the gap between media and literary SF needn't be as wide as it often is. However, its message for today's would-be spacefarers is one that remains just as timely as it was then: if you can't convince people that it simply *has* to be done, it won't be.

OUR BATMAN

There are not many film characters who constitute their own genre. When we talk of "Tarzan movies" or "James Bond movies," we're talking of a character who spans decades on film, and who has been tackled by a variety of filmmakers and actors. Other characters in the pantheon would include Superman, Sherlock Holmes, King Arthur, Dracula, Frankenstein's monster, and Zorro. For the most part, though, a movie character is usually associated with a particular actor, so there is no Rocky without Sylvester Stallone and no Dirty Harry without Clint Eastwood.

Watching the eight live-action Batman films—ranging from 1943 to 2005— becomes a journey through more than sixty years of American life. Some of the ways times have changed are obvious, as with a '40s dress code which has even the thugs in suits, ties, and hats, and others are less so, as in the evolving depictions of the life of Batman's alter ego, Bruce Wayne. In exploring the movies, one thing becomes clear: each age gets the Batman it deserves.

Certain characters, because they are so endlessly adaptable, prove to be mirrors of their times. The Sherlock Holmes who asks Dr. Watson for "the needle" in the 1939 *The Hound of the Baskervilles* is merely bored at having solved another mystery. The cocaine-abusing Holmes of *The Seven-Per-Cent Solution* (1976) is someone with a drug problem. The Batman of the 1940s is an uncomplicated hero for children to cheer, just as their parents cheered President Roosevelt, a heroic wartime leader whose confinement to a wheelchair was largely kept from the public. The notion that someone could be a hero *and* have problems was left for more serious works.

Things changed with the Baby Boom, a generation that famously refused to grow up, at least not on the terms of their elders. Where their parents learned to put "childish things" aside as they took on adult responsibility, the Boomers didn't want to make a choice. One could be responsible and yet still have fun with the things they enjoyed when they were younger. Comic book readers turned to "graphic novels," and filmmakers adapting Batman to the '80s and '90s assumed that adults who had grown up with the character would be a part of their audience.

Now we were ready to accept a complex and flawed Batman, because the other once-simple heroes of our past had proven similarly complex. Sports stars use steroids. The rock star/actor/public figure going into rehab and emerging a changed person is part of our everyday culture. Perhaps that explains why the public ultimately lost faith in George W. Bush. He was trying to be a '50s politician who never has doubts and never asks questions in a 21st century world where doubts and questions are all we have.

Things have changed, and following Batman shows us just how far we've gone.

That the first two Batman films—*Batman* (1943) and *Batman and Robin* (1949) —were serials reveals much before a single frame is viewed. Although movie serials go back to the silent era, by the 1940s they were firmly established as kiddie fare. The fact that Batman was deemed fodder for the serials as opposed to a feature length film shows how the character was dismissed by the studio executives and the adult world. Batman was not a masked avenger, like Zorro or the Scarlet Pimpernel, he was merely a comic book character. Like Superman, Flash Gordon, and Buck Rogers, the serials were good enough for him. With the comic book series itself only four years old in 1943, the filmmakers—already constrained by the usual tight budgets of a serial—didn't bother to look too closely at the young Batman mythos. Instead, Batman (Lewis Wilson) and Robin (Douglas Croft) are out to prevent a criminal ring headed by the Japanese Prince Daka (J. Carroll Naish) from getting the radium they need to complete a super weapon. In chapter after chapter, Daka learns of some new source of radium, only to be thwarted by "the Batman."

The 1940s' Batman reflects 1940s America. By definition, white, male Americans are the center of the universe, and anyone who is non-white, non-male, or non-American is inferior. In the 1943 film at least some of that, shocking though it may be today, is understandable. It was wartime, and movies demonized the enemy, especially when he was Japanese. When the action shifts to Daka's lair for the first time, the modern viewer is likely to gasp at the narration: "This was part of a foreign land, transplanted bodily to America and known as Little Tokyo. Since a wise government rounded up the shifty-eyed Japs, it has become a virtual ghost street..." Over the course of the serial, Daka has to put up with being called a "Jap murderer" and a "Jap devil" before meeting his inevitable doom.

Such wartime propaganda aside, what may be most surprising is how dumbed down this Batman is. Heroes who had to keep their identities secret were not unusual. The Batman mythology was built on previous vigilante heroes who had civilian identities that they kept separate from their masked roles. However in the serials, security is surprisingly lax. Robin repeatedly calls Batman "Bruce" after they escape danger ("Are you all right, Bruce?"), and they even change into their costumes in Bruce's car. Since Batman was merely a "comic book" hero for kids, the filmmakers were under no obligation to think through anything beyond the surface action. What was needed in 1943 was someone whom young viewers—particularly boys—could cheer on in fighting the Japs. Even the choice of villain is revealing. Were Batman to fight the Nazis, we might have to explain why our values were better than their values. Fighting "slant-eyed devils," however, required only a cartoon hero to fight a cartoon villain, the latter of whom could be dismissed as alien. (After all, those Americans who might have identified with Daka—even if they remained loyal Americans—had been sent to detention camps, at least on the West Coast.) Batman had been reduced to the barest minimum: a white male vigilante protecting us from the 1940s version of the "Yellow Peril."

Six years later, the war was over, and the Batman comic book was well-established. The 1949 *Batman and Robin* (with our heroes now played by Robert Lowery and Johnny Duncan) borrows more heavily from the comic book, introducing the characters of Commissioner Gordon and photographer Vicki Vale, and giving the Dynamic Duo a masked foe, the Wizard. Even if he wasn't in the comics first, he was easily recognizable as another megalomaniac with plans for Gotham.

If the second serial is somewhat more sophisticated, the filmmakers still agree that, like Superman, Batman's secret identity is merely a cover. This is an odd decision. In the case of Superman, he really *is* Kal-El, the survivor of Krypton who has gained super powers on Earth. Clark Kent is simply a disguise he assumes so he can pass among Earth people. Bruce Wayne, on the other hand, is the heir to the Wayne fortune and survivor of the tragic murder of his parents. Batman is the disguise he puts on for his crime-fighting chores. In the serials, though, Batman is the real person, the solid citizen who can be counted on to fight evil, support the establishment, and work with the authorities. Bruce Wayne, on the other hand, is a cowardly lay-about. It's one thing to throw people off the track—although, as noted, he doesn't do a particularly effective job of it—but it's quite another to be so sniveling and unreliable that Bruce becomes little more than a disguise that Batman adopts.

It is Batman, not Bruce Wayne, who stands for the values of 1940s white male prerogatives, and this becomes clearer in the 1949 film. In the first serial, he protected us from the Yellow Peril. Now, besides fighting bad guys, he also makes sure that uppity women get put in their place. When photographer Vicki Vale (Jane Adams) grows suspicious of Bruce, even noting that Batman seems to get around in Bruce's car, Batman takes Vicki's own car keys to try to prevent her from following him. There's no romance here. Batman is what a later generation would call a male chauvinist. In one scene he airily dismisses her, saying, "Don't worry about her. She's always taking pictures no one ever sees." Bruce is more polite, but we're invited to regard him as a shallow wimp who is merely Batman's mask. It's Batman we're cheering, and he lets us know that women need to be disciplined. This is the same year that Spencer Tracy and Katharine Hepburn would do *Adam's Rib*, and it's an interesting contrast. The Tracy/Hepburn battle of the sexes seems years ahead of its time, and still feels modern today. *Batman and Robin* may offer a more authentic view of contemporary attitudes in Batman's patronizing of Vicki, which is why it seems so odd to us now.

Batman and Robin also shows us a world coming to grips with having entered into a technological age. There is fear about new powers being unleashed. The Wizard has a stolen weapon allowing him to control all means of transportation in Gotham, and he communicates with his gang via two-way radio. He even manipulates the media through the person of a radio reporter who drives Batman and Commissioner Gordon mad with his ill-timed scoops. By contrast, the good guys are still playing catch up. Tipped off to a criminal plot while outside of Gotham, Batman and Robin hurry back to the city, with Batman instructing his partner, "Commissioner Gordon needs help. Watch for a phone."

By the late 1940s, America was what would soon be called a superpower, but we couldn't be sure that we had the upper hand. The Soviet Union had dropped what Winston Churchill dubbed "the Iron Curtain" across Eastern Europe, and they had their first successful atomic test in August of 1949. Although the serial began spinning out its chapters months before, it reflects that unease America felt in a world it did not fully control. Batman's frantic search for a pay phone reveals much about American anxieties at the time—the fear that we were being out-thought and outmaneuvered by our enemies—providing a context for the rise of Joe McCarthy and his Red-baiting witch hunt the following year.

The launch of the *Batman* television series in January 1966 was a sensation. Obviously modeled on the old movie serials, each episode in its first season ran in two parts on consecutive nights, the first part always ending in a cliffhanger. Adam West and Burt Ward were the Dynamic Duo, and much of the mythology from the comics made it to the small screen: the eccentric villains, the Batmobile, the numerous gadgets and devices developed for fighting crime. What was new was the camp element. Batman still wasn't being taken seriously. Now he was an earnest hero trapped in an ironic Roy Lichtenstein painting, complete with "Pow!" and "Biff!" captions during the fight scenes and appropriately arch dialogue. That first season, both weekly episodes made the top ten in the Nielsen ratings, and the series became a precursor to *The Love Boat* as a place for slumming actors and has-beens to pick up a paycheck, in this case playing villains.

The 1966 *Batman* movie had originally been conceived as a launch for the series (as it would be in Europe), but when ABC ordered the show rushed into production, it would be released the following summer. It features a diabolical plot by four of the show's most popular villains: the Joker (Cesar Romero), the Penguin (Burgess Meredith), the Riddler (Frank Gorshin), and the Catwoman (Lee Meriwether). The casting of Meriwether instead of Julie Newmar, who had played Catwoman in the first season, was because Newmar was already committed to making another film and wasn't available.

The mid-1960s was a time when Hollywood was doing a lot of spoofing. *Get Smart* was sending up the spy genre on TV, while *Cat Ballou* (1965) lampooned the Western. This was exactly the wrong time to make the argument that Batman should be considered a dark vigilante, fighting crime in a way that society was unwilling or unable to handle. It wasn't an argument made in the comics, and it would turn out to be an argument ignored on the big and small screens as well. So Batman is treated even more as a cartoon character than he had been in the movie serials. The best-remembered moment in the movie is Batman trying to get rid of a bomb—it's the cartoon bowling ball with a sparkler fuse—and everywhere he turns he is stymied: by nuns, by a mother with a stroller, by young lovers, even by ducklings. "Some days you just can't get rid of a bomb," he complains, with viewers invited to see him as a clown. He's a heroic clown to be sure, as compared to villainous clowns like the Joker and the Penguin, but a clown nonetheless.

Given the cartoonish nature of the movie, you might miss that it's taking some of the issues of the Batman universe much more seriously. He's been deputized by the police and thus now operates under color of law. For youngsters—and those not yet disillusioned—this might be reassuring. Batman was official now. For those who, in a just a few years would be labeled part of the "counterculture," it indicated that our heroes had sold out and were reduced to being posturing fools in costumes. Indeed, for those starting to grow cynical of the government which had gotten us into a war in Southeast Asia, it made perfect sense that this heroic buffoon was now firmly tied to the Establishment.

Ironically, the 1966 *Batman* allows Adam West to portray the best Bruce Wayne on film. He certainly looks the part with his square-jawed good looks, and although Bruce is still a playboy, he's also more of a philanthropist now. We're told he's a "do-gooder" and a "square citizen." West's wry performance makes clear that he is in on the joke. Batman may be a clown, but Bruce Wayne is not. Almost by accident, the film understands that Bruce Wayne is the real man and Batman is the disguise.

By making Batman such a ridiculous figure—reflecting an era in which we would soon be questioning everything—it suggests that Establishment values had all the depth of a comic book panel. While real life battles were raging over civil rights and Vietnam, this Batman distracted us with a dream world, defending America against cartoon villains.

The four "Batman" films from 1989 to 1997 are a series, despite the fact that three different actors played Batman and two different directors helmed the movies. While there's an obvious break between the first two and the last two, from Hollywood's perspective this was a textbook franchise. The movies are what are known as "tentpoles," released at the start of the summer season in the hopes that they could sustain the studio's (Warner Bros.) fortunes.

The first one did just that. In more than twenty years as a professional film critic, this writer can remember only one time he was stopped going *into* an advance screening by a TV camera crew and asked for an opinion on the film not yet seen. That was for the 1989 *Batman*. The hype had been building for months, and audiences were primed to be blown away. Director Tim Burton did not disappoint. Although the casting of Michael Keaton as Batman was controversial among fans, he completely won them over with his earnest, deadly serious portrayal of the Dark Knight. He's less successful as Bruce, perhaps because we can see his face and it was hard at the time to take the star of *Mr. Mom* (1983) and *Beetle Juice* (1988) in a serious role. As Batman, though, he is a creature of the night, striking fear into evildoers, and perhaps the only one who can stand up to Jack Nicholson's Joker.

The casting of a star of Nicholson's magnitude was a signal this would be a very different *Batman*. Aided by production designer Anton Furst, Burton shows us a dark and evil Gotham City. This Batman is not a goofball, but a tightly controlled vigilante, doing what is necessary to fight crime. Burton had the clout to treat Batman seriously, and by 1989, the world of comic books had changed as well. Frank Miller had done *The Dark Knight Returns* in 1986, and fans—if not the general public—were primed for a Batman who felt real human emotions. No longer a clown or a character simply to thrill children, this Batman was a pained guardian, *driven* to fight crime. He donned the cape and cowl not merely as a disguise, but because he *had* to. Such psychological motivations were no longer beyond the grasp of the audiences for comic book films. Other genres, like westerns and cop movies, had offered us revisionist heroes in the '60s and '70s. Finally, the comic book film was ready to take the plunge. Now no longer kiddie fare, *Batman* was a movie squarely pitched to adults who had knew full well the ambiguities and compromises of real life, and could handle a dark fantasy figure whose problems were merely shadowy versions of their own.

For Burton, the 1989 *Batman* was merely testing the waters. Would audiences accept a comic book hero—and a villain—who acted out of psychological motivations? Could they relate? That they did. In the years after Watergate and Vietnam and, for that matter, the Iran hostage crisis, we no longer accepted our leaders or our heroes as perfect. It was enough if they could get the job done. As Bruce, Keaton is conflicted and vulnerable, finally revealing his secret identity to Vicki Vale (Kim Basinger), whom he also gets to take to bed, proving him a grown-up Batman indeed. You had troubles opening up to a lover? Look what *he* had to go through. Earlier Batmans were so tightly controlled they didn't even go to the bathroom. This one would get laid even as he finally defeated the villain in the end.

It wasn't until *Batman Returns* three years later that Burton and Keaton felt fully comfortable really delving into Batman's psyche. It's one thing to learn the Joker killed your parents and want revenge. It's another to find yourself attracted to someone similarly motivated and even less in control. The transformation of Catwoman (Michelle Pfeiffer) into a fetishistic vinyl creation complete with whip shows us the continuum that Batman is on. Bruce saw his parents killed. Selina Kyle (Pfeiffer) is killed by the evil industrialist Max Shreck (Christopher Walken), only to mysteriously come back to life as the Catwoman. Is she good or is she evil? Batman is drawn to her, and even reveals his secret identity to her to try to shock her out of killing Shreck. He fails, but it's clear that she's got her claws in Batman and won't let go.

The film is complicated by the inclusion of the Penguin, turned into a bizarre, malformed character played by Danny DeVito, who was abandoned as an infant by his parents. The Penguin threatens to turn the situation with Batman and Catwoman into triangle, but while she toys with him, she has no real interest. Someone obviously feared that neither villain had the star power of Nicholson as the Joker, but together they might carry it off. They did, but it was largely on the strength of Pfeiffer's Catwoman.

By 1992, women had come a long way. Where Vicki Vale had to put up with Batman's putdowns in the 1949 *Batman and Robin*, *Batman Returns* is clearly a different world. Rescuing a woman being menaced by an assailant, Catwoman taunts the would-be rapist, "Be gentle. It's my first time." Later battling Batman, she momentarily upsets him—and gains the upper hand—by playing to old stereotypes, "How could you? I'm a woman." She then uses Batman's courtliness against him, telling him, "Life's a bitch. And now so am I."

It's a brilliant, sexy performance by Pfeiffer, who may have haunted more twisted fantasies as a result than any actress since Diana Rigg in *The Avengers*. Whether it's licking herself because she "feels dirty" or assuring Bruce that normal guys have let her down—and then pouncing on him for a steamy kiss—she's a woman who will no longer allow herself to be victimized. That Batman accepts this says much about how times have changed. He's not threatened by Catwoman; he's turned on. A strong, fiercely independent woman is not a challenge, even if she's on the kinky side. It's not surprising to find such a film the same year that America elected Bill Clinton president. He would be impeached for a fling with a White House aide and not only be acquitted, but retain the support of the country in the process. If we hadn't quite turned into France, we had become increasingly willing to forgive the sexual peccadilloes of our heroes, so long as they weren't hypocrites. Clearly what was needed was a follow up film focusing more on the Batman and Catwoman relationship, which was hinted at the end of *Batman Returns* when the Bat signal brings out Catwoman, who had been presumed dead. Instead, Keaton hung up the cape, and Burton turned over the director's chair to Joel Schumacher.

The Batman series continued, but it would now reflect not the sociopolitical *Zeitgeist* in America. Instead, it demonstrated how Hollywood had changed from being the 1930s "Dream Factory," which had turned out an unending stream of escapist fare, to the 1990s assembly line that manufactured blockbusters to order. Schumacher is not a critics' favorite, in spite of such respectable films as *Lost Boys* (1987), *Falling Down* (1993), *Tigerland* (2000), and *Phone Booth* (2003), and he is certainly not a stylist like Burton. His two Batman films, *Batman Forever* (1995) and *Batman & Robin* (1997), demonstrate that he learned exactly the wrong things from the Burton movies. He keeps them dark, but where *Batman Returns* is practically a study in black and white, Schumacher makes his films much more cartoonish.

Batman Forever gives us both Two-Face (Tommy Lee Jones) and the Riddler (Jim Carrey), as well as the addition of Robin (Chris O'Donnell). *Batman & Robin* keeps Robin, adds Batgirl (Alicia Silverstone), and offers up Mr. Freeze (Arnold Schwarzenegger) and Poison Ivy (Uma Thurman). Watching the two movies back to back makes it abundantly clear that they are virtually the same film, only the villains have changed. Robin's costume even gets the same fetishistic rubber/leather makeover as the Batman outfit, although it's interesting to note that when Batgirl arrives on the scene, her costume lacks the superfluous nipples that the Batman and Robin suits have.

What became clear with the Schumacher films is that the series couldn't hold on to a Batman. After Keaton left, Val Kilmer and George Clooney each took the role for one film apiece, with Kilmer faring better, perhaps because he got to explore Bruce's dual personality with sympathetic psychiatrist Dr. Chase Meridian (Nicole Kidman). The problem with the latter two films of the series is that they reflect the economic boom times of the '90s. They are all too aware that they are entries in a big studio franchise. When Two-Face invades E. Nigma's big party, Nigma—the Riddler's real identity—complains that Two-Face should have warned him so he could have pre-sold the movie rights. When, in *Batman & Robin*, the young crime fighter asks for his own car, there's this exchange:

> Robin: "I want a car. Chicks dig the car."
>
> Batman: "That's why Superman works alone."

It's like they can't make up their minds if they're in the *noir*ish world of the Burton movies, or if they've slipped over into the wisecracking mode of an Arnold Schwarzenegger action film. The casting of Schwarzenegger as Mr. Freeze signaled which direction they were going when he made his entrance by declaring, "The Iceman Cometh."

The Batman of the Schumacher films is like the Johnny Depp of the *Pirates of the Caribbean* sequels. No one is interested in character and nuance any longer. Now it's about feeding the public what they want. Trot out the wacky villains, do the action set pieces, and resolve everything so the next product can be put on the assembly line. There's a reason the momentum in Hollywood swung from the DC comic book heroes to those of Marvel (particularly *X-Men* and *Spider-Man*). The Schumacher "Batman" films told us more about '90s Hollywood and what it thought audiences wanted than it did about the audiences themselves.

What the '80s-'90s quartet of "Batman" films are about, in the end, is the power of the box office. The first film was a blockbuster hit, taking in over $250 million in domestic receipts. *Batman Returns* proved a bit too weird for some, dropping to "only" around $160 million. To Warner Bros., it must have seemed that Schumacher got the series back on track, with *Batman Forever* boosting the take to $180 million. Thus you can imagine their disappointment when *Batman & Robin*, which fully accepted the lessons of the third film, topped out at $107 million. On an estimated budget of $125 million, that made the film a certified flop, even if overseas box office and subsequent video and cable sales eventually balanced the books. It would be eight years before the Caped Crusader appeared again on screen—outside of animation—and then it would be a reinvention that scraped away nearly everything that had come before.

Batman Begins (2005) is the best and most serious Batman put on film to date. Director Christopher Nolan seems to have asked, "What if this was real? How would it be done? Why would it be done this way?" The result is a movie that gives us credible explanations for every aspect of the Batman legend, from the armored suit, weapons, and Batmobile, to where he got his fighting skills, why he wears a cape, and the source of his special bond with Alfred, Bruce's long-serving butler and the only one who is supposed to know that Bruce is Batman.

Indeed, by the end of the quartet, the question could be properly asked: who *didn't* know Batman's identity? He had revealed it to Vicki Vale, Selina Kyle, and Dr. Chase Meridian. It had also been figured out by the Riddler, Dick Grayson, and Barbara Wilson/Batgirl. Here his childhood friend Rachel (Katie Holmes) guesses the truth, but it's not a big revelation scene. Instead, it's a confirmation for both as to why a serious relationship between them has become impossible.

Nolan opens the film in a completely unexpected manner, showing Bruce Wayne (Christian Bale) as an inmate in a Chinese prison. Slowly we get the story of how and why he is there, and how it leads him to the League of Shadows, where he receives his training from Henri Ducard (Liam Neeson). In answer to the Joker's famous query in the 1989 film, "Where does he get those wonderful toys?" we see him slowly acquire them from the basement of Wayne Enterprises, where military prototypes that never went into mass production are his for the taking.

For a movie that dispenses with Robin, it makes some astute observations about male bonding. As the "women's lib" of the '60s and '70s became a given for the next generation, the pendulum had swung back and forth for men as well. The ideal man of the early 21st century was now expected to be *both* macho *and* sensitive, which our hero turns out to be. Bruce is tortured by guilt over his parents' death—they left the opera and were gunned down after young Bruce freaked out seeing bats on stage—forcing him to work out his roles as both businessman/philanthropist Bruce Wayne and the dark crime fighter Batman. He has only two people to turn to, Alfred and Sgt. Jim Gordon (Gary Oldman). Alfred (Michael Caine) became Bruce's foster father, in practice if not in actuality, after he was orphaned. Their bond is expressed in typical male fashion, in the little jibes that make it clear that affection is being expressed by other means. When Alfred informs the newly returned Bruce he has been declared dead, Bruce remarks that at least his property—which went to Alfred—has remained in good hands. Alfred drolly replies, "You can borrow the Rolls. Just bring it back with a full tank." Later, Bruce is hosting a birthday party at Wayne Manor, but has to run out as Batman just as the guests are arriving. Alfred wonders what he should do, and Bruce archly advises, "Tell them that joke you know."

Times had changed, and though the widespread cynicism toward the "wartime" leadership of President George W. Bush was not yet underway when the film was in production or initial release, the movie certainly pointed the way.

The system is corrupt, whether it's the military industrial complex (represented by Rutger Hauer, as the head of Wayne Enterprises), law enforcement (with Sgt. Gordon being the notable exception), the civil authorities (under the thumb of Tom Wilkinson's gangster), or even the educated elite, such as the duplicitous doctor played by Cillian Murphy. Where once we had faith that those in charge could be trusted, and thus Batman worked closely with them, now it was taken for granted that anyone with power could *not* be trusted, which is why a Batman became necessary. Outside the *film noir* genre, we wouldn't have hailed someone taking the law into his own hands during the complacent '50s under Dwight Eisenhower, or even the idealistic early '60s under John F. Kennedy. However in 2005, a Batman who made his own rules and saw those in charge as corrupt and venal required no explanation. It was the way American moviegoers were increasingly seeing the real world.

Batman's relationship with Gordon is significant, and will likely be developed in subsequent films. Gordon is the beat cop who comforts young Bruce after his parents are murdered. Later, Gordon is the rare honest cop on the force who defends Batman and is sought out by him for assistance. Their big bonding moment occurs late in the film. Batman needs Gordon's assistance, and asks him if he can "drive stick" before sending him off with the Batmobile, which we heard Gordon admire earlier. Married and a parent, Gordon is not interested in the car because it's a chick magnet. These are two men who, though taking different paths, are determined to fight the corrupt system and do what's right for Gotham. Batman recognizes Gordon as an honest cop, and Gordon recognizes Batman as a vigilante who, nonetheless, feels constrained by the law. In a world of corruption, standing for the ideals the Establishment once espoused becomes an act of rebellion for them both.

When, at film's end the newly promoted Lt. Gordon informs Batman of a mysterious new criminal who has left a Joker playing card behind at the scene, their friendship is cemented:

Gordon: "I never said thank you."

Batman: "And you'll never have to."

Modern men don't have to express emotions. They merely have to acknowledge them. Batman/Bruce Wayne's bonding—with Alfred, with Gordon—is all implied. If they are worthy of his trust, and they are, they don't need to say anything or ask anything. Their actions speak louder than any words.

What the eight Batman films demonstrate is a slow but certain journey from treating the character as a child's fantasy to making him a fully adult character. It's interesting that in the wake of the success of *Batman Begins*, two other movie icons were similarly reinvented in 2006: Superman in *Superman Returns* and James Bond in *Casino Royale*. In each case, but particularly in *Batman Begins* and *Casino Royale*, there was a conscious attempt to eliminate the camp and the cartoonish elements so that instead of the special effects, we're focusing on the characters.

If each age truly gets the Batman it deserves, perhaps we're finally ready to accept a Batman struggling with the problems of what it means to be a man in the modern world, even if he has to wear a costume to do it.

ATOMIC ANTS

The ending of the 1954 shocker *Them!* could sum up not only numerous science fiction films of the era, but also the underlying fear of the decade. As the good guys finally wipe out the remaining stronghold of the giant ants—base to the queens whose egg-laying prowess threatens to eradicate humanity—the last word goes not to the heroic FBI agent Robert Graham (James Arness) or fatally wounded police sergeant Ben Peterson (James Whitmore), but to aged scientist Dr. Harold Medford (Edmund Gwenn): "When man entered the atomic age, he opened a door to a new world. What we'll eventually find in that new world, nobody can predict."

In the popular imagination, the 1950s were a time of complacency and conformity. Things that challenged that conception needed to be tamed. Beatniks, rebellious youth, Commie subversives... they could be dealt with, if not in reality then certainly in our pop culture. The atomic bomb, on the other hand, would prove to be another story. Numerous science fiction films addressed our fears of this primal energy that was now let loose on the world. Although there were some movies that tried to deal with our atomic fears directly, as in the post-apocalyptic *The World, the Flesh and the Devil* and *Five*, more often than not we preferred to deal in metaphors. It's not surprising that the Japanese *Gojira* (released in the U.S. as *Godzilla*) featured a monster whose path of destruction was reminiscent of the wreckage of Hiroshima and Nagasaki, the only cities to have actually faced atomic weapons. American movies gave us monsters, alien rays, and other sources of mass destruction, but *Them!* took this unease in unexpected directions. The "atomic age" itself seemed to become a metaphor for this modern age in which regular guys like Graham and Peterson could no longer rely on eternal verities. Giant ants were not the only thing that emerged as part of this new world order.

Them! was a classy production from Warner Bros. with a better-than-expected cast. Edmund Gwenn, for example, had won the Oscar for his Kris Kringle in *Miracle on 34th Street*, and Whitmore was on his way to becoming a veteran character actor, already having notable roles in *The Asphalt Jungle* and *Kiss Me Kate*. James Arness, who was the monster in *The Thing* and was getting increasingly bigger roles, was still a year away from his most famous part, that of Marshal Matt Dillon on TV's long-running *Gunsmoke*. As for director Gordon Douglas, he was one of those journeymen whose career spanned four decades and included "Our Gang" shorts, westerns, crime dramas (including several in the '60s with Frank

Sinatra), comedies with Jerry Lewis and Bob Hope, and the spy spoof *In Like Flint*. Douglas may not have been an *auteur*, but he was a respected professional, and his appearance at the helm made it clear that this was not some throwaway B-picture. "Sci-fi" movies were in, and Warners wanted a piece of the action.

What they got was a film where, in a little over 90 minutes, we would not only learn a lot about ants and why letting them turn into a gigantic atomic mutations might not be such a good idea, but a catalog of many of the other fears of the era. The story opens as a mystery. Sgt. Peterson finds a young girl wandering in the desert in her pajamas and she's in a state of shock, unable to speak. The ensuing investigation leads to the discovery of odd footprints, as well as a dead body that is suffused with formic acid, but no sign of theft or any other understandable motive. The FBI doesn't have much of an idea either, but when agent Graham sends a model of the footprint to Washington, it leads to the arrival of Dr. Medford, an authority on ants.

His arrival immediately raises two concerns. If Peterson and Graham are the regular guys, Medford is the scientific expert. In earlier films, such experts were wiser than the officials (as in *The Day the Earth Stood Still*) or not (as in *The Thing*), but in neither case did they call the shots. Now the authorities are forced to defer to scientific expertise for the simple reason that he understands the situation and they don't. At first he refuses to tell them what his theories are, for fear of starting a panic. Later, when they know what they're facing, they still defer to him not only in terms of what the public is told, but in how they will fight the ants. When one of the generals suggests simply bombing the ant's nest that night, Medford has to calmly explain that these ants stay out of the desert sun and come out at night to search for food. If they were to follow the general's idea, most of the ants would be away from the nest during the attack. In previous battles the generals were the experts. Now they not only don't know what to do, but they might actually make things worse if they don't listen to the scientists. When Peterson and Graham finally encounter one of the ants, it is Medford who has to tell them to shoot for the antenna, which renders the creature helpless. It's not the sort of information that would have been immediately available to the cop and the G-man.

Then there's Pat Medford (Joan Weldon), who is a scientific expert in her own right, and the daughter of the older scientist. She's clearly here as the "sex interest," and her entrance into the movie is of her shapely leg as she climbs down from the plane where her skirt gets caught on the ladder. Asked if she needs help, she demurs, saying she'll handle it herself. This is actually a sign of things to come, but agent Graham can't quite get used to the idea of a lady scientist, noting that if she's a doctor, he wants to get ill.

Later, when Graham and Peterson go exploring one of the nests to discover the full scope of the situation, she prepares to go underground with them. Graham, however, is having nothing of it. Clearly this is no place for a woman. But it is she who has little use for his misplaced gallantry. She points out that only she and her father have the expertise to know what they're looking for, he's too old to do it, and there's no time to give the lawmen a crash course in the subject. In fact, what we keep hearing from these regular guys is that they need to have things explained to them in plain language. When it's pointed out that the elder Dr. Medford is one of the world's leading "myrmecologists," Graham sighs that that's exactly what he means about not being able to follow all the technical discussion. The younger Dr. Medford wins the argument, and Graham comes to see that being smarter than him—at least about ants—isn't necessarily a drawback to a relationship.

From the perspective of more than half a century later, what might be most disturbing is the matter-of-fact way the film accepts not only government secrecy, but seems to endorse outright repression. When they realize that some queen ants have escaped and have set up new nests, the authorities have to figure out how many, where they are, and how to make sure they destroy them all. To track the ants, they have people monitoring the wire services for any stories involving UFOs, mysterious deaths or disappearances, or break-ins where sugar was a factor. Meanwhile, no information is going out. Reporters harangue one government official who offers only "No comment," even when he's asked, "Has the Cold War gotten hot?" Apparently, allowing wild speculation leading to possible panic about World War III is better than warning people about the actual danger of giant ants invading Los Angeles.

A man (Fess Parker) who saw what he described as UFOs that looked like giant ants, is locked up and questioned. He knows his story sounds insane, but he also knows what he saw. The doctor who is holding him is ready to release him, recognizing that he is neither mentally ill nor dangerous, but agent Graham urges the doctor—without explanation beyond invoking national security—to continue to keep the man locked up. This is not seen as an egregious violation of civil liberties, but as a necessary evil in the battle against the ants. When a ship at sea is taken over by the giant bugs, killing everyone on board, a naval vessel is able to sink the ship, destroying the nest. We're assured that the Navy will keep their own ship at sea until the emergency is over, since letting it return to base with its crew, who saw what happened, risks letting the story get out.

It is these last incidents that are more troubling than the giant ants. The movie is arguing that not only must authorities defer to scientific experts, since they lack the knowledge to do the job properly themselves, but that the general public should be kept in the dark because they would go out of control if they knew the facts. Indeed, the only way to ensure this is to permit innocent people to be locked up in mental wards when they stumble onto the truth. The excuse for such secrecy in *The Thing* was because the alien was at a remote polar installation. Here, two boys are trapped by the ants because they had no way of knowing that there was any danger in the first place. When one of the military figures argues the boys are probably dead already, and they should just burn out the nest, he's dismissively told to go tell that to the boys' mother, whom Graham has allowed to come to the site. Finally, at least one person in authority has begun to treat the people as citizens with something at stake, rather than simply another aspect of the mutant ant problem.

Amid all this, the ants become a gigantic metaphor for a modern age where nothing can be assumed. What sets up Dr. Medford's speech at the end is the observation that these ants were apparently created as a result of the initial atomic tests. It's noted that in the nine years since, there have been many more tests. Might there be more dangers in store? Dr. Medford's admission that "nobody can predict" what future threats may arise is a pessimistic note on which to end the film. Throughout the story, we've been asked to defer to authority and to recognize that the scientific experts know much more than we laypeople. We ignore them at our peril. Yet when he admits that this is beyond the scope of even the experts, we are left in the position of that little girl at the beginning. She finally regains her speech when Medford brings some formic acid to her hospital room and allows her to smell it. She leaps up screaming, "Them!" In the context of the movie, it's clear she means the giant ants, but for viewers at the time, it might just as well have been women scientists, experts speaking in indecipherable technical language, the government keeping secrets from us about dangers in our own communities, and the queasy feeling that the world had become so unsafe and unpredictable that we really couldn't be sure of anything anymore. The door had indeed been opened, and those ants might prove to be the very least of our problems.

THE BARE NECESSITIES

It's a story at least as old as the Bible. A man or a group of people is lost in the wilderness and has to figure out how to survive. Moses, of course, had divine assistance in providing for the wandering Israelites, obtaining manna from the heavens and water from a rock.

Daniel Defoe's novel *Robinson Crusoe* dates back to the early eighteenth century with its tale of a man fending for himself on a remote island inhabited only by savage cannibals. A century later, Johann Wyss would offer up *The Swiss Family Robinson*, about a family traveling to New Guinea and ending up shipwrecked on an uninhabited island. Even with multiple TV and movie adaptations of both stories, the genre still fascinates, as demonstrated by the Tom Hanks film *Cast Away* (2000), about a Federal Express executive trapped on another of those conveniently well-stocked, but out-of-the-way desert isles.

For some reason, the 1960s was a time when this type of saga was especially popular. The most enduring example is, of course, *Gilligan's Island*, the legendarily silly sitcom that spawned numerous reunion movies, documentaries, memoirs, and even a reality TV series. Disney would do a 1960 adaptation of *Swiss Family Robinson* with Tommy Kirk and his elders fighting off pirates. What may be most interesting is that the early '60s saw both the Robinson family and Crusoe adventures recast in the future, with those desert islands being transformed into other planets.

First would come a comic book series remembered, perhaps, only by comic aficionados: *Space Family Robinson*. Then would come the TV series *Lost in Space*, about a completely different but equally lost Robinson family. The stories were essentially "space opera," with little regard for reality or scientific speculation. As with *Gilligan's Island*, the emphasis was on entertainment and adventure, not on practical problem solving. It's something of a joke, regarding *Gilligan*, that the Professor (Russell Johnson) could make a short-wave radio out of coconut shells, but couldn't figure out a way to get the castaways home. Neither of the Robinson families managed to match the achievement of their literary forebears, with both the comic and TV runs ending with them still lost among the stars.

The notable exception to this was the 1964 film *Robinson Crusoe on Mars*. If the solutions the film comes up with in terms of air, water, shelter, and food seem like cheats, it helps to remember what our practical knowledge of life in space, and on Mars in particular, was some forty years ago. Looked at now, it's not the solutions that are interesting, but the problems. If manned landings and bases are hoped for on the moon and Mars in this century, then a study of this film by prospective astronauts seems worthwhile. Could you survive under these circumstances? Could anyone?

The story opens aboard Mars Gravity Probe One. Its two-man crew consists of Col. Dan McReady (a pre-*Batman* Adam West) and Col. Christopher "Kit" Draper (Paul Mantee). There's also a monkey named Mona. When we see what passes for high-tech equipment—Kit checks the reading on what looks like a spinning odometer with its faceplate removed—and hear the astronauts joking about their fancy space dinners ("I like mine in paste form, you know, in a tube"), it doesn't look very promising.

Then a meteor hits the ship, and Mac and Kit have to eject separately. They plan to meet up on the Martian surface and figure out what to do next. Out of contact with Mac, and with much of his equipment ruined in the crash, Kit is now alone on an alien planet where he needs to find some solutions fast or he will die. What does he need to do first?

Obviously, oxygen is the top priority. If there's not enough to breathe, nothing else matters. Kit discovers there's oxygen in the Martian atmosphere and tests it by lifting his visor. One could quibble about his risk of infection, but if one is doomed to die by asphyxiation, the prospect of possibly contracting Martian influenza might seem an acceptable risk. The air, however, is too thin for him to breathe, and he must rely on his dwindling reserves.

One can imagine a team of scientists examining the film and trying to figure what they should do to avoid the situation. Plant caches of oxygen tanks on the surface? Terraform the planet? Genetically alter astronauts to be able to breathe in the thinner atmosphere? As we drift more into the realm of truly speculative science, the film's solutions may not seem as far fetched, although they rely a bit much on wishful thinking.

Kit stretches his supply through calculation. He can breathe the Martian air and take short "boosters" from the tanks every fifteen minutes or so. He can sleep for an hour before requiring a booster. He sets up an alarm system to rouse him from sleep to take the needed oxygenated breaths, but this is a stopgap, simply staving off the inevitable. So the filmmakers provide the convenient discovery that certain rocks seem to spontaneously combust and, in fact, contain oxygen to feed their flames. In short order, he is replenishing his supply from the abundant rock piles.

It serves the requirement of the story, since if Kit chokes to death, it's not going to be much of an adventure. However, it raises the interesting question of how to provide for planetary explorers. There are supplies aboard Kit's still-orbiting ship, but his radio controls prove ineffective. The supplies might as well be back on Earth, for all the good they do him.

Let's grant the film its solution and move on to the next necessity. He's found a convenient cave, so shelter isn't a concern at the moment. After oxygen, it's his water supply that is at issue. In a touch of gritty realism, Kit's supplies include educational tapes prepared for the astronauts. He views one about searching for water, and is warned against drinking seawater or his own urine, no matter how desperate the situation. The problem in both cases (besides taste or, indeed, disgust) is the salt. Salt goes into the blood stream, where it draws out water. So drinking saline solutions would simply exacerbate the problem of dehydration.

Once again, the film provides a fanciful and convenient answer. Kit has found Mac's escape pod, but Mac is dead. He buries his comrade, but then discovers that Mona the monkey has survived. In a major plus for the film, Mona is not merely a cute pet, but proves the key to the water problem. Kit notices that Mona refuses his offers of water, and deduces she has found her own supply. He denies her water for several days while restricting her movements, then lets her go. He then pursues her to see if she has found a water supply.

Indeed, she has been imbibing from an underground pool. Mona isn't writhing in agony from drinking from it, so he figures what does he have to lose? The more fastidious of us might want to boil it first. Monkey germs aside, there's no telling what microorganisms might exist in it. The fact that there's plant life in the water becomes another convenient solution (hey, it's edible!), but it does raise the question of what else is there, and what the plants are feeding on.

However we react to the discovery (with willing suspension of disbelief or a rolling of the eyes), it's not the answer that's interesting but the question. Is there a way to prepare oxygen and water for emergencies on the moon or Mars? Are there natural resources already there that can be utilized? This has to be one of the major factors in planning any long-term exploration or settlement of space.

In keeping with the Robinson Crusoe theme, Kit's extended stay has him adapting to his primitive existence. The plants in the waters prove amazingly versatile. "This is manna from heaven," he declares. "You eat it, you weave it, and you wear it." (Kit proves amazingly versatile as well, as weaving was presumably not part of his training. Oddly, there is no scene of him improvising a way to shave or cut his hair, yet he retains his military look throughout.)

There is one more survival issue with which the film has to deal before it gets to the alien space slavers in the final part of the story, and that is Kit's loneliness. Sure, he has tapes and he has the monkey, but nothing like real companionship. One night he makes a stew of the strange Martian plant, and it is implied that it has some hallucinogenic chemical. Whether from the plant or oxygen deprivation, Kit imagines that Mac is alive and visiting him in the cave. It is an eerie sequence in that Mac does not react to anything Kit says or does. When Kit awakens and realizes it was a dream, we understand that after months in what amounts to isolation, the strain is taking its toll.

This being *Robinson Crusoe on Mars*, the solution to this problem is the arrival of Friday (Victor Lundin), a humanoid alien who is not native to Mars, but has been brought there to work by aliens from another system. The film cleverly avoids focusing on the aliens by simply having scenes of their ships appear in the sky as they attempt to track Friday through his manacles. They dart through the sky in a method suggesting either a limited knowledge of physics by the filmmakers, or else an alien science far in advance of our own. Both assumptions are arguably correct.

Friday's solution to the oxygen problem is the pills he takes that allow him to survive in the thin Martian atmosphere. He offers to share them with Kit but the astronaut, heretofore showing no reticence in breathing Martian air, drinking Martian water, or eating Martian plant life, suddenly decides to play it safe and declines. Later, when Kit is nearly buried alive, Friday rescues him and makes him take a pill. By film's end, Kit becomes one of the few '60s castaways to make it home, when an Earth ship arrives to rescue him and, presumably, Friday.

It's no surprise that *Robinson Crusoe on Mars* is as thoughtful as it is about the difficulties in surviving on an alien world. Director Byron Haskin was no novice to the world of SF, having directed such movies as *The War of the Worlds* and *The Conquest of Space* for producer George Pal, and then working on the early '60s TV series *The Outer Limits*. Ib Melchior, who originated the script, co-wrote and directed the quirky 1964 feature *The Time Travelers*, and has other SF credits to his credit, including the original story for the '70s cult classic *Death Race 2000*. It was Melchior who thought of using Death Valley as the location for the film, being inspired to write the film after a visit there.

Ultimately, this movie might be classified as an intelligent but minor effort. It simply isn't equal to the pantheon of great SF films of the era that were about big ideas and which challenged the imagination. In a way, that's its strength. Kenneth von Gunden and Stuart H. Stock, in their useful (and, alas, out-of-print) 1982 volume *Twenty All-Time Great Science Fiction Films*, compare the film to the sorts of stories that John Campbell, Jr., was running in *Astounding*. It posits a realistic problem that can be solved through scientifically trained minds applying "reason, knowledge, determination, and a little luck." As such, it remains fascinating viewing because of the issues it raises about the potential problems for space explorers in the twenty-first century and beyond.

BEING AND NOTHINGNESS: THE MOVIE

French existential philosopher and writer Jean-Paul Sartre had nothing at all to do with the 1957 movie *The Incredible Shrinking Man*, but it's fun to imagine what he would have made of it. The film is remembered for its still-impressive special effects, but it is even more notable for being a science fiction film that not only addressed the anxieties of its time, but steadfastly refused to pander to its audience. There's no last-minute "cure." Its protagonist doesn't wake up and discover it was all a dream. The movie takes its premise to a conclusion that is more philosophical than climactic.

Indeed, when one looks up the meaning of "existentialism," it sounds like a description of the movie: "A philosophical movement embracing the view that the suffering individual must create meaning in an unknowable, chaotic, and seemingly empty universe." In this case, the suffering individual is Scott Carey (Grant Williams) who seems like a nice guy and loving husband, but whose life is about to go seriously off course. While on vacation with his wife Louise (Randy Stuart), he's exposed to a mysterious mist that may be a pesticide. Several months later, he is similarly exposed to some sort of radiation, and the combination somehow causes him to start shrinking.

What's interesting about that opening scene is that it's the only time we get to see Scott and Louise as a "normal" couple. Their playfulness—he orders his "wench" to get him a beer, she tells him to get it himself, they negotiate the terms in which she'll get the beer and he, in return, will get the dinner—suggests that Scott is sure of himself and secure of his place in the world. He's not threatened by Louise asserting herself. He understands how the world works and is comfortable about his own role in it—a complacency that might also describe America in the 1950s.

In Richard Matheson's script, based on his novel, Scott begins a losing battle in which he will be confronting every aspect of modern life. It starts when he realizes his clothes don't fit. He assumes either his wife or the dry cleaner has made a mistake. It's almost played as a joke, as if this was a suburban sitcom of the era, but Scott isn't laughing. It's a petty annoyance: the sleeves of his shirt are too long, the collar is too loose. However, it's the first sign that things are not working the way they're supposed to, challenging the conformity and stability he's taken for granted.

Scott does what people are supposed to do when something physical is wrong: He goes to see his physician, who assures him that people don't shrink and there has to be a rational explanation for what he's been experiencing. Of course there does. We turn to the men and women of science for reassurance. (When they don't reassure us in our beliefs, by talking about evolution or global warming, some people decide the problem is not with their beliefs but with the scientists.) Scott is momentarily ready to accept this explanation from his doctor, but he continues to shrink. Who is he going to believe, the expert or his own eyes? When Scott and Louise can no longer deny the obvious, they turn from the family doctor to the scientific experts in their lab coats, who are now able to confirm what Scott already knows. See, science works. Now all he needs is the cure, and his life can get back to normal.

However in this movie, that normalcy will occasionally be held out in front of Scott, only to be snatched away from him again. Science has identified his problem, but is unable to come up with an answer. He continues to shrink until, at three feet, his wife is now more like his mother. Where they once had an equal relationship, now her job is to shield him from the increasingly hostile outer world. In one scene they are so inundated by the media that Louise tries to get them an unlisted phone number. Apparently this is a task far beyond her capabilities, because when the phone company gives her a runaround, she feels she has no choice but to cancel the phone service and go on the waiting list for a new number. Scott is furious and tells her she should have insisted it was for him, since he is a "big man" now that the story of his shrinking has gotten out. His bitterness causes him to lash out at Louise, but it is really his frustration at his own impotence. He shouldn't have to rely on her ineffective protection. One can imagine how emasculating this must have seemed in this pre-feminist time. It's one thing to negotiate getting a beer. It's another for him to be physically inferior to and dependent upon Louise.

If his home is no longer his castle, Scott finds that science has also failed him. They come up with a "cure"—a shot which will stop his shrinking—but they can't restore him to his original size. This is a devastating admission in an era where science could seemingly do anything. Polio had been cured. The power of the atom had been unleashed. That same year Sputnik would be launched. Yet the scientists are forced to admit they are stymied by his condition. For all their vaunted breakthroughs, they are forced to admit that they are as powerless as he is.

Feeling hopeless, Scott heads out from his home to see if there's something in the outside world that will help ease his pain. In a bar near a carnival, he meets a woman who is a midget. She recognizes him and backs off for fear of intruding, but he's starved for human contact. If Louise has turned into a mother figure, this woman puts him back on an equal footing. Suddenly he's not alone. For a brief while, he has someone to talk to and share the burden with who can truly understand what it's like to see the world as he does. These moments allow the "normal" Scott to come back. In a different story, he might leave his wife and start over again with this new woman. However, that is not to be. After this agonizingly brief respite, he starts shrinking again. When he realizes he is now smaller than her, he is humiliated and runs off. In short order, he will find himself stripped of all the vestiges of his former life.

We next see him as he is forced to live in a doll house. He is now so small there is no way he could deal with normal chairs or beds. In one of the film's big scenes, he is attacked by the family cat. Scott is no longer the owner—if anyone can truly be said to "own" a cat—but has become the prey. He barely escapes to the cellar. In the film's cruelest twist, his wife comes home to discover a bloody scrap of cloth, and assumes that the cat has eaten Scott. We keep waiting for the moment when she will discover her mistake, but she never does. Now Scott is truly alone.

The final portion of the film is his life in the cellar. Having lost everything else, he is now stripped of the veneer of civilization. His existence is reduced to finding food, water, and shelter, and avoiding being consumed by something higher up the food chain, in this case a spider. It is a primitive existence, but one he is ready to master, even if he has regressed to the prehistoric life of a hunter/gatherer. By film's end, his situation is hopeless. His wife is gone, assuming him dead, and he is so tiny that he can't possibly get the attention of any other person, much less interact with them. Worse, he's continuing to shrink. It is a horrible fate. Will he soon find himself fending off complex molecules? The film ends here and, even more incredibly, it ends on a hopeful note. Scott, who had earlier been seen writing an account of his misadventure, continues to narrate his story and finds, in the end, he isn't alone after all. Rejecting the existentialism that has permeated the rest of the story, Scott gets religion, embracing the notion that God takes notice of all things great and small, and decides that applies to him as well, no matter how small he may get. After all, what are we full-size humans in comparison to the galaxy or the universe? It is on this note that the film ends.

The movie was a success at the box office, and Matheson was commissioned to write a sequel entitled "The Fantastic Little Girl," in which Louise starts to shrink, but it was never made. (It was published in his book *Unrealized Dreams* in 2005.) In the years since, the premise has been revisited in a number of films, but almost always as a comedy, from *The Incredible Shrinking Woman* (1981) to *Innerspace* (1987) to *Honey, I Shrunk the Kids* (1989). It was the chance to play with special effects, of having normal things look gigantic next to the miniature characters, that seemed to attract the filmmakers. It's no surprise that an announced remake of *The Incredible Shrinking Man* is to star Eddie Murphy in what will be, no doubt, another comedy. The rare exception to this was *Fantastic Voyage* (1966), where the miniaturization was part of a thriller plot taking place inside the body of someone needing delicate surgery.

The Incredible Shrinking Man takes its science fiction straight up and serious, ready to tackle some heavy issues. It's the rare film of any sort that confronts the issue of "what is the meaning of life?" Yet this one wants to take away every convention and support of civilization and still find hope. The contrast with a nihilistic movie like the recent *The Road* is stark. *The Road* posits a doomed world of hopelessness. Some people may mistake that bleakness for profundity, but when asked if there's any positive message at all, its defenders would have the characters unwittingly quote Monty Python and say, "I'm not dead yet." By contrast, *The Incredible Shrinking Man* is closer to the Biblical book of Job in arguing that just because you don't know why you are suffering doesn't indicate that there is no meaning in the universe. Even if you only have a glimmer of the larger picture, a God who sees the whole thing takes notice of you as well.

That's all well and good for people of faith, but what about the non-believers? Is the film to be dismissed as an exercise in existentialism that ultimately falls short and sells out? Perhaps not. The argument the film is making in the end is that Scott's life has meaning and significance no matter how small he gets. He has a role to play in the universe, even if he's not quite sure what it is. To paraphrase another philosopher, René Descartes, "I think, therefore I matter."

However you come out, what can't be denied is that science fiction films at their best give us something to think about beyond the thrills and effects. It's why, more than half a century after its release, *The Incredible Shrinking Man* is worth viewing and talking about, while less than a year after *its* release, the top grossing US movie of 2009—*Transformers 2*—is not.

(NOTE: The Library of Congress apparently agrees. At the end of 2009, *The Incredible Shrinking Man* was one of twenty-five films selected for preservation as part of America's film heritage.)

MY BLOODY VALENTINE

For science fiction fans of a certain age, seeing *Destination Moon* or *Forbidden Planet* or *This Island Earth* was the moment when they first experienced that "sense of wonder." These movies took young viewers off to the Moon or into deep space and alien worlds, making it seem incredibly real even as viewers knew it was all Hollywood legerdemain. With disbelief duly suspended, one could imagine being part of a future where space travel and other such superscience was possible. Think of a young 21st century teen seeing *Avatar* for the first time, and you get some sense of what it's like to be swept off your feet into a world of imagination and future possibilities.

For those of us who were children of the '60s rather than the '50s, a movie like *Forbidden Planet* was something first encountered on TV or perhaps, much later, at a revival house or, even later, back on TV via home video and cable. Marvelous as the movie is, we were simply too young to appreciate it in its day. For budding science fiction fans in 1966, the sense of wonder movie wasn't about outer space at all. *Fantastic Voyage* was a movie that sent its miniaturized crew into *inner* space: inside the human body. Watched today, the Cold War era plot seems contrived, and the effects could probably be done better by computer, but the movie has a charm that endures.

The story opens with U.S. government operative Charles Grant (Stephen Boyd) escorting Jan Benes (Jean Del Val), a scientist who is defecting to the United States. Benes, we learn, has solved a problem occurring in top secret programs run by both the U.S. and the Soviet Union. He wants to make sure that his solution, which has important military implications, is divulged only to us. En route to his rendezvous with American officials there is an assassination attempt. Benes suffers brain damage which proves to be inoperable... by ordinary procedures. As Grant discovers, the secret program Benes has been involved with has to do with miniaturizing people and things to microscopic size. An army can be reduced to fit inside a bottle cap. The problem for the military is that the effect only lasts for a single hour. Benes has solved this problem, which is why it is crucial to save the scientist's life.

Grant's arrival at CMDF headquarters is right out of James Bond. He's told to stay in his car, which is then lowered from the surface to a vast underground complex. How vast? People need carts and scooters to get around. One might wonder what city has so much empty space underground that this huge facility could be built without disrupting water mains, sewer lines, cables, etc. Our attention is not on such mundane matters. Instead, like Grant, we need to be briefed by General Carter (Edmond O'Brien), who explains that CMDF stands for "Combined Miniature Defense Forces." Grant is being drafted to be part of a select team that will be injected into the scientist in order to operate on his brain. The first step, of course, is that they must be shrunk to cellular size.

There's some more blather before the mission finally gets underway. Grant is being sent along in order to prevent any sabotage. The rest of the crew is essential, but not all of them are trustworthy. These include: Dr. Duval (Arthur Kennedy), a brilliant but erratic brain surgeon; Cora (Raquel Welch), his assistant; Capt. Owens (William Redfield), the pilot; and Dr. Michaels (Donald Pleasance), the commander of the mission who, it turns out, suffers from claustrophobia. At the briefing, Col. Reid (Arthur O'Connell) is apoplectic that "girls" do not belong on such a mission, but Cora looks so good in a wet suit he is overruled. The mission is simple: they will be shrunk while aboard a specially prepared submarine, which will then be injected into an artery in the scientist's neck. They'll travel to his brain, use a laser to destroy the blood clots, and then get out before the hour's up. If they're still inside and start growing, they will attract the attention of white corpuscles and be treated as foreign invaders of the scientist's body which, obviously, they are. The more blatant problem—if they're inside the scientist's brain and start rapidly growing, his head will explode—isn't mentioned.

Finally, all of the exposition is out of the way and the crew boards their ship. They carry with them a radioactive particle that can't be shrunk, which will power the sub's atomic engine. It's at this point that the engineers and biologists in the audience may throw up their hands and start picking apart all the scientific flaws in the premise, such as what happens to all that mass when the miniaturization occurs. The tiny sub in the hypodermic is treated as if it weighs nothing. Legendary author Isaac Asimov knew it was scientific claptrap, but he agreed to write the novelization of Harry Kleiner's script, itself based on a short story by Otto Klement and Jerome Bixby. Asimov had nothing to do with the film, but the book, originally issued in hardcover, proved so popular and enduring that many years later he wrote a sequel novel where he was able to put his own spin on the science (or pseudo-science) of the story.

Meanwhile, after a methodical sequence depicting the miniaturization, the now-tiny crew are in Dr. Benes's bloodstream. There may be problems with the science, but the filmmakers made some effort to create what people might actually see inside the human body if they were to be shrunk to that level. What's amazing is that everything we see had to be actually created for the camera and filmed.

There's some trickery involving blue screens which allows them to combine images, but this is decades before such work would be created via computer. The "blood stream," for example, was actually a tank filled with unmixable fluids along the same lines of a lava lamp. The camera pointed down into the tank so that the "corpuscles" bubbled up. When that image was then placed in front of the ship's view screen, it made it appear as if they were traveling along the artery. To a preteen viewer, this was way cool, even if it wouldn't have been put that way at the time.

When the ship gets diverted from its path into the carotid artery, things start getting dicey. They end up having to go through the heart (briefly stopped so the ship can get through it in one piece), and then they replenish their air supply by tapping into the lungs. How the miniaturized and unminiaturized oxygen will mix, or whether at the atomic level it doesn't matter (as with their power source), isn't clear, but having to deal with attacks by platelets—which nearly strangle Cora—provides plenty of excitement. In the most inventive sequence of the film, they're forced to access the brain through the scientist's ear, and we're told that slightest sound in the operating theater will so reverberate that there could be terrible consequences for the crew while they're there. Naturally, someone drops something, and we get to see our heroes buffeted around.

Finally, they make it to the brain, which proves to be another amazing location with electrical charges racing along synapses. Dr. Duval attempts to operate with a jury-rigged laser, hastily repaired after it was mysteriously sabotaged along the way. The saboteur is revealed—it's unlikely that even 1966 audiences were surprised at who it turns out to be—and subsequently suffers a horrible death by white blood cell. The survivors cleverly exit the body through a tear drop, and the operation is a success. How the white blood cells manage to remove all of the parts of the destroyed sub—not to mention the dead saboteur and the miniaturized saline solution—before it all reverts to full size is also not explained.

What that summary should tell you is that *Fantastic Voyage* is a combination of a boy's adventure story with a biology lesson. The details are fudged, but then they're fudged whenever we have time travel or faster-than-light spaceships. What we're left with is that sense of wonder at how complex and wonderfully strange our bodies are, which not even Dr. Duval's dramatic bloviating can ruin. When Grant says he thought that blood was red, it's pointed out that oxygenated red blood cells are, but much of the blood stream is more akin to seawater, carrying the various blood parts on their journey through the body. That concept seems a lot more real from inside a tiny sub traveling through an artery than it does in a dry textbook.

Looked at as an adult, other things are more likely to be noticed, such as when Cora is being wrapped by the clinging platelets and the men are all pawing at her body as they try to remove them. Maybe Col. Reid was right about what happens to boys when girls are around. On the other hand, Reid is also the one who responds to the report that the crew has reached Benes' brain by saying, "Imagine, they're in the human mind." No, characters entering someone's dreams or thoughts can be said to be in someone's mind. These guys are in the physical brain. They have no access to what the scientist is thinking.

Such silliness aside, it's clear that the movie is celebrating a fascination with the human body quite unusual for Hollywood. When they first notice some phenomenon in the bloodstream, Dr. Duval says, "I think we should stop and investigate." Of course they shouldn't. The clock is ticking and they've got a job to do. It's all so interesting, though, that we sympathize, and we're glad when they get thrown off course and have to take a detour. This is much more exciting than anything on *This Island Earth*'s Metaluna ever was.

In the end, that's what that sense of wonder is all about. It's not about thinking like a child or leaving your critical faculties at the door. It's about being open to knowledge and experience that may change the way you look at the world. There's a running joke about General Carter guzzling coffee with plenty of sugar throughout the film, and late in the story he's looking at some of the sugar he's spilled which has attracted an ant. He's about to crush it under his thumb and then stops, suddenly making the connection between the tiny living thing and the miniature crew he's sent on a do-or-die mission. Col. Reid suggests that Carter is turning into a Buddhist, seeing all life as interconnected. Carter denies this, but this moment just might be the summing up of the film. Whether you take it from a religious perspective or not, being aware of the miracle of life and, indeed, of the universe, engenders a sense of wonder. For at least one young viewer, this movie would be an entryway into not only the world of imagination, but a way of looking at the real world as well.

LOVE IN THE TIME OF PARADOX

Romantic comedies are a hardy genre. It's been crossbred with everything from mysteries (*The Thin Man* movies) to coarse frat boy comedies (*There's Something About Mary, Knocked Up*), but what about the science fiction film? Putting aside the movies where the "love interest"—meaning the hero's girlfriend—is put there just to have someone to scream at the monster, SF films where we have to take the romance seriously tend to be dramas, like *Time After Time* or David Cronenberg's remake of *The Fly*. These are films where the romance is important, but not the primary thrust of the film. In *Time After Time*, the hook is H.G. Wells (Malcolm McDowell) traveling to the present day of 1979 in pursuit of Jack the Ripper (David Warner). In *The Fly*, the doomed romance between Seth Brundle (Jeff Goldblum) and Veronica Quaife (Geena Davis) adds to the tragedy of the story, but our focus is Seth's mutation into "Brundlefly."

Is there a film where the romance is front and center that is also undeniably both a comedy and science fiction? It turns out there's at least one. *Happy Accidents* is a charmer that passed quickly through theaters in the summer and fall of 2001, and now awaits rediscovery on DVD.

(Note to the "no spoiler" fascists: If you are the type who screams at someone for telling you that Hamlet dies or that the Allies won World War II because now the story has been "spoiled" for you, stop reading now. While not revealing the big surprises, I will be discussing something not disclosed until about twenty minutes into the film. It's also revealed on the back of the DVD cover. Life must be very difficult for you.)

Ruby Weaver (Marisa Tomei) is a thirty-something living in New York. She's just broken up with her latest loser boyfriend. She and her girlfriends put pictures of their rejects in a shoe box they call the "Ex Files," which should already be a tip-off that writer/director Brad Anderson is one of us. Ruby doesn't ask much of the men she meets, just that they not be drug addicts or Jesus freaks or fetishists who wear rubber gloves... In short, she wants someone she can have fun with, enjoy talking to, who's engaged with her and with the world.

One day in the park, she meets Sam Deed (Vincent D'Onofrio), who's all that and a bit more. On the one hand, his taste in music is a bit strange (he likes polkas), but on the other hand, he follows her to her new job as an English as a second language instructor and introduces himself to each of the students in their own native tongue. There's clearly something odd about Sam, but he's kind and sweet and obviously adores her. Ruby loves being with him, but she keeps waiting for the other shoe to drop. When he finally reveals why he seems different, Ruby has to decide whether to believe his outlandish story or simply throw him out.

See, Sam is from the future. Not only is he from the year 2470, but he was born on the Atlantic coast of Iowa, so you know things are quite different from the world as we know it. He explains that one day he found a picture of her in a curio shop and fell in love. Naturally, he decided that he had to go back into the past to meet her. Is this a love story that spans the centuries, as he wants her to believe? Is it an elaborate, intimate role-playing game, as her friend suggests, where she's being invited to share in his fantasy? Or is Sam really from present day Iowa, despondent over a family tragedy, and seeking refuge in a delusion? The film keeps dropping hints first one way and then another, before tying everything up in a satisfying bow at the end. How Anderson accomplishes that you'll have to see for yourself, but suffice to say that couples with a shared fondness for SF who rent this for Valentine's Day will not be disappointed.

What makes this work as a hybrid is that the film fulfills the requirements of both the romantic comedy and the time travel story. In the former, the classic plot outline—boy meets girl, boy loses girl, boy gets girl—is followed, but more importantly, so is the emphasis on character. In most of the best examples of the genre, we want the couple to learn from each other and discover they belong together. Ruby has been drifting from job to job and from boyfriend to boyfriend in a fruitless pursuit of perfection. When it doesn't fall into her lap, she gets restless and moves on or gets fired. As she learns from her mother (Tovah Feldshuh), perfection is not to be had in this world. In an illuminating conversation about her father (Richard Portnow), a recovering alcoholic, her mother is glad he's stopped drinking, but then adds ruefully that he was a lot more fun back then. So what if Sam is a little strange? If he makes her happy isn't that enough to stop her from tossing him aside?

As for Sam, the story he tells Ruby keeps shifting and changing, but just when she thinks she's caught him in a lie, he has a perfectly rational—for him—explanation. He is looking for stability and family, something he has lost in the world of 2470. With Ruby's help, he's ready to settle down and commit. Is he stable enough to do it? Her therapist (Holland Taylor) isn't so sure, and so Ruby is at a loss what to do.

While all this is going on, the SF elements are not getting short shrift. The discussions of time travel lead to several conversations about the paradox of traveling into the past and whether it is possible to change things once there. One hilarious scene at an art gallery has actor Anthony Michael Hall (playing himself) convinced that Sam is having a great "improv" moment as he explains how scientists have solved the apparent problems inherent in, say, going back and killing one's own grandfather. One odd side effect of time travel is that he occasionally experiences brief spasms of time flowing backward, as if his body had still not come completely to rest in the "present."

There's the additional problem that Sam could not bring anything back with him, so he has no "proof" of what he says except his own memories. The details that are dropped about the future and how time travel is managed all play out, such as the idea that rival factions in the future could be working at cross-purposes in our time. One character even claims to have moved to the past "for tax reasons."

Happy Accidents manages to succeed as both a romantic comedy and as an SF film without any special effects necessary. It's such an unusual hybrid, however, in a field where SF is pigeonholed as movies with robots or aliens or mad scientists, that IFC Films (the company that released it) had no idea what to do with it. It was sold as a straight-up romantic comedy, and though both excellent actors, neither Tomei nor D'Onofrio were big enough names to attract much attention. It was too mainstream to get much of a launch out of the Sundance Film Festival (where it premiered in 2000), and too weird for general audiences to get any appreciable word of mouth going. It was a flop, grossing less than $700,000 in its theatrical run.

As readers of my past essays know, I am a regular at the annual 24 Hour SF Film Marathon held President's Day Weekend in Somerville, Massachusetts. After *Happy Accidents* died, I urged the director of the festival to book the film for the next event. It ended up playing at the marathon in February 2002 to enthusiastic response from an audience that was barely aware of its brief run in general release. This is a small, quirky, and delightful movie ready to be discovered.

There's an interesting P.S. to the story, which the fest director shared with me and which tells you a lot about the way the movie industry works. He had contacted the distributor to book the film, which was already at the end of its theatrical run. He explained this was for a single showing at a science fiction film festival. According to the director, there was a long pause at the end of the line.

Finally the person on other end said, "Hmm... science fiction. Maybe if we had sold it that way..."

IRONIC, ISN'T IT?

The release of a newly restored print of 1975's *A Boy and His Dog* is a cause for celebration. Until the arrival of *Star Wars* in 1977, the decade was not considered a golden age for science fiction movies. There were *Planet of the Apes* sequels, Charlton Heston action films, and the occasional surprise like *Westworld* or *The Man Who Fell to Earth*, but for the most part, these were lean years for science fiction on the big screen.

What makes *A Boy and His Dog* interesting is that it is an uncompromising adaptation of Harlan Ellison's story. From the title to the ending, it's a movie that fairly demands *not* to be taken at face value. Those who do—which is to say, the irony-impaired—will end up being baffled by a movie that delights in breaking the rules.

We meet Vic (Don Johnson), a young man trying to survive in a post-apocalyptic world. Vic is a fighter, but not the sharpest knife in the drawer. He's aided by his dog Blood, who is not only intelligent but also telepathic. We see them trying to avoid being killed in their survival-of-the-fittest world above ground, and then we see Vic lured into an underground community, which is a parody of small town America from a century earlier. In spite of the veneer of civilization provided by the town's leaders (headed up by an unexpectedly cast Jason Robards), life is just as brutal for Vic down below. Vic finally escapes along with young Quilla June (Susanne Benton), the strong-willed woman who had lured him to the town in hopes that it would allow for her own ascent to power. Once out, they are reunited with Blood, who has barely been hanging on after having suffered severe injuries. Vic has to decide which one of his companions to sacrifice for the other, and the title ought to give away his answer.

What does it all mean? Director L.Q. Jones (who also adapted Ellison's story) doesn't give us any easy moral for the story. This is not a Michael Crichton adventure where technology is the problem, nor is it a message movie like *Soylent Green* or *Silent Running*. Jones simply presents Vic and Blood's adventures and leaves us with what used to be thought of as a happy ending involving man and his best friend. The fact that we don't sit back and smile at the end ought to make us think. This is not a movie about surviving the apocalypse. It's a movie that asks us whether the apocalypse will be worth surviving.

The title brings to mind the works of the quintessential illustrator of American life, Norman Rockwell, who actually did a painting called "A Boy and

His Dog." The movie then proceeds to turn everything on its head. Vic is little more than an animal. He can think and talk, but he's primarily concerned with survival, food, and sex, and not necessarily in that order. Blood (voiced by Tim McIntire) is the strategist of the team, looking at the big picture. While Blood needs Vic to survive, it's even more obvious that Vic needs Blood.

We're then presented with two distinct post-apocalyptic worlds. Aboveground is a Darwinian nightmare, with the strong exploiting the weak. Life is reduced to a matter of brawn, not brains. When Vic goes for an evening's entertainment at an encampment where some entrepreneur is showing scratchy prints of old porno films, he cheats the gatekeeper by palming off unwanted canned vegetables as something else. He gets away with it because in spite of his power, the guy collecting admissions is illiterate. While Vic is a good fighter, as we see when he faces attack from some nomads, it is Blood who knows how to spook them by making them think the "screamers" are upon them. The "screamers" are nothing more than the air raid sirens that have now lost all meaning except as an omen of impending death.

Often in these kinds of stories, the goal of our hero is to reach some stronghold of civilization where wise people are trying to start anew. Thus we're not quite sure what happens when Quilla seduces Vic, and then lures him into Topeka, an underground community. There—except for the lack of sunlight and the odd makeup the people wear—we seem to be in a Norman Rockwell world. Everything seems so wholesome, and we see that the Committee (headed by Robards) is genuinely pleased with Vic's arrival. The problem is that the world down there is just as corrupt and brutal as the one aboveground. Those with power use it ruthlessly and are loathe to relinquish it. As for Vic, he's needed because he's virile and, more important, fertile. He's there to "marry" all the young women—one at a time—and then impregnate them. That sounds fine to Vic, except that this "moral" community can't have the bestial Vic pawing their women. Instead, he will be strapped down and "milked," and the women will be artificially inseminated. It's only a matter of time before Vic, with the help of a now disillusioned Quilla, bust out.

It's hard to imagine that anyone could miss the dark, satiric nature of the film. This is a surreal vision presented as if it's a boy's adventure. Yet people continue to misread the film, almost as if they think that Jones (and Ellison) *approve* of what occurs in the movie. Eric Henderson, in a 2003 review for *Slant*, calls it "the 1975 cult classic for boys who hate women." One might wonder how he came to that odd conclusion, except he's not the first to totally misconstrue the film as a misogynist fantasy. One might more properly call it misanthropic: it despairs of the human condition in general, not women in particular.

A little over thirty years ago, I was an undergraduate at the University of Rochester when the film played on campus. Over the next several days, the letters column of the school paper was filled with a debate over the film, with some very humorless people insisting that the movie, and particularly the ending where Vic favors Blood over Quilla, was not only anti-woman but actually *advocating* violence against women. After a week or so, someone had the wit to collect all these newspapers and mail them to Harlan Ellison for a reaction. The writer is known for having a legendary temper when he feels he's been wronged, which is what made his reaction all the more surprising. He said that if his expenses would be paid, he'd waive his speaking fee and fly across country to debate the film's critics.

He did just that. It's hard to say if any minds were changed that night, but Ellison made it clear that things expressed in satire are not to be taken literally, and that he certainly was not suggesting that a dog's life was more important a woman's. For those of us (male and female) who "got" the film, the uproar was a little baffling. It would have been like picking up the *National Lampoon* and thinking it was *Time* magazine. Yet, for the literal-minded, *A Boy and a Dog* seemed to be a movie that was endorsing rape and murder, instead of simply turning a jaundiced eye at societies where such things are able to take place.

You may have heard the old theater expression, "Satire is what closes on Saturday night." That's because most consumers of plays and movies (and TV shows and books) aren't equipped to handle nuance or layers of meaning. For them, *Life is Beautiful* is a movie that says the Holocaust was fun, *Dexter* endorses serial killing, and *Romeo and Juliet* is pro-teenage suicide. Goodness knows what they make of movies like *A Clockwork Orange* or *Blade Runner* or *The Truman Show*.

Maybe it's just as well that science fiction doesn't often succeed with the mainstream. As another expression has it, "Reality is a crutch for people unable to handle science fiction."

THE ULTIMATE BOOK MOVIE

As a science fiction fan and a movie buff (later a professional film critic) I was exposed to *Fahrenheit 451* fairly early. It was one of the earliest "grown up books" I read, around the age of 11 or 12, and unquestionably the first Francois Truffaut film I saw, at no more than 14 or 15.

Ray Bradbury's novel is the ultimate statement on censorship, positing a society where the fire department's mission is to locate and burn books. It was that theme that was so attractive to Truffaut, a filmmaker who loved books but never got to write any. His bibliography during his lifetime (he died in 1984) consisted of his published scripts, his collected film reviews (he was a critic before he became a filmmaker), and a book-length series of interviews with Alfred Hitchcock. Not too shabby for someone primarily remembered as a director. While Truffaut's works are noted for his love of film, those who know his films well soon realize Truffaut was also in love with books.

It was apparent right from his first feature, *The 400 Blows* (1959). His alter ego, Antoine Doinel (Jean-Pierre Leaud), nearly burns down his parents' apartment when he builds a shrine to his favorite author, Honoré de Balzac. Several Truffaut films are adaptations of novels, including his 1961 classic *Jules and Jim*, while his *The Man Who Loved Women* (1977) lingers over the process of the protagonist's book being published.

However, his love affair with books had its fullest flowering in a film that was difficult to shoot, was maligned by critics upon release, and yet has managed to retain a definite appeal. He first became interested in filming *Fahrenheit 451* in the early '60s, and would subsequently see it through a long and difficult process.

Truffaut faced several challenges: it was his first film in color, and also his first film in English, a language in which he was less than fluent. He cast Julie Christie in a dual role, and then had a falling out with Oskar Werner, who played Montag—the fireman who starts taking books home with him. The director and star had differing ideas about the character, usually not a good sign for a film, and were reportedly not on speaking terms by the end of the production.

However, if you come to the 1966 movie without any preconceptions, it has a number of things to appeal to the bibliophile. Start with the opening credits, which are spoken rather than printed. This is a world where the printed word has been banned, and the film establishes that from the very beginning.

Then there are the scenes of the firemen at work. Clearly, they are supposed to be horrific, echoing the book burnings of the Nazis. Truffaut had to face the question of which books get burned on screen. It's an interesting selection. The expected mix of classics and "controversial" books are there, many of them favorites chosen by the director himself, including a copy of *Cahiers du Cinema*, the French film magazine where Truffaut first made his name. Also fed to the flames is a paperback collection from *MAD* magazine, a bit of juvenile satire that really hit home to this viewer who, at the time, was still reading it.

For people who love books but know they are never going to write one, Truffaut provides the next best thing at the movie's end. Montag has run away from the burners and finds a hidden community of readers. It is illegal for them to keep their banned volumes, so they do the one thing open to them: they memorize their favorite books, locking them inside their heads until such time as the world comes to its senses. In effect, they have become living books. One man is nearing death and is teaching his nephew the work he is preserving so it won't be lost. The final shots of the film, of the book people walking in the snow, reciting their texts so as not to forget, is among the great tributes to literature on film.

Of course you should read Bradbury's novel—and many other books as well. But if you're really a book lover and have never seen Truffaut's film, have I got a movie for you.

(NOTE: This was written for the Quality Paperback Book Club desk calendar, in which I had a limited space at the bottom of two pages—covering one week—to expound on my topic. The club continues but, alas, the annual desk calendar does not.)

THE MYSTERY OF *THE WOMAN IN THE MOON*

For those of us enamored of science fiction movies, studying their early history is limited to a finite set of "classics" and a few oddities for the more ambitious. Of course the science fiction masterpiece of the silent era is *Metropolis*, directed by Fritz Lang and released in 1926. The historical curio one is obliged to see (and usually ends up enjoying) is Georges Méliès' 1902 *A Voyage to the Moon*. It's the one that includes a chorus line of cuties seeing off the cannonball-like rocket that lands right in the eye of the man in the moon.

After that? Some include *The Cabinet of Dr. Caligari*, Robert Wiene's 1919 expressionistic masterpiece. It's more of a psychological horror tale, but we can afford to be inclusive. There's the startling art deco *Aelita: Queen of Mars* (1924), a Russian comedy about a detective chasing an inventor turned murderer all the way to the Red Planet. Throw in a few other Méliès shorts and the 1925 *The Lost World* (complete with special effects by Willis O'Brien, who would go on to do *King Kong*) and that's about it. Most of what we know about the remaining science fiction movies of the silent era comes from reading about them, rather than actually seeing the films.

Part of the reason for this is that many of them are lost. Those rarities that still exist in archives are rarely shown. Collectors may prize them, but they don't turn up on TV. Video and DVD releases—when they happen—are sporadic and limited. It's unfortunate but inevitable. SF readers aren't clamoring for reprints of all the uncollected stories written for pulp magazines in the first part of the 20th century either. There may be some forgotten gems to be found that have yet to be anthologized, but for the most part it is material best left forgotten except, perhaps, by historians and critics.

Yet every once in a while, a fresh assessment is important. Something that seemed ordinary or uninteresting to one generation may have things that engage another. Such is the case with *Frau im Mond* (*Woman in the Moon*), a 1929 science fiction epic that has been given short shrift for years. It's time for another look.

Director Fritz Lang was at the top of his form when he undertook the project. He had completed *Metropolis* and *Spione* (*Spies*), the latter considered the cinematic precursor to the James Bond and other superspy movies. This space adventure would be his farewell to silent movies. His following film would be a talkie: M, the landmark thriller starring Peter Lorre as a child molester hunted by both the police and the criminal underworld.

If you go by what is written about it, *Woman in the Moon* is a dull movie with a few minor elements of note, but really not worth exploring. Indeed, it has such a lackluster reputation, that even this writer confesses to passing up opportunities to see it over the past twenty years. Leonard Maltin, not the most reliable critic when it comes to science fiction, dismisses it with two stars: "slow and way overlong." The more reliable John Clute uses words like "silly" and "ponderous" in describing the movie. Frederik Pohl and Frederik Pohl IV (in their *Science Fiction Studies in Film*) can't do more than mention the film in passing while focusing on *Metropolis*. So, though the film remains available, including on video in lengths varying from 90 minutes to some two and a half hours, it is usually ignored.

With a build-up like this, you might expect the revelation that the movie is, in fact, a lost masterpiece. No such luck. However, it turns out to be far better than its reputation would allow, mixing uncanny scientific predictions with absorbing melodrama, as well as extremely impressive special effects. Of course it gets things wrong, too, but only people outside the field focus primarily on SF's predictive powers.

The story begins with Professor Georg Manfeldt (Klaus Pohl), a renowned astronomer, presenting his views at an academic conference. His theory that "the moon is rich in gold" is greeted with hails of derisive laughter. Manfeldt expected to be challenged, perhaps, but not humiliated. "Gentlemen, laughter is an argument of idiots against every new idea," he tells them, to no avail. His career is ruined.

Years later, a now bedraggled Manfeldt gets his chance. Wolf Helius (Willy Fritsch) and Hans Windegger (Gustav von Wangenheim) are planning their own rocket to the moon. A mysterious Finance Committee is eager to bankroll them in order to get monopolistic control over the moon's riches. They send Walter Turner (Fritz Rasp) along to guard their interests. Joining them is the beautiful Friede Velten (Gerda Maurus), whom Helius loves, but who has just become engaged to Windegger.

It's pure soap opera, of course, complete with the rocket being named for Friede, but look at the moment when Helius pleads with her to get off the ship. Friede, a modern woman, stands up for her place on the mission: "Are you trying to say we women are not brave enough to try this venture?" Helius backs down, but in the real world, it would be more than fifty years before a woman would finally get the opportunity to show her abilities in space.

For space adventure fans, the first half of the film is fascinating as we realize that many of the things we're seeing were being put on screen for the first time.

An earlier rocket—it's the classic Hugo-shaped silver cigar with tail fins—has been sent on a test mission, with its lunar impact being photographed from Earth. Now the *Friede*, a much larger rocket, is readied for a manned journey. Through the use of animation, we see the planned trip, and it looks awfully familiar to those of us who lived through the Apollo missions. The multistage rocket will blast off with great acceleration, which must then be cut off. The path will take them in a figure eight around the moon and then back to Earth.

Where did Lang get these ideas? The film's writer (and Lang's then-wife) Thea von Harbou, wasn't a rocketry expert, so Lang brought in those who were: Willy Ley and Hermann Oberth. Ley would later flee the Nazis, as did Lang. Oberth would work on Hitler's rocket program, but after the war he, too, ended up in Hollywood for a stint as technical advisor on *Destination Moon* (1950). Their advice was so good that part of the film's legendary reputation is based on the fact that it was withdrawn from circulation by the Nazis, who feared it revealed too much about their actual rocket program. The models used in the film were supposedly destroyed.

The movement of the rocket on the ground by derrick also provides a sense of déjà vu decades before the reality of our space program, although its immersion in a pool of water—due to the "delicate materials" from which it was made—seems strange. Then comes the moment for which the film is best known: the countdown. The title cards flash the final sequence ("5, 4, 3, 2, 1, Now!") in a manner that filmgoers may not realize was invented for the film.

Willy Ley recalled years later (in his book *Rockets, Missiles, and Men in Space*) that he was startled to realize that this was the first countdown in a movie. He contacted Lang and asked him if Lang had perhaps picked this up in military practice during World War I, but Lang told Ley he had made it up himself for dramatic purposes. Little did they realize that this bit of stagecraft would have a lasting impact.

Meanwhile the crew goes through the trauma of high G forces (referred to as the "critical eight minutes... of acceleration, which can be deadly"). Helius turns off the power in time, but the entire crew passes out, and hours go by before they re-awaken. When they do, they discover what would become a clichéd plot device but seems surprising here: a stowaway. Forget Dr. Smith, this is more like Will Robinson: young Gustav (Gustl Stark-Gstettenbaur) has hidden in one of the spacesuits.

Gustav announces that he has "studied the moon problem very carefully," and wishes to participate in their expedition. He then opens his knapsack and withdraws his research materials, which turns out to be a bunch of pulp magazines. We notice a "moon vampire" on one, and a gigantic cow (the one that jumped over the moon?) chasing a man on another. Is there any SF fan for whom that youthful desire for space travel does not strike a chord? Friede, however, is taken aback by an image of a spacesuited figure parachuting to Earth as she suddenly realizes that they have no idea where they are.

In fact the ship is right on course, as a look out the window demonstrates, and this brings the film to its most incredible sequence. As the ship goes into lunar orbit, the detailed and cratered surface rolls beneath them. In the distance, Earth can be seen against the star field. Not until *Destination Moon* more than two decades later would space travel be depicted with such awe and excitement.

There's also the usual movie hokum about weightlessness, and again viewers must remind themselves that these bits would become clichés, but were not yet. Gustav bounces upward through a hatch without touching the ladder. Friede tries to pour some water and nothing comes out. Her fiancée shakes some water globules out of the pitcher (through an animated effect) and then collects them in a glass so she can drink it down.

Once on the moon, the film leaves reality as we know it completely behind. First, Manfeldt tests the moon's "atmosphere" by lighting matches. He then removes his space helmet and finds the air breathable. The gold plot comes to the fore, with Turner willing to kill anyone who comes between him and the riches he was sent to claim for the Finance Committee. By the time Turner is himself killed, the ship has lost half its oxygen and can not return with all of the remaining crew. It's a variation of a bit that would provide the climax of *Destination Moon* as well, but Lang is a lot less sentimental than George Pal would prove to be. The ship really can't take everyone back, and someone will have to be left behind. How that is resolved will not be revealed here (you want to have some surprises left, don't you?) but it's an ending that has surprising impact.

Watching *Woman in the Moon* was a revelation. Although *Metropolis* is clearly the better film, it is also more of a parable about a dystopia with a robot and a mad scientist thrown into the mix. Science fiction fans have no problem embracing it, but it's less about "What if?" and more about "Beware!" Here, Lang and his collaborators are trying to excite viewers about the real possibility of traveling to the moon, and the ideas are presented as plausible and not the least fantastic. Some critics who object to the melodramatic elements of the story often give such things a pass in non-SF films, while others—perhaps not having seen the film in a long time, if at all—are prepared to simply repeat the received wisdom: long, boring, silly, not worth the effort.

In fact, *Woman in the Moon* is well worth the effort. Indeed, it deserves recognition as the first serious science fiction movie about space travel, filled with images and ideas about such exploration that would not fully flower until many years into the future.

1953

(One of the highlights of the World Science Fiction Convention is the announcement of the Hugo Awards, given by fans to the outstanding science fiction achievements of the past year. Under one of the many rules governing the process, a convention is allowed to give out "Retro Hugos" if it is the anniversary of a year in which the awards were not given out. To date it has only been done three times. In 2004, the convention gave out awards for both 2003 and 1953. As fans have several sources to turn to for advice on whom to nominate for the Hugos in the two-stage process, the organizers of Noreascon 4 provided a helpful guide to fans wanting to be brought up to speed on the potential candidates for the Retro Hugo ballot. The following was my overview of all the potential "Dramatic Presentation" candidates from 1953.)

Voters for the 1953 Retro Hugos understand that it's impossible to duplicate the experience of having lived through 1953 and then calmly considering the best of the year. Fifty years later, our take is inevitably colored not only by what has endured and stood the test of time, but also what is readily available. That is particularly true in the Dramatic Presentation category.

Under Hugo rules, nominations will take place under the current category breakdown, which includes "short form" and "long form" dramatic works. The Hugo administrators have some leeway to move items from one category to another within certain time limits, as well as to collapse the two categories into one if there are insufficient nominees. With most, if not all, of the feature films qualifying as "short form," it is going to be a Solomonic task. In order not to prejudice the voters or the administrators, this breakdown is by medium rather than length.

TELEVISION

The year 1953 is well before the heyday of classic SF TV like *The Twilight Zone* and *Star Trek*. What's more, most of what was on is not readily available for viewing, if it was preserved at all. Thus *Captain Video* (the space serial starting in 1949) and *The Secret Files of Captain Video* (a second, non-continuous series that started in 1953) were both on the air, but it will be hard to track down and promote single episodes from 1953 as Retro Hugo-worthy items. The same can be said of other 1953 series that were geared to kids: *Atom Squad*, *Rod Brown of the Rocket Rangers* (starring a young Cliff Robertson), and *Space Patrol*.

In prime time science fiction showed up rarely, but 1953 did have episodes of *Tales of Tomorrow*. Other anthology series, notably *Suspense*, may have run episodes that year that would be eligible, but lots of luck tracking them down and then getting people to see them. (Radio presentations were beyond the scope of this article, but will have the same sorts of availability issues.)

The one TV series with 1953 episodes that meets the test of accessibility to fans today is the syndicated *The Adventures of Superman*, which starred George Reeves as the Man of Steel. Twenty-four episodes of the series aired in 1953. Among the more notable episodes that year were "The Runaway Robot" (a stolen robot is used to rob banks), "Shot in the Dark" (a photographer gets an infra-red shot of Clark Kent changing into Superman), "The Defeat of Superman" (a bad guy discovers the power of Kryptonite), and "Superman in Exile" (our hero becomes radioactive and removes himself from humanity).

CARTOONS

The major studios were still producing shorts for theatrical exhibition, and 1953 produced a bumper crop of eligible cartoons. The late, great Chuck Jones created two of his masterpieces that year: "Duck Amuck" is a surreal effort where Daffy keeps getting redrawn by an unseen hand that changes the background, the foreground, his body, and the very nature of the cartoon film we're watching. "Duck Dodgers in the 24th and a Half Century" is a space opera spoof where the dashing duck is sent to Planet X in pursuit of the rare "shaving cream atom," setting a planetary course of "due up." Bugs Bunny and Elmer Fudd got their turn at SF with "Robot Rabbit," a Friz Freleng offering where a mechanical bunny wreaks comic havoc.

Over at MGM, Tex Avery did "T.V. of Tomorrow," one of a continuing series of gag-driven films about some aspect of the future. Meanwhile, Disney produced the half-hour "Ben and Me," the story of a mouse who becomes friends with Benjamin Franklin and helps him with his experiments.

Paramount was producing several common series, including ones with Popeye, Casper the Friendly Ghost, and Herman and Katnip (a smart mouse and a not so smart cat). Popeye starred in his only 3D offering, "Popeye, the Ace of Space," where he's kidnapped by Martians and shows them the true meaning of spinach. Presumably all of Casper's outings are fantastic enough to qualify for consideration, including such titles as "Frightday the 13th," "Spook No Evil," "By the Old Mill Scream," and "Little Boo Peep." Herman and Katnip were more mundane characters, but were in two films of interest that year: "Of Mice and Magic" and "Herman the Cartoonist." The plot for the latter sounds suspiciously like "Duck Amuck." Rounding out the studio's offerings was "Invention Convention," a follow the bouncing ball sing-along about fantastic devices.

Finally, Terrytoons had their superhero Mighty Mouse in three entries in 1953: "When Mousehood Was in Flower," "Hot Rods," and "Hero for a Day." All these cartoons might make for some interesting convention programming.

SERIALS

Fellow fan and serial buff Thomas Chenelle—my go-to guy on movie serials—checked his references and came up with only four movie serials for 1953, a year very much at the end of the genre. Although Republic's *Canadian Mounties vs. Atomic Monsters* sounds promising, it's just the Mounties versus foreign spies who want to steal atomic secrets. Two others are even less likely, a pirate swashbuckler (*The Great Adventures of Captain Kidd*) and another uranium chase, this time through the jungle (*Jungle Drums of Africa*).

The only truly SF offering is Columbia's *The Lost Planet*, which turns out to be the last SF movie serial produced. As might be expected, it suffers from poor production values and a "who cares?" attitude toward the material.

FEATURE FILMS

As a film critic, I have strong feelings about many of the films and their worthiness for consideration. Retro Hugo voters, of course, are invited to see the films for themselves. Phil Hardy's eminently useful *The Encyclopedia of Science Fiction Movies* lists 20 titles for 1953. Let's start with the seven major contenders.

The Beast from 20,000 Fathoms: A giant beast menaces New York City in an exciting and intelligent monster movie with impeccable credentials. Director Eugene Lourie had previously worked with famed French filmmaker Jean Renoir. The script was based on a Ray Bradbury short story called "The Fog Horn." The special effects were the premiere effort of Ray Harryhausen, and the cast includes Cecil Kellaway, Lee Van Cleef, and Kenneth Tobey (who had starred in 1951's *The Thing*).

Donovan's Brain: The second, and some consider the best, version of Curt Siodmak's novel about a scientist who keeps a human brain alive with unpleasant results. Lew Ayres starred, and his wife is played by Nancy Davis, who would go on to become Nancy Reagan.

Invaders from Mars: One of the scariest of the "aliens take over human bodies" movies, with the story seen through the eyes of a young boy who sees all the trustworthy figures of adult authority subverted, including his parents and the police. William Cameron Menzies (*Things to Come*) directed and the visuals are nightmarish. This was, according to Hardy, the first alien invasion movie shot in color.

It Came from Outer Space: Besides providing the SF debut for director Jack Arnold, the movie provided another paycheck for Ray Bradbury, since it was based on his short story "The Meteor." Aliens land and no one will believe journalist Richard Carlson when he tries to warn them. Russell ("The Professor") Johnson is also in the cast.

The Magnetic Monster: Richard Carlson appears again in what was to have been a pilot for an *X-Files* type series. Carlson plays a scientific investigator on the trail of a radioactive isotope that eats energy and grows bigger and bigger. Curt Siodmak directed and co-wrote the script with Ivan Tors.

The Twonky: A real curio, this was based on a Henry Kuttner story about a man whose life is taken over by an intelligent TV set. Hans Conried is the man trying to escape from the dictatorial tube. Arch Oboler wrote and directed.

War of the Worlds: One of the best of the George Pal productions, based on the H.G. Wells novel. Gene Barry is the scientist who tries to figure out how to combat the invading Martians when they start tearing up the country in sleek, manta ray-like spaceships. Byron Haskin directed.

Although it is likely the feature films nominated will come from the above list, let's take a quick look at the other thirteen SF releases that year. They can be divided into the bad and the obscure.

Bud Abbott and Lou Costello appeared in two features that year, and neither is worth considering. *Abbott and Costello Go to Mars* is generally recognized as one of their worst films. *Abbott and Costello Meet Dr. Jekyll and Mr. Hyde* does have the advantage of Boris Karloff and some neat effects, but it's a far cry from their glory days of such films as *Abbott and Costello Meet Frankenstein*.

Cat Women of the Moon featured Sonny Tufts and a lot of moon vixens in black leotards running around sets left over from other movies. *Killer Ape* offered Johnny Weissmuller as Jungle Jim, looking for a mad scientist using experimental drugs on the apes. *The Mesa of Lost Women* has a pre-Uncle Fester Jackie Coogan as a mad scientist who is trying to create warrior women. *The Neanderthal Man* has Robert Shayne (Inspector Henderson from *The Adventures of Superman*) as a scientist trying to regress animals—and people—into prehistoric form. *Phantom from Space* has the authorities searching for an invisible alien. Producer/director W. Lee Wilder was the brother of the much more prominent filmmaker Billy Wilder.

1953 is also the year of one of the worst movies ever made, *Robot Monster*. This is the one where the alien is a guy in a gorilla suit with a diving helmet on his head, and where he communicates with the home world with a device that looks like a cross between a ham radio and a bubble machine. If this makes the ballot, look for mandatory drug testing for Hugo voters in the future.

Among the obscurities—which could mean they are ripe for rediscovery or else deservedly forgotten—are *Alert in the South*, a French spy movie featuring Erich von Stroheim as yet another mad scientist, this one with an atomic death ray, and *Four Sided Triangle*, a Hammer entry about a scientist who clones an unfaithful girlfriend and finds the duplicate doesn't care for him either. Mexico's first important SF film, *El Monstro Rescitado*, included a mad scientist bringing the dead back to life.

Project Moonbase has a script credited in part to Robert Heinlein, and was patched together from the busted pilot for a proposed TV series. *Silver Dust* is from the Soviet Union and the mad scientist in this one, who is experimenting on people with atomic dust, is an American. He's being pursued by greedy businessmen, the military, and an ex-Nazi scientist. *Spaceways*, another Hammer entry, has American actor Howard Duff as a scientist accused of murdering his wife and her lover, the latter being a Soviet spy. Duff and *his* lover take off into space to prove his innocence.

The dramatic category was easier the last time around for the Retros, since, whatever its merits or faults, *Destination Moon* was clearly the outstanding dramatic SF presentation of 1950, and a landmark in a movie genre that was just in the process of being reborn. By contrast, one is hard pressed to pick any one 1953 release as the definitive SF dramatic presentation, but there's a much wider choice.

(NOTE: When the nominations were closed, the dramatic categories were collapsed into a single one. The four runners up were "Duck Dodgers in the 24th and a Half Century," *It Came from Outer Space*, *The Beast from 20,000 Fathoms*, and *Invaders from Mars*. The winner was George Pal's production of *War of the Worlds*.)

RETRO ROBO

One of the highlights of the month of February for me for nearly thirty years now is the annual Boston Science Fiction Film Festival. It's a 24-hour marathon of SF movies that was renamed a "festival" when it started snagging the occasional premiere. Over the years, I've been introduced to many of the classics on the big screen, revisited favorites, and also seen some of the worst movies ever made. This year's discovery was the hilariously inept *Frankenstein Meets the Space Monster* (1965), a movie I fell in love with the moment I learned that it was also released under the alternate title *Mars Invades Puerto Rico*. (Guess where the producer spent his vacation.)

The annual event gives attendees who have already seen many films the chance to take a fresh look at titles they may not have seen in quite a while. Some, like *Forbidden Planet*, clearly stand the test of time. Others are not so fortunate. This year there were several films that I had seen first-run in the theaters, but hadn't watched in ages. The one I was most interested in taking a fresh look at was *Robocop*, which I had reviewed when it came out in 1987 and then seen maybe once more in the twenty years since then. How had it held up?

Memory had dimmed, perhaps because the two theatrical sequels were so mediocre, and I never really paid attention to the subsequent TV series and miniseries. I was surprised to learn that there have been several. However the first film (which, though R rated, is slightly less gory than the unrated "director's cut" on DVD), turns out to feel fresh and original. The only thing that really dates it is that we now know some of the then-unknown cast from their subsequent work:

* The sadistic villain Clarence Boddicker is played by Kurtwood Smith, an actor who had been working on TV and in small film roles, here getting his first real standout part on the big screen. Although he is an absolutely vicious thug here, taking pleasure in the pain and death he causes, it's hard not to be reminded of his best known subsequent role, as "Red" Forman on *That '70s Show*.

* Ray Wise, who plays corporate executive Leon Nash, would go on to a variety of memorable roles, including that of Leland Palmer on *Twin Peaks* and Vice President Hal Gardner on the fifth season of *24*.

* Slimy executive Bob Morton was played by Miguel Ferrer. He also turned up on *Twin Peaks*, as FBI agent Albert Rosenfield, and more recently has been Dr. Garret Macy on *Crossing Jordan*.

* Paul McCrane was Boddicker's henchman Emil, who comes to an especially gooey end involving toxic waste. He's been seen more prominently in recent years on the small screen as Dr. Robert Romano on *E.R.* Last year, he had a short but notable run on *24*, as Jack Bauer's duplicitous brother Graeme.

* And, of course, there's Peter Weller. Already a fan favorite from *The Adventures of Buckaroo Banzai* (1984), his title role in *Robocop* would solidify his SF stardom. It's a genre he would return to on occasion (such as in *Screamers* or guesting on *Star Trek: Enterprise*). He would also make the *Robocop* alumni association's obligatory appearance on *24*, playing Jack Bauer's mentor-gone-bad Christopher Henderson. For the actor, taking the title role in *Robocop* was a daring choice. During most of the movie, he is almost completely encased in his robotic costume, and his "performance" is limited to his voice and his lower face. There's only so far a heroic chin can take you.

The story, for those who have somehow missed all its incarnations, is set in a near-future Detroit. Crime is out of control, and drug dealing and murder are only the most obvious felonies. We see that the corporate powers-that-be like it that way, since it presents new business opportunities, some of them even legitimate. Alex Murphy (Weller) is a good cop newly assigned to a particularly gruesome precinct. He's paired with Anne Lewis (Nancy Allen), who may be a woman but is as tough as nails. It's not racism or sexism that plagues this future Detroit, it's lawlessness and anarchy. Murphy finds himself trapped by Clarence Boddicker and his gang of plug-uglies, and they sadistically toy with him, brutally maiming him before Boddicker finally puts a bullet in his head.

Enter OCP. This is a megacorporation that has won the contract to start providing robotic policing to the city. Their hope is the ED-209, one of those robots obviously unfamiliar with Asimov's Three Laws of Robotics. Brought out for demonstration at a board meeting, it goes horribly wrong, killing a hapless junior executive who had already complied with a demand to put down his gun. Bob Morton sees his chance, sucking up to the "Old Man" (Dan O'Herlihy) by proposing a different remedy: a half-man, half-machine cyborg. The half-man part will be provided by Murphy, who is legally dead and beyond help.

What's most interesting here is Murphy's legal status. The plot of the film has him slowly recovering his memories and Officer Lewis realizing who he is. There are questions here the film doesn't resolve, though there were attempts to do so in later entries. For one thing, Murphy has a wife and child. When Robocop enters his old house—which his widow has departed—he starts to recollect happy times there. Is Robocop merely Murphy with prosthetic body armor, or has he become a new being with residual memories from his human past? The film seems to lean in the latter direction, which is in keeping with its cynical, take-no-prisoners attitude.

However, if Murphy is now a new being, is he to be considered a citizen—a sentient, living being, with all that implies? Or is he, as Morton seems to feel, merely property of OCP with no more "rights" than a computer keyboard? The contempt the scientists and executives have for their machine is seen through his "eyes" in a series of shots where Murphy/Robocop regains consciousness. No attempt is made to help Murphy adjust to his new situation, and the food created for him (the human part still needs nutrients) resembles nothing so much as raw sewage. Clearly, they don't care in the slightest about him.

Why should they? The world we see here shows a culture where life is cheap and meaningless. For all the glimpses of Murphy's happy pre-Robo home life—and the satirical images we see on TV screens such as a family enjoying a nuclear war-themed board game—this is a world where one executive thinks nothing at all of hiring a contract killer to take out a rival. Director Paul Verhoeven and screenwriters Edward Neumeier and Michael Miner even make us complicit in this violence when Robocop tracks down the people responsible for his fate. It's one thing to watch Clarence Boddicker get his well-earned death. It's quite another for audiences to cheer—as they did in 1987 and again this year at the film marathon—when slimy executive Dick Jones (Ronny Cox) takes a hostage knowing that Robocop's programming ensures he can't harm any OCP employee. The Old Man's "Dick, you're fired," freeing Robocop to act, is immensely satisfying. It also means we accept a world where violent action is the remedy.

At film's end, Robocop is accepted by his police colleagues and, seemingly, the law-abiding public (of whom we have seen very little). We are led to believe that with the deaths of Dick Jones and Bob Morton—note the bland names—the rotten eggs at OCP have been removed. There's no real reason to believe this, given that the corporation has obviously rewarded these men with promotions and power along the way, nor is there any reason to believe that the Old Man and the other executives have any more scruples.

We're left with the most honest and trustworthy character in the film being the cyborg Robocop, where both humans and robots have fallen short. *Robocop* is a great action film and remains hugely entertaining, but one can't watch without wondering if its dark vision of our future offers even the slightest glimmer of hope.

THE CRANKY PERSON'S GUIDE TO THE 2009 "BEST DRAMATIC PRESENTATION, LONG FORM" HUGO NOMINEES

I don't have a good relationship with the Hugos. When I started casting Hugo ballots in the '90s, I tried to be very conscientious, reading as many of the nominees as I could. I discovered a lot of authors who became favorites. And then I watched as the stuff I ranked *beneath* "No Award" went home with the prize.

Then there are the "lost years," that awful time a few years back when it was pointless to even vote in the Dramatic Presentation category because that horrible Tolkien crap was going to win. Every year. Even the year after, when Gollum's appearance at an awards show won. I don't know why I'm immune to the supposed charms of these overrated books and movies, but I'm very glad they're long behind us now.

Which brings us to this year's [released in 2008] long form nominees. When the dramatic category was split, I was in the camp which wanted what most people wanted: a movie category and a TV category. However, revising the Hugo rules is like herding cats or sculpting in Jell-O: it's exasperating, and the results are going to be far different from what was intended. Crazed nitpickers—or more properly, our fellow fans—insisted we had to broaden the category to include plays, slide shows, podcasts... in short, all sorts of performances. In addition, why should a miniseries compete with a single episode when it's more like a movie? So we have the "long form" and "short form" categories. I haven't seen the "short form" nominees this year, hence this essay focusing solely on the long form. With any luck, this will appear after the voting has ended and have no impact whatsoever.

Three of the nominees are features films based on comic book (excuse me, "graphic novel") characters. These were actually three of the most entertaining films out last summer, and I gave them all good reviews. But are they Hugo-worthy? *The Dark Knight* was the follow-up to the brilliant retooling of Batman in *Batman Begins*, and while hugely entertaining, was a little too busy for its own good. Did we really need the Joker and Harvey "Two-Face" Dent in the same film? I think not. However, there's no question that the late Heath Ledger's turn as the Joker was a memorable and unsettling capstone to his all-too-short career. While some cynics think his untimely death made people overreact, there is no doubt that this is a performance that would have been noticed even without the real-life tragedy.

That said, what exactly is it that makes it a science fiction movie? Sure, there are people running around in various disguises and costumes, but while they might be copied at a convention masquerade, there's nothing inherently science fictional or fantastical about doing so. (Odd, yes. "Sense of wonder" unusual? No.) I'd be disappointed if this film won the Hugo. I accept that fantasy and horror are often included in our awards, but I don't see any of those elements playing much of a role here.

Which brings us to *Hellboy II: The Golden Army*. Okay, here we have demons and mutants. This qualifies. I did have a lot of fun with this film, but I thought the story was too complicated and it overreached. Thinking back now, I'm not sure I could describe what the story was about without rereading my review. On the other hand, the scene where Hellboy and Abe Sapient get drunk on Mexican beer and sing along to a maudlin Barry Manilow song was well worth the price of admission. There was a real twisted sense of humor at work here. Which is to say, my kind of humor.

What is there to say about *Iron Man?* Great film. The birth of a new franchise. Robert Downey, Jr., was a standout, and if he'd agree to come to Montreal [where that year's World Science Fiction Convention was being held], that would be reason enough to give it to this film. As the author of a book about romantic comedies, I also loved the by-play between Downey and Gwyneth Paltrow as his trusted assistant. Let the twelve-year-olds geek out over the suit. My favorite moment was when Downey said he could do very well without her and Paltrow replies, "Really? What's your Social Security number?" Not a perfect film, though, and the climactic battle reminded me of nothing so much as the excesses of *The Transformers* as the two mechanical suits battled it out. (Were the actors even there that day?)

The last actual movie on the list is *WALL-E*. Pixar has become the gold standard of animated features, and their film for this summer, *Up*, will be on many ten best lists at the end of the year, including mine. They've only failed once—artistically, not financially—with *Cars*. (The only thing worth watching in *Cars* is the final few minutes with an absolutely delicious joke involving John Ratzenberger, who is in the voice cast for all the Pixar films.) *WALL-E* is a touching parable about consumerism and standing up for one's self, and if the robots were sometimes too cute, well, this *is* a cartoon being released by Disney. Clearly the most SFnal entry on the list, it would be a worthy Hugo winner if the voters so decree.

But wait, there's one more nominee. *METAtropolis* is an audio book presentation edited by my dear pal John Scalzi. Well, not quite a pal. We did a couple of panels together at Denvention [the Denver Worldcon] last year, and he signed a book for a friend of mine. I love his writing, and he was delightful in person, but I doubt he could pick me out of a police lineup. Scalzi and four other writers (Elizabeth Bear, Jay Lake, Tobias Buckell, and Karl Schroeder) each wrote a novella for a shared universe about a future urban dystopia. I bet it's wonderful. I bet I'd love it if it came out in book form. However, even for free, there was no way I was going to devote 547 minutes to find out. Maybe you folks who commute 4 ½ hours each way to work have the time to listen in. You're probably the same people who want to know if you can give more Hugos to the "extended editions" of *Lord of the Rings*. Come Judgment Day, I will no doubt have a lot to answer for, but I don't think that not devoting nine hours of my life to an audiobook nominee is going to be one of them.

So the curmudgeon in me is rooting for the adorable *WALL-E* and hoping that the youngsters who enjoyed it will become the convention-going fans of tomorrow. And John, if you should win instead, congratulations in advance. When next year brings a 400-hour audiobook nominee from Neal Stephenson, we'll all know whom to blame.

(NOTE: This was written in advance of Anticipation, the Montreal Worldcon, for Chris Garcia's long-running fanzine *The Drink Tank*. When the awards were announced at the convention, the winner was, indeed, *WALL-E*.)

THE FUTURE IS NOW

Although George Orwell wrote *1984* before I was born, I remember the *frisson* people felt as the real calendar year approached. The specter of Big Brother had been with us for years, *1984* having become synonymous with the concept of a totalitarian dictatorship. Of course for those of us in the western world—even with Ronald Reagan in the White House and Margaret Thatcher at Downing Street— Orwell's nightmarish vision of a Stalinist society had not come to pass. In fact, it can be argued that Orwell had helped prevent that future with his cautionary tale.

The next year we "knew" long before it arrived was 2001. Back in 1964, filmmaker Stanley Kubrick and author Arthur C. Clarke began collaborating to create what Kubrick called "the proverbial good science fiction movie." Four years later, the result was *2001: A Space Odyssey*, arguably one of the greatest of cinematic achievements. Like *1984*, it remains so despite its "failure" as a predictor of the future. They couldn't even convince people that the 21st century wouldn't start in the year 2000. Today, the actual year is remembered for 9/11, rather than the landmark movie.

In late 1984, a bumper crop of new science fiction movies arrived. I know because I was completing my first year as a film critic, and I ended up doing a round up of five major feature films opening that season: *Dune, Le Dernier Combat, Runaway, Starman,* and *2010.* (Luc Besson's 1983 *Le Dernier Combat/The Last Combat* had arrived in the States a year later.) The first four films will have to wait for future essays. Our focus is the arrival of *2010* which was considered a major event... and then a major disappointment. Twenty-five years later, with the real 2010 upon us, it is time for a fresh look.

The rap on the film is that it couldn't possibly be any good because director Peter Hyams is not Stanley Kubrick. One doubts that Hyams would dispute it. (Hyams, who wrote the script, is also not Arthur C. Clarke, but he did have Clarke's novel to adapt.) Kubrick is one of the few filmmakers for whom the word "genius" is not inappropriate. His *2001* is a film that continues to be debated precisely because, while his storytelling is straightforward, his meaning is obscure. A mysterious monolith appears in prehistoric times, and gives a group of apes a nudge into learning how to wield tools. Thousands of years later, spacefaring Americans find a monolith on the moon, which sends a signal off to Jupiter. After a series of misadventures involving the HAL 9000 computer and the death of nearly everyone on board the spaceship *Discovery*, astronaut David Bowman (Keir

Dullea) discovers yet another monolith orbiting Jupiter. He leaves the ship and disappears—at least, as far as folks back on Earth are concerned.

We see him go into the monolith and through some sort of space warp, eventually being transformed into what would be known as the "Starchild," which many have interpreted as the next evolutionary step. As with the apes learning to use tools, mankind was now being nudged forward again. The final image of the film, of the Starchild contemplating Earth, raised all sorts of questions. Now here was *2010* to answer them.

In fact, the answers prove to be the least important part of the movie. Considered as fanfic (fannish slang for stories written by fans to further explore the worlds of their favorite stories), *2010* proves to be much more interested in exploring the details of the Kubrick/Clarke universe than in solving its mysteries. As with much SF, its predictive value is minimal. We still don't have any moon bases, and Pan Am is still defunct. The most obvious thing the film gets "wrong" is that its main conflict is an impending showdown between the United States and the Soviet Union. (Let's take a moment as younger readers Google "Soviet Union.") This reflects the fears of 1984, where it seemed President Reagan was ready to heat up the Cold War with his Strategic Defense Initiative, which was popularly known as "Star Wars."

There are all sorts of references that reflect when the film was made, including a scene where Heywood Floyd (Roy Scheider) is trying to convince his successor as head of the space program to allow a joint US/Soviet mission to the abandoned *Discovery*. When Floyd offers the argument that if the Americans don't join in, the Russians will get there first by themselves, it's noted that having American "spies" on a Russian mission would appeal to the unnamed reactionary president. (The idea that we would have an African-American moderate Democrat in the White House would *really* have been considered science fiction back in 1984.)

What stands out watching the film now is that Peter Hyams stepped up his game, knowing he would never be able to withstand comparison to Kubrick's original, but trying to do it justice anyway. Hyams has done numerous genre movies, some of them decent, like *Timecop*, and some of them horrendously awful, like *A Sound of Thunder*. Along the way, there were also movies like *Capricorn One*, *Outland*, and *End of Days*. Hyams is an ambitious filmmaker, often writing, directing, producing, *and* serving as cinematographer, and one wishes the resulting films were masterworks rather than disposable entertainments. However, with *2010* the very look of the film is different from a typical Hyams effort. The lighting is softer and more diffuse, with characters often appearing backlit. The sets are not as austere as in the Kubrick film, yet great efforts were made to recreate the pod bay of the *Discovery*, the original set being long gone. Watching *2010*, you are not conscious of this being a recreation.

In *2001*, we knew little about the characters. We had a few details, like Dr. Floyd leaving a message with his young daughter via "picture phone," but most of the conversation was small talk and arguably the most "human" character in the film was the HAL 9000 computer. Now a decade has gone by (in film time) and Dr. Floyd has remarried and has a young son, briefly mentioning his grown daughter in passing. By making him the central character and casting Roy Scheider, we know we will learn much more about him. He pretty much disappears from *2001* after the lunar monolith sends its signal toward Jupiter, but now we see that he was so wracked by guilt over the deaths of the crew—Bowman is presumed dead as well—that he has left the space agency and taken a position with a university. It is the opportunity to find out what happened that motivates him when his Soviet counterpart comes up with the offer of a joint mission. The Russians have the means to get there first, but the Americans have the knowledge of what happened and the ability to restart the *Discovery*. In a sense, Floyd will get the chance to see that the men *he* sent off into space did not die in vain.

The film wisely avoids giving us any explanation as to what happened to Bowman. Keir Dullea appears as Bowman at various ages, clearly manifestations created to convey messages to humans who could not comprehend him in his present form. However, other than warning the Russians and Americans that they must leave the space around Jupiter sooner than they had planned, he is basically there to promise us that "something wonderful" is about to happen. It might seem as if he was thrown in to foreshadow the film's climax for viewers who need lots of explanations, but one might just as well consider that the transformation of the solar system for humankind's benefit *would* need a lot of preparation if people were not to assume it was the end of the world and go stark raving mad.

Besides Floyd and Bowman, there's one other character from the original who needs to be redeemed, and that's HAL (voiced, once again, by Douglas Rain). The computer expert Chandra (with an oddly cast Bob Balaban in the role) treats HAL with respect and sympathy, as if HAL is a colleague and not simply a collection of hardware and software. Chandra spells out for us what went wrong with HAL's programming. When the computer is "awakened," it has no memory of the event. Instead HAL is given closure, told by Chandra that its mission was successful.

2010 could not hope to match *2001*'s landmark status for cutting-edge special effects, nor could it hope to provide another deep dish statement of the human condition. On those points, it was doomed before it began. Knowing that, Hyams goes with Clarke's message that scientists can reason together in ways that politicians cannot. (In a nice little in-joke, we catch a glimpse of the cover of *Time* magazine with, presumably, the Soviet and American leaders depicted, bearing a striking resemblance to Kubrick and Clarke.) Where Hyams makes his most daring break with *2001* is in wanting us to care about the *people* in the story. In one scene, the Russian ship is braking to a halt near Jupiter, using a process that works fine in theory but has never been tested. Floyd has no role to play, and huddles for safety with a Russian—a young female, naturally—who also is not needed. The easy thing would have been to have a scene where they share their fears and hopes. Instead, lacking a common language, they merely hold each other. At the end of the scene, she kisses him on the cheek before going off. It is a moment that provides an ironic echo of the apes in the cave in *2001*'s opening "Dawn of Man" sequence, who also lacked verbal communication but huddled together.

Likewise, when ship designer Walter Curnow (John Lithgow) nearly loses it during a space walk from the Russian ship to the *Discovery*, both Floyd and one of the Russians talk a lot, but what they're saying can be reduced to "There, there." They're trying to distract and comfort Curnow, who isn't really prepared to be an astronaut, but is crucial to the mission. For all the talk in the movie, there is a real effort not to reduce this to the level of a mere thriller. Even the Russian commander (played by a 39-year-old Helen Mirren) isn't treated as the "heavy" of the story. Like Floyd, she's trying to negotiate the scientific mission during extremely troubled political times.

Watching *2010* now, away from the hype of it being the long-awaited *2001* sequel, one sees a decent movie made by a filmmaker whose SF efforts have not always been jewels of the genre. Yet here Hyams does some of his best, most serious work. No, it's not *2001*, but it is no more unworthy of being part of the post-*2001* conversation than Clarke's *three* sequel novels (*2010*, *2061*, and *3001*). And while I hesitate to criticize a film that, at this writing, I have not yet seen, I suspect *2010* has a lot more to say to us as we enter the real year of 2010 than *2012* will have to tell us about the real or imagined end of the world.

(NOTE: Having since seen the film, it still seems a safe bet that 2012 will be nothing like Roland Emerich's film.)

WE'RE SCIENTISTS, TRUST US

On the border between science fiction and horror films is the figure of the "mad scientist." In the most dystopian stories, we're often in awe of the technological breakthroughs, even if they're being misused. It's notable that the makers of the most prominent dystopian films of the last twenty-five years (*Brazil*, *1984*, *Dark City*) chose a decidedly retro look to avoid the inevitable "sense of wonder" that speculation about future technology usually brings.

That's what makes the films based on the novels of the late Michael Crichton (and several that he wrote and/or directed himself) so schizophrenic. Crichton was the anti-Arthur C. Clarke. In novels like *The Terminal Man* and *Jurassic Park* (both made into movies) he came up with scientific extrapolations and then told stories about how they went horribly wrong. Where Clarke saw science and reason as the hope for the future, Crichton saw only danger. If he wasn't quite a Luddite, he certainly wasn't a tribune for science. His pessimism is made even clearer when contrasted with Stanley Kubrick's. In Kubrick's science fiction films (*Dr. Strangelove*, *2001: A Space Odyssey*, *A Clockwork Orange*) it's not the technology that fails but the human beings. To take but one example, the HAL 9000 computer isn't the film's monster. It's the victim of bad programming (by people) which required it to a) protect the mission at all costs and b) keep that mission secret from the crew for the time being. The two commands come into conflict with deadly results, but it's *not* because HAL is "evil." It's because HAL is reconciling the bad commands as best as it can.

The Andromeda Strain was the first movie based on a Crichton novel, and one already sees the seeds of his future "science gone wrong" stories; although, as directed by veteran filmmaker Robert Wise, it plays out as more of a thriller than an indictment. Wise was an eclectic American director whose credits included editing *Citizen Kane*, and directing *West Side Story* and *The Sound of Music*. He also directed two SF film landmarks, *The Day the Earth Stood Still* and *Star Trek: The Motion Picture*. Wise did not have an affinity for SF films the way, say, Steven Spielberg does, but he didn't treat such assignments as if he was slumming. In *The Andromeda Strain* he wants us to be fascinated by the details as dedicated scientists prepare to solve a deadly mystery.

The story opens when a satellite sent from Earth to collect material in space crashes in a small Arizona town. Appallingly, it has brought back *something* that has killed everyone in the town. Most dropped dead where they stood. A few had time to go mad and take their own lives. A team of scientists is assembled, and we see their lives disrupted as armed men come to their doors to announce that there's been a "fire," the code for the arrival of some sort of alien invasion. In this case they are microscopic, but no less deadly.

Wise (and screenwriter Nelson Gidding) are going for a documentary-like feel, even starting with a disclaimer that no classified information has been revealed in the film, and that the actual documentation will soon be released, as if this was a true story. The first job is the recovery of the satellite itself, and so team leader Dr. Jeremy Stone (Arthur Hill) and Dr. Mark Hall (James Olson) go in hazmat suits and explore the carnage. (There is a wholly gratuitous shot of a nude young woman among the victims, almost as if Wise was acknowledging he could now get away with such things under the then-relatively new rating system. Nevertheless, the film was rated G.) The scientists find the satellite, which a local doctor has foolishly opened, and they make two other discoveries. First, whatever it is that happened has caused its victims' blood to turn into powder. Second, there are two survivors: a colicky baby and an old drunk.

Stone and Hall are joined by two other colleagues, Dr. Charles Dutton (David Wayne) and Dr. Ruth Leavitt (Kate Reid). Now their work is cut out for them. They have to figure out what's causing the deaths, and they have to figure out what the baby and the drunk have in common that make them seemingly immune. However, before they can get to work, they have to go to a secure site that, at Stone's urging, had been built for just such an eventuality. It is a five-level underground facility that becomes increasingly sterile as they descend. The film spends a great deal of time establishing just how thorough the cleansing process is, including radiation, inoculations, examinations, suppositories, and a color-coded change of clothing at each level. The clothes from the previous level are summarily burned.

There's another twist that will provide the necessary suspense late in the film: the facility is equipped with a nuclear device. Should the infectious material escape, the place will self-destruct before it can get out. Once the device is triggered, it can only be stopped by one man, who will have only five minutes to get to one of the turn-off points to use *his* key. That key is entrusted to Dr. Hall under a theory that a single man with no children is most apt to look at the situation objectively, rather than assume the risk of infectious outbreak because of emotional attachments on the outside.

It's a bit of hokum you can buy or not, but while it leads to the inevitable race against the clock late in the film, the real point of the movie is watching the scientists at work, realizing that they are both professionals and fallible human beings. One scientist turns out to have epilepsy, but has been keeping it secret to avoid losing government clearances. Another is aware of the real nature of the facility—which has more to do with creating offensive capabilities for the military than in research. At one point, crucial information is withheld from the team because a bell signaling an incoming message has been inadvertently disabled by a piece of paper.

However, for all that, what comes across is that these are dedicated experts doing the best they can to avert a crisis. The screw-ups are overcome. The secret government agenda is almost a footnote to the story. (If this had been made just a few years later, post-Watergate, the film might have ended with one of the scientists dropping a dime on the project by tipping off the *Washington Post*.) The discovery of the nature of the infectious agent and how to combat it is almost elegant, requiring no major weapons—or major special effects—but some basic knowledge of chemistry. Only at the very end do we get the cynicism about science that would soon become a hallmark of Crichton's film legacy. The virus has mutated into a form that no longer affects humans, and action is taken to destroy the invader once and for all. Yet a computer tracking the mutation soon starts flashing the number "601," which we have earlier been told is code for the computer being overloaded with too much information. *Something* has happened to the virus that is beyond the computer's ability to track. The end.

The Andromeda Strain is probably the closest we will ever get in a film by or derived from Crichton in which scientists are essentially the good guys, and their work averts rather than creates a catastrophe. The satellite project is attributed more to civilian and military officials in the government, and the downbeat ending is as much of a throwaway as is the revelation of the lab as a possible biological warfare facility. This might be attributed to the fact that Crichton's anti-science bias was not yet really developed in a body of work that was just getting underway. Additionally, Wise was a director who, more often than not, told stories that were more hopeful than bleak, even when dealing with corporate greed (*Executive Suite*) or capital punishment (*I Want to Live!*). In his science fiction films, he at least allowed for the potential that humanity would eventually do the right thing, even if they stumbled along the way.

The Andromeda Strain stands out as a truly unusual film for its era. The personal histories of the scientists are largely backstory. The one woman scientist is decidedly older and not involved in any contrived romantic subplot. It is an intelligent, well-made movie speculating about a scientific problem we may well face in the future and seem to have already confronted with several potential plagues originating here on Earth. Scientists without any inherent sex appeal are our heroes. Later Crichton himself, as well as his adaptors, would make scientists and technicians the bad guys in movies like *Westworld*, *The Terminal Man*, *Runaway*, *Coma* (based on the Robin Cook novel and directed by Crichton), *Looker*, *Sphere*, *Jurassic Park*, and *Timeline*. Whether by accident or design, science became part of the problem. For the moment though, in *The Andromeda Strain*, science was still part of the solution.

A FUNNY THING HAPPENED
ON THE WAY TO THE FUTURE

The old joke is attributed to various sources. The actor is on his deathbed, and he's asked if dying is hard.

"Dying is easy," comes the reply. "*Comedy* is hard."

When it comes to science-fiction, comedy is doubly hard. There are authors who could handle it, like William Tenn, Rudy Rucker, and Robert Sheckley. There are TV shows that pull it off, like *Red Dwarf* or the famous "The Trouble with Tribbles" episode of the original *Star Trek*. On the big screen, though, it's few and far between.

The best SF comedies are usually spoofs, like Mel Brooks' *Spaceballs* or the affectionate send-up of *Star Trek* and fandom that is *Galaxy Quest*. Sometimes you'll get movies pitched to kids or teens that appeal to adults as well, like *Lilo & Stitch* or *Back to the Future*. There are also dark satires containing sufficient SF tropes that we claim them for our own, like *Dr. Strangelove* or *The Truman Show*.

One of the best SF comedies ever made, however, is dismissed by its director as one of his slighter efforts, which only goes to show that the author of a work is often not the best judge of its value. Woody Allen's *Sleeper* is the work of an outsider dabbling in a genre not his own and to which—fantasy elements in a few of his later films notwithstanding—he has never returned. Give him credit for respecting the genre enough to get it right. When he and co-writer Marshall Brickman finished their script, he sent it to no less a personage than Isaac Asimov to get his reaction. Allen wanted to get both the science and the science fiction right. He knew little of the genre and didn't want to do something that was novel for him but old hat to people well-versed in the field. Asimov was a fan of the filmmaker, and told Allen not to change a thing. When Allen asked Asimov to be official consultant on the project, which would be shot in Colorado, Asimov declined, as it would have involved too much travel. Instead, he recommended his friend and fellow author Ben Bova, who did advise on the film.

When it was released in 1973 it was a hit. Artistically, it was probably the most successful of his pre-*Annie Hall* movies, after which Allen shifted gears away from gag-filled comedies to more dialogue-driven romances. Along with the more recent *Men in Black* movies, it remains the rare example of a wholly original SF comedy that is intended for grown-up audiences.

The story involves Miles Monroe (Allen), who runs a health food store in Greenwich Village in 1973 and who goes into the hospital for a routine procedure. Complications develop, resulting in his being put into suspended animation. When he awakes, it is 2173, there's a world dictatorship, and the "Underground" has brought him back because he is unique in that he has no records within the police state. The film follows his misadventures in the future, which include having to disguise himself as a robot, getting reprogrammed by the authorities when he is caught, and finally plotting the assassination of the leader who, at present, is just a nose awaiting cloning.

Watching *Sleeper* today is like taking a time machine into the past, rather than the future. For younger viewers, some of the topical jokes may not even make any sense. Fortunately, Google is your friend. Take the most celebrated line in the film, when scientists explain to him that they've lost most records of the past after a war which was started "when a man named Albert Shanker got hold of a nuclear device." When I saw this film first run in a Manhattan movie house in 1973, I couldn't hear the next several lines because the audience was laughing so loud. Today's viewers may wonder who Albert Shanker was, and they wouldn't be alone. The actor who said the line didn't know either, and Allen told him not to worry about it. Shanker was, at the time, the combative head of the New York City teacher's union.

That's the problem with topical humor. Time marches on, and what was once current now needs footnotes. Hopefully, viewers will recognize that Bela Lugosi—whom Miles identifies as a former mayor of New York—was in fact the actor who played Dracula, and that French leader Charles DeGaulle *wasn't* a famous French chef. If you don't know who the acerbic sports commentator Howard Cosell was, you should still be able to figure out by context that the scientist's theory that citizens who were caught in criminal acts "were forced to watch this" wasn't actually the case. Perhaps the most obscure reference is a simple sight gag: Miles comes out of a McDonald's which boasts "100,000,000,000,000,000,000,000,000,000,000,000,000,000,000,000 served." This may not seem very funny given that the signs currently read "Billions and billions served," but they used to contain a frequently updated count of the actual number of burgers sold, and Allen merely took it to the absurdly logical extreme.

His technology gags are less of a problem. Here he plays with the expected SF props: artificially enhanced food, robots, ray guns. There are no space monsters, but Luna (Diana Keaton)—the bubble headed "poet" who ends up his hostage—refers to him as "the alien." There's also a pudding with a mind of its own (and which Miles has to fend off with a broom), gigantic fruit (which, naturally, leads him to slip on a gigantic banana peel), and the mind-altering "orb" (which gets him high as, disguised as a robot, he passes it from guest to guest at a party). Perhaps the best joke is the "Orgasmatron," which is how people in the future apparently have sex, since the men are all impotent and the women are all frigid. A couple steps into the tiny chamber together, the door closes, and in short order both achieve orgasm. Eventually Miles has to hide in one by himself to try to escape the police, emerging as a drooling basket case.

Sleeper is a reflection of its times disguised as a look into the future, often the case in science fiction. We see this when Miles and Luna stumble onto the home of the sort of stereotypical gay characters—complete with a mincing, lisping, effeminate robot named Reagan—that ought to strike us as offensive today. We also see it when one of the scientists offers Miles a cigarette and urges him to draw the smoke deep into his lungs. It turns out everything we currently think is bad for us—like tobacco, sugar, and fatty foods—science has since proven are the most healthful things we can consume. Then there are the jokes about the increasingly impersonal and automated society of the future. Miles goes to confession, and the computerized device simultaneously absolves him and offers up a kewpie doll. There's also Rags, the robotic talking dog, which he is issued to be his companion. Miles asks if it's housebroken or will be leaving little batteries around the house. These are things that make us laugh, but it is a laugh of recognition, as these seemingly far-fetched gags reflect all-too-present anxieties.

The payoff for the story is when Miles and Luna, now operating in the Underground, go in to assassinate the Leader's nose before the dictator can be cloned and reborn. Here is the subtlest commentary of all in this broad, slapstick comedy. Instead of the Utopian ideal of progress, this technological Eden is, in fact, a repressive society, and the outlook for liberation is bleak. Miles succeeds in destroying the nose (under a conveniently placed steamroller), but he tells Luna it will make no difference if Underground leader Erno (John Beck) assumes power. Power corrupts, and in a few years they'll be stealing Erno's nose.

Made in the era of Watergate and Vietnam, it is a bleak statement of the ability of government to solve problems, an attitude not all that alien to today's culture. Miles similarly dismisses science and religion as having answers and closes with another famous line, where he states he believes in only two things in life, "Sex and death—two things that come once in my life, but at least after death you're not nauseous."

All too often, writers or filmmakers come to our science fiction playground and act as if they're slumming. What they're doing isn't really science fiction, they tell interviewers, it's about ideas and people. All this demonstrates is how clueless they are about science fiction. Allen was a visitor to the genre, but he showed it sufficient respect to get it right, and to get advice when he thought he needed it. The result is not only a favorite among Woody Allen fans, but a science fiction comedy that remains a model for future filmmakers.

NOT COMING TO A THEATER NEAR YOU

(This review requires a bit of explanation. It is for a film that I would love to see but which doesn't actually exist. In 2001 Steven H Silver was launching his fanzine Argentus *and asked a number of professional and fan film critics to write a film review for a movie adaptation of a book they'd like to see filmed. I chose Greg Bear's* Blood Music, *a novel that was key to renewing my interest in science fiction books as an adult. I once had the opportunity to recommend it to film director David Cronenberg when I was interviewing him, and noted I had no connection to Bear. I simply thought he'd be the perfect director for it. Cronenberg replied that I was not the first person to suggest the book to him. Alas, the film has yet to be made. I cast Adam Sandler as the lead as a personal joke. I despise much of Sandler's film work, and it's something of a running gag with several of my colleagues. I had changed my mind about Jim Carrey and I wondered if such would be possible with Sandler. That, too, has yet to happen.)*

BLOOD MUSIC
produced and directed by David Cronenberg, written by Andrew Niccol, based on the novel by Greg Bear. A Dimension Films release.

With Adam Sandler, Christina Ricci, James Woods. Rated R

**** (4 stars)
   Vergil Ulam (Adam Sandler) is a geeky scientist working on an experimental process that combines living cells with computer chips. His goal is to make cells that can learn and transfer that knowledge when they reproduce. At the start of *Blood Music*, the financing for the work is pulled and Ulam is told to destroy his samples. Instead, he smuggles them out of the laboratory the only way he can think of: he injects himself with the "smart" cells.
   Such is the nature of this truly bizarre film that the above description of the film's opening is the most easily understood part of the story. Director David Cronenberg (*Videodrome, The Fly*) and writer Andrew Niccol (who wrote *The Truman Show* and wrote and directed *Gattaca*) have easily created one of the most astounding and intelligent movies of the year. As one might expect, it doesn't stand a chance at the box office.
   What happens once Ulam leaves work is the start of an adventure that begins with the "noocytes," as he calls them, correcting various problems he has, from his

vision to his receding hairline to his sex life. However, as the story progresses we see that the cells are more than intelligent—they have developed their own agenda. Ulam quickly goes from being their creator to being their agent, as they proceed to reorganize and perfect the world to form a new social order.

It was a big risk putting comedian Adam Sandler in the role, given that his fans are likely to be annoyed that there's little of the bodily function humor they expect in a typical Sandler outing. Apart from a shower scene where he realizes just how much the cells are doing to turn him into the world's greatest lover, there's little of that sort of humor here. Clearly, he is here for insurance, much as Jim Carrey was used in *The Truman Show*. Fortunately, as with Carrey, Sandler doesn't disappoint, and shows there may be an actor inside him struggling to get out.

Other cast members handle their roles well, but are upstaged by the special effects, especially in the second half of the film, when the cells literally take over the world. Christina Ricci has a nice turn as a troubled young woman whose life is changed as the noocytes expand their influence, while James Woods finds the sympathetic side to the role of Ulam's boss. As he realizes Ulam has created, in effect, a communicable disease that can think for itself, his character remains the scientist rather than an administrator looking to fix the blame.

However, the end results of this adventure are so mind boggling that audiences who refuse to suspend their disbelief are likely to respond with laughter or disgust rather than awe. Cronenberg and Niccol have remained faithful to Greg Bear's novel (itself an expansion on Bear's award-winning short story) and have made what is, in fact, an optimistic movie about life as we know it coming to an end. It's not going to be for every taste. Cronenberg was precisely the right director here, given that several of his films have had to do with characters discovering that they are at war with their own bodies (*The Fly*, *The Brood*, *Scanners*). Here he finally gets to tell that story on a grand scale.

See *Blood Music* fast. It isn't likely to be in theaters very long, and you shouldn't have to wait for the video release to catch what will undoubtedly be one of the most provocative movies of the year.

WATCHING ME, WATCHING YOU

The notion of discovering that your life is a lie—that everything you've seen and known is false—is such a powerful one that it has been used in countless stories and movies. From *The Wizard of Oz* (1939) to *The Matrix* (1999) we've seen characters awaken only to learn that what they have been experiencing was all a dream or an illusion. Usually these stories are about the experiences of their protagonists. *Donnie Darko* (2001) and *Eternal Sunshine of the Spotless Mind* (2004) are about characters who, by chance or by choice, have become disconnected from the world. Sometimes these stories are not science fiction or fantasy at all, but the stuff of thrillers. Movies like *The Lady Vanishes* (1938) or *Gaslight* (1944) have characters whom, for various reasons, people are trying to trick into believing that what they know to be true is really false or vice versa. Even the notion of one's life being a work of fiction in someone else's reality has been done more than once, from Paul Bartel's classic short "The Secret Cinema" (1968) to the strained Will Ferrell comedy *Stranger than Fiction* (2006).

So there's nothing new under the sun. Why then did *The Truman Show* strike such a chord in 1998, and why does the film still seem brilliant a decade later? I can still recall sitting at the press screening for the movie—oddly, shown a few months rather than a few days before the opening, as if they knew we would need time to digest it—and thinking I had just seen what was likely one of the best films of the year. Although it was only March, my judgment stood, and I easily placed it on my year's end ten best list. What impressed me then and impresses me now is just how complex a film it is.

As noted, typically such stories focus on the protagonist. Yet while Truman (Jim Carrey) is clearly *one* of our concerns here, his situation and reactions is not the only thing on the film's agenda. There are at least three viewpoints the film wants us to consider in telling its story of a man whose whole life is a lie, and his is only one of them.

A corporation has adopted baby Truman while still *in utero*, and his entire life has been turned into a reality television show. Of course "reality" is a misnomer, just as it is with *Survivor* and *American Idol*, in that there is some manipulation planned behind the scenes determining what occurs on camera. One of the things the film explores is how much of an effort must be put into creating the illusion of reality that Truman experiences as his daily life. It's not a supercomputer or a dream or drugs. No, it's a vast conspiracy involving literally hundreds of people.

They include the actors playing everyone from his parents to his best friend to his neighbors to his wife. They include behind-the-scenes workers who monitor his every move and ensure that nothing happens to Truman that might break the illusion. This involves quickly responding to the inevitable glitches—like protestors sneaking onto the "set"—so that Truman doesn't get wise to his situation. Most important of all, the conspiracy of running Truman's life is headed by Christof (Ed Harris), the creator of the show and the mastermind controlling every aspect of the project.

For Truman, the story of the movie is about discovering the truth of his existence. It begins in small ways, as a klieg light unexpectedly crashes in front of his house, and then his car radio unexpectedly picks up chatter from the show's control room. Slowly he begins to see beyond the charade, and comes to understand that his whole life has been a fraud. There can only be one way for this story to have a happy ending, and that is for Truman to break free. He does so in a completely satisfying way, allowing us to feel that the human spirit is indomitable.

Yet Andrew Niccol's script—directed by Peter Weir—gives us two other perspectives that are not so happy, and not so reassuring. Christof, brilliantly played by Harris, is the creator of a TV show who has gotten to experience what it's like to be Creator of the Universe. So far as Truman is concerned, Christof (with his not so subtle name) is God. Christof has determined every facet of his life, and pulled the strings to get the results he wanted. To ensure that Truman won't want to travel, he gives him a fear of water caused by the drowning of his father in a boating accident. When the actor playing the father unexpectedly shows up, Christof has to figure out how write the "dead" father's return into the script.

Many an author or director has felt godlike in creating a fictional world, but Christof has gotten to take it much further. He can make the "sun" shine at night. He can call a storm upon a calm sea. When he addresses Truman at the end of the film, he is a disembodied voice speaking from the sky. Truman's rejection of this "god," who promises to take care of him and to protect him in ways that the real world can't, might seem like a statement of atheism, and it certainly can be read that way. However, it might also be read as a rejection of the false god represented by Christof, a man who has robbed Truman of his free will.

Throughout the story, Christof has decided what Truman must do, and then arranged things accordingly. When he falls in love with Lauren (Natascha McElhone) instead of Meryl (Laura Linney), cast for the role of Truman's college sweetheart, Lauren is physically removed from the show. Truman is told her family has moved to Tahiti. However, while Truman dutifully falls in love with Meryl, he keeps trying to put together a composite picture of Lauren's face so he won't forget her.

The Truman Show verges on a theological debate between the forces of pre-destination, led by Christof, and the notion of free will, expressed by Truman's desire to think and act for himself. The woman who "played" Lauren protests Truman's situation as enslavement, no matter how nice his prison may be. She wears a button that reads, "How's it going to end?" The logical implication of *The Truman Show* is that if Christof has his way, the cameras will follow Truman to the grave without him ever being aware that his entire life has been a hoax.

As if that wasn't enough, the film also critiques us in the audience, the consumers of "reality" TV fare. In many ways, it's the most cartoonish aspect of the film. We keep returning to the same people, including a man who, improbably, spends all his time in the bathtub. However, what we see is that for fans of the show, it has become a vicarious life. Truman's day-to-day existence is nothing out of the ordinary: he goes to work, greets neighbors and colleagues, visits his mother. Yet for the viewers, even this is preferable to their own apparently mundane lives where what they share with each other is their concern for Truman. Of course since this is television, the film acknowledges concerns for ratings and keeping advertisers happy. When Truman escapes and Christof orders a "technical difficulties" card put up on screen, he wryly notes that the card is getting even higher ratings than they usually do. This separate track of the lives of the viewers makes this distinct from similar stories, and leads to the devastating closing line of the film where we see that the passive audience may cheer Truman's moment of liberation, but seems to have learned nothing from the experience.

Not presented or sold as a science fiction film *per se*, *The Truman Show* is one of the very best modern examples of the genre, providing plenty of food for thought while keeping us entertained with its creative variation of a recurring premise. After watching *The Truman Show*, it's hard to look at our TV sets—and our relation to them—in the same way. We can only resolve to do what we can to make our own lives as "real" as possible.

THE TIME TRAVELER'S MOVIE

For those of us who toil in the field of genre, the "problem" of science fiction films is getting people to take it as seriously as *film noir*, the western, and the romantic comedy. Fans may not care, but for critics and academics, genre is not merely a marketing tool, but a key to approaching a given work. *The Time Traveler's Wife* provides us a perfect example for examining how we define the science fiction film. When the novel by Audrey Niffenegger came out, it was positioned as a mainstream novel, and ended up on the best seller list. What are we to make of the movie adaptation? Does it transcend science fiction, or is it an SF film dressed up in mainstream drag?

My knee-jerk reaction is to argue that, of course, it has to be science fiction. One of its main characters, Henry DeTamble (Eric Bana), is like Kurt Vonnegut's Billy Pilgrim in *Slaughterhouse-Five*: he has become "unstuck in time." He will suddenly disappear and emerge elsewhen, without the ability to bring along any evidence of where he came from, including his clothes. That should settle it right there, since the time travel story is one of the staples of science fiction. Yet the fact that this is entirely involuntary—that he has no control as to when he travels or to what time he goes—underscores the point that this is primarily a story not about the paradoxes that ensue from his journeys, but about something else entirely.

Why then are we so quick to embrace it? One only has to look at the history of how science fiction has been ghettoized in mainstream culture. Science fiction films may clean up at the box office, but you rarely see them up for Oscars for anything except makeup and special effects. Unlike other genres, science fiction remains a stigma to be avoided. Actors, writers, filmmakers, and critics often strive to put distance between a work and this suspect genre.

Robert Schwentke, director of *The Time Traveler's Wife*, insisted it wasn't a science fiction film at all but rather "an epic love story." John Anderson, writing in the *Washington Post*, liked the movie, but insisted that its SF trappings were merely a ruse: "[F]rom a marketing perspective, it's a chick flick disguised as science fiction—which, presumably, will mean girls can get guys to go see it." On the other hand the *Sunday Times* (of London) critic had no problem classifying the movie as SF, but that was only because he *didn't* like it: "This is silly sci-fi tosh that tries to play itself out as a serious and heart-rending love story, but *Ghost* it ain't."

See, if it's any good, it *can't* be science fiction, but if it's bad, it's easy enough to put in the "sci-fi" dumpster. In reaction to such absurd prejudices, fans and sympathetic critics are quick to embrace mainstream works such as *Frankenstein*, *1984*, and *The Handmaid's Tale* as science fiction. The result is that with both the book and the movie of *The Time Traveler's Wife*, given their mainstream success, we want to be able to assert it's one of ours. Here is a popular romantic drama, yet it's about time travel. It *has* to be science fiction, whether mainstream critics are willing to admit it or not.

But is it, really? While those who work in the SF ghetto have grown hardened calluses allowing them to ignore mundane critics so they can move on to other topics, for critics and academics who focus on genre issues the discussion is just beginning. If science fiction is worthy of study—and this critic and academic thinks that it is—claiming a film for a particular genre requires that we explain *why* it belongs in that category, and not simply fly its banner from the ramparts. What *is* a science fiction film, and why should *The Time Traveler's Wife* be included? Let's be strict for a moment and say that science fiction movies are defined as stories where, if you removed the real science, you wouldn't have a story. The imaginative qualities of the film have to build on scientific fact and go on from there, as with *2001: A Space Odyssey*. This is what is usually called "hard science fiction." If we take that line, then it is *The Time Traveler's Wife* that falls short, not the other way around. The only explanation we get for Henry's abilities is that there is some sort of mutation in his cell structure. It's highly implausible, but even hard SF allows its creators to engage in some "what if" flights of fancy. Once done, however, what follows has to make scientific and logical sense, and it doesn't here.

Henry seems to be traveling along his own time line. He doesn't appear before he was born, say during the Civil War, and his actions don't seem to change things even though he clearly is interacting with people in his past. He doesn't return and find the Earth is under Martian control or that George W. Bush was never president. So it's not clear what time travel does other than disrupt his own life. *The Time Traveler's Wife* tries to have it both ways, with Henry's travel clearly having an impact on him and his circle, yet his being unable to change things when they really matter.

Then there's the fact that it doesn't seem to be much of a secret. His wife Claire (Rachel McAdams) obviously knows, as do their closest friends, one of whom learns of this when he discovers a time-traveling Henry in an alley fight. There's even a scientist he goes to for help who eventually publishes his findings. So where are the government officials demanding that Henry come in for questioning? In fact, where's the media? Why isn't this the lead story in every newspaper and on every channel on the planet? It's almost as if Henry is simply the quaint fellow next door who pops in and out of time.

Finally, there's the identity of another time traveler he meets (whose identity I will not reveal, so as to not "spoil" the story). Just the fact that there *is* another suggests that Henry is not unique. Why aren't there several others? Why don't more people report meeting time travelers? None of the issues one would expect in an SF time travel story comes up. Indeed, strictly speaking, a hard SF story could never be about time travel. Unless you're a subatomic particle or move fast enough to be approaching light speed, you're traveling through time the same as the rest of us: second by second into the future. So where does that leave *The Time Traveler's Wife?*

For those of us wanting to claim this as SF, we have to admit it is "metaphorical" science fiction: a romance that uses time travel as a metaphor to explore the relationship between Henry and Claire—it might as well have been an exotic disease. His comings and goings are beyond his control, as is their duration. She has to decide whether she can make a commitment to a man who, literally, may not be there from one moment to the next. It's not hard science, yet it is recognizably science fiction. SF is a genre that has numerous ways to explore issues, with scientific realism being only one of them. This is where the conversation between those of us who are serious about SF and those who feel they're slumming in having to review a science fiction film inevitably breaks down.

It's sad that most film critics don't know this, but SF movies *aren't* about the future, even when they're set there. They're about us in the here and now. They think the special effects are the *point* of such movies instead of recognizing that in a serious SF film, they're merely the window dressing. It ought to go without saying that movies like *Alien Nation* or *District 9* or *E.T.* aren't really concerned about how we'll be treating visiting space aliens when they get here. These films use their alien visitors to reveal something about *us* and how we react to people we perceive as "other." Science fiction has a long history of using its tropes as metaphors. For every *Destination Moon* trying to imagine what a future moon landing would actually be like, there are movies like *Them!* and *Invasion of the Body Snatchers* that use giant ants and space pods to explore '50s paranoia about atomic weapons or the threat of Communism. Is *Blade Runner* a movie that wants us to worry about runaway replicants, or is it using those replicants (and Deckard, for that matter) as symbols of alienation?

The Time Traveler's Wife shows itself to be quite original in playing with some of the conventions of the time travel story as it applies them to its romance. Claire first meets Henry as a little girl in the woods (raising some icky questions about a naked adult male and a child by herself) and subsequently reappears to her as she gets older. When she finally meets him in *his* present, she's already in love with him and knows they will marry. Meanwhile, he's meeting *her* for the first time and doesn't know who this woman is. Who's stalking whom now?

On the day of their wedding he disappears before the ceremony but a future, older Henry shows up in his place. There are some murmurs about why he suddenly has gray hair, but the more interesting question is whether she's cheating on Henry with another version of himself. This becomes even more pointed after she has a series of miscarriages, and then Henry gets a vasectomy without telling her. She proceeds to get pregnant anyway, and the ethics of the situation are mind boggling. Is sex truly consensual when she knows beyond certainty that his future self will be against it?

The movie ends differently from the book, but thematically it's pretty much the same. It's the notion that our love for others outlives our lives, in this case made literal. It remains moving because the movie spotlights the fact that even with this strange ability, Henry has no guarantees in life. He can use his "advantage" to play the lottery without too many qualms, but he can't avoid the fate of every human being: you're born, you live, you die. It's his fate as well. He just gets to live it in a different order.

As with the book, this is a movie that takes a classic science fiction concept and plays with it a bit, but keeps our main focus on the characters. Critics who think that's what proves it isn't science fiction are missing the point. Special effects and art direction aside, that also describes the original *The Day the Earth Stood Still*, the remake of *The Fly*, *Gattaca*, and many other films that are unquestionably science fiction. The difference is not between character-driven "serious movies" and science fiction "trash." The difference is between *good* science fiction and *bad* science fiction. As it turns out, *The Time Traveler's Wife* is pretty good science fiction.

PART III. BARGAIN BIN

Let's admit it. Not all science fiction films are great. If they were, there never would have been a *Mystery Science Theater 3000*. As a rule, I haven't written a lot about bad SF movies because why would I want to sit through them again? Occasionally, though, I have written about such films outside of my normal reviewing chores, or dissented from the critical pack. The secret among film critics is that while, of course, we'd prefer to *watch* good movies, writing about bad ones can be a lot more fun. Writing these pieces often proved much more entertaining than the movies themselves.

REMAKE LOVE, NOT WAR

As soon as the remake of the 1951 classic *The Day the Earth Stood Still* hit the theaters, the knives were out. The movie failed on numerous levels, but not because it was a remake. Like the snap judgment on a film adaptation that the book has to be better, the notion that remakes are automatically bad is demonstrably false; some of those remakes are good, or even great.

Often remakes are done simply because a studio owns a property and thinks that if an idea worked before then it will work again, as in the proposed remakes of *Logan's Run* and *Westworld* currently in development. That may make good business sense, but it's the wrong reason to tell a story. A good remake needs a valid purpose to justify retelling the story.

One such reason is when someone sees the opportunity to correct and revise a flawed original. Take *The Fly*. Based on a George Langelaan story that had originally appeared in *Playboy*, it was a melodramatic potboiler about a scientist (Al [David] Hedison) whose experiment goes horribly wrong. His teleportation device leaves him with the giant head and arm of a fly, while the fly, discovered at the end, has a tiny human head and arm. It was good for some screams in the 1950s, even with Vincent Price in a relatively sedate role but, as future director David Cronenberg noted, the story made no sense. If the machine simply swapped body parts, shouldn't the scientist have a tiny fly head? Where did all that extra mass come from?

In his brilliant 1986 remake, Cronenberg attempted to address those issues. The film takes advantage of three decades of scientific advances to make the combination of man and fly more credible, if not actually believable. As Seth Brundle (Jeff Goldblum) notes, his transporter has turned into a gene splicer, merging the DNA of man and fly. Some chose to read Seth's deterioration into "Brundlefly" as symbolic of AIDS, but Cronenberg explicitly rejected that notion, arguing that it would imply he somehow caught it from science journalist Veronica Quaife (Geena Davis). He preferred to see it as the equivalent of the aging process, something Baby Boomers were just beginning to experience as they started to find that their bodies didn't work like they used to.

Simply revising the science of the story might have been reason enough to do a remake, but the film goes further, becoming a chamber piece in which Seth, Veronica, and her editor/ex-lover Stathis Borens (John Getz) are caught up in a complex series of betrayals and misunderstandings. In the '58 film, the key job of the wife (Patricia Owens) was to scream at the big reveal of her husband's transformation. Veronica is much more of an active player. As a reporter, she is the one who stumbles on to the story of Seth's research and then aggressively pursues it, even over his objections. She successfully negotiates access to his experiments as the price for sitting on the story. She deals with both Stathis and Seth as equals, not always prevailing but not taking a passive role, either. In the film's final act, her ordeal is every bit as important to the story as Seth's. She realizes she is pregnant by him and seeks an abortion. It is Veronica who is the pro-active character in the film's climax, with both men finally overwhelmed by events. Coming five years before Davis's role in the overtly feminist *Thelma and Louise*, it's a powerful reflection of just how different women in the '80s were from their mothers in the '50s.

The lesson here is that, while jazzing up the special effects may be part of the process of doing a remake, the focus has got to remain on the story and characters. John Carpenter knew that when he set forth to redo another '50s classic, *The Thing*. The original was directed by Christian Nyby and produced by Howard Hawks, himself a major director. In it, American scientists and military personnel at a remote Arctic location discover a spaceship whose vegetable-based passenger thrives on our blood. The arguments between the scientist, who wants to seek knowledge for its own sake, and the colonel, who wants to shoot first and ask questions later, is the mirror image of the debate in the original *The Day the Earth Stood Still*, which came out that same year, only this time the military is proven right. The movie is fondly remembered for several "sense of wonder" moments, including the closing warning to "Keep watching the skies."

For his remake, Carpenter largely ignored the Nyby film. He instead focused on *Who Goes There?*—the short story by Don A. Stuart (a pseudonym for legendary SF editor John W. Campbell) that served as its source. As good as the 1951 film was, it used very little of that story. Instead of turning the film into another Cold War parable, Carpenter's version is an exercise in paranoia. The scientists and military men, now in Antarctica, are isolated by a storm when the alien starts to attack. As in the short story, the alien is not a giant carrot but a shape shifter. Who can you trust when one of your colleagues—or even a sled dog—might be the alien in disguise? The movie provided scares (courtesy of make-up effects wizard Rob Bottin) that would never have been permitted in a movie three decades earlier but, more importantly, it transformed the political and intellectual dilemmas of the '51 movie back to the psychological and existential unease of Campbell's story.

Some stories are so timeless they can be told again and again, with new variations and interpretations introduced each time. Consider the variations on a theme in the three versions of Richard Matheson's "I Am Legend." The 1964

Italian film *The Last Man on Earth*, starring Vincent Price, is a melancholy tale of loneliness and futility as the last survivor of a plague fights vampiric zombies. Seven years later, Charlton Heston starred in *The Omega Man*, in which numerous changes were made so that Heston's heroic stature could be preserved. The zombies were transformed into strange and deadly cultists; other survivors were found; and, most importantly, the macho Heston saw plenty of action. The 2007 *I Am Legend* ups the ante even more with amazing effects of an abandoned Manhattan slowly returning to wilderness. It makes its hero (played by Will Smith) into a combination of Price and Heston. The loneliness is slowly driving him mad, but he gets to kick some zombie butt while also trying to find a cure for the plague.

While one can have preferences among the stylistic or narrative differences of the films, or the fact that Smith's film had much more money to play with than either of its low budget predecessors, what's interesting is that none of these films is universally hailed as the definitive adaptation of Matheson's story or a masterpiece in its own right. Just as no one complains when a show is revived on Broadway, and different performers and directors bring their own ideas and interpretations to older plays, the "I Am Legend" films demonstrate that a good story can be told again and again, provided that no one version completely overshadows the others.

The key question for any director contemplating a remake is figuring out why you want to tell this story now. Consider *Invasion of the Body Snatchers*, which has been filmed four times. The 1956 original, based on Jack Finney's novel, is a classic that still has the power to shock audiences. Miles Bennell (Kevin McCarthy) returns to his sleepy California town of Santa Rosa to find that numerous people are complaining that imposters have replaced family members. We learn of pods from space, which absorb the lives and memories of humans, killing off the real people in the process. It's a scary take on conformity in 1950s America, whether you see the pods as stand-ins for Communist infiltrators or for the witch hunters. For his part, director Don Siegel said it wasn't really about politics at all, but about letting others do your thinking for you.

The film was remade in 1978 by director Philip Kaufman, and was greeted with initial skepticism by fans of the original. However both McCarthy and Siegel did cameos in the remake, implicitly giving their blessings. The new film was still about conformity, but it now reflected the concerns of the "Me Decade." Bennell's psychiatric colleague (Leonard Nimoy) became the author of pop psychology self-help books. The action had moved from Santa Rosa to San Francisco, with the anonymity of big city life aiding the pods in their conquest. When McCarthy showed up for his cameo, he was shown running down the street shouting,

"They're here! They're here!" almost as if he had been screaming out warnings since the end of the last film. Indeed, the close of the '56 film, in which Miles is finally believed, was added only after the distributor freaked out over the original downbeat ending. Twenty-two years later—after assassinations, Vietnam and Watergate—moviegoers had grown more cynical, allowing Kaufman to offer a chilling conclusion in which one of the remaining humans is outed by the pod people. Rather than simply rehashing the original film in color and with bigger stars and effects, Kaufman's version reflected the malaise of the late '70s.

The two subsequent remakes provide counterexamples of how not to do it. Abel Ferrara's 1994 *Body Snatchers* sets the action at a military base, which is also being taken over by the invaders. As Don Siegel might have noted, if you set this story in a situation where everyone is supposed to conform and obey orders, how can you tell who the pods are?

Even more disappointing is the 2007 *Invasion*. Directed by Oliver Hirschbiegel (the German director of *The Experiment* and *Downfall*). It was defeated by the real life pod people at the studio. Much of the film is a thoughtful retelling, with the renamed Carol Bennell (Nicole Kidman) now a psychiatrist and mother living in Washington, D.C., with her young son. Instead of pods, the film posits an infectious goo transmitted by one person to another, almost as if it's a sexually transmitted disease. However, the downbeat film Hirschbiegel intended was never released. Instead, James McTeigue was brought in to do reshoots, including new scenes written by the Wachowski Brothers (of *Matrix* fame), providing a wholly unbelievable happy ending. The studio was less interested in what story was being told than in giving the public what they wanted. As it turned out, the public didn't want it.

So, with so many examples of how to do a remake the right way or the wrong way, why did the new *The Day the Earth Stood Still* fail? The 1951 film featured Michael Rennie as the alien Klaatu who arrives on Earth with a message he wants to deliver to all of Earth's leaders. The problem is that getting all of Earth's leaders in one place proves impossible. Instead, after numerous difficulties, Klaatu delivers his message to a group of the planet's great scientists and thinkers, led by Professor Barnhardt (Sam Jaffe channeling Albert Einstein). His message is this: there's a vast interplanetary union out there that lives in peace which has no intention of letting Earth export its wars. Humans can kill each other, but once we start putting our weapons into space, they will have no choice but to destroy us. Coming in the midst of the Cold War, with the atomic bombing of Hiroshima only six years in the past, *Day* was a cautionary fable about the choices in front of us: war or peace, life or death.

The new film keeps the framework of the original, but now has Klaatu concerned about pollution and global warming. That makes it timely, but the filmmakers seem never to have asked why *this* story was necessary to address those issues. The political content of *Day* is not simply a modular chip that can be replaced by an upgrade. The fear and suspicions of the Earth authorities in the 1951 film were reflective of the anxieties of the time. We get little sense that the authorities in the new film are in a post-9/11 world. When the new Klaatu finally delivers his message, it is that he's come to destroy all human life on Earth. Mankind is not given the chance to make a choice. Where's the educational value of that? Indeed, if the whole point of his mission is to destroy humanity, why even bother to land? Just send a drone ship with the new robot Gort and be done with it.

By turning the alien's warning into a special effects attack on the planet, it defeats the whole purpose of the tale. The original movie is about humanity being given a chance to change before it's too late, to see if the wise scientists and thinkers can overcome the paranoia and defensiveness of the political and military leaders. When Klaatu wins the trust of a widowed mother and her young son, we know there's hope. Although these elements are retained in the new version, the meaning is lost. The boy, now her stepson, is simply a brat, while her goal is no longer helping Klaatu complete his mission but trying to convince him to abandon it. Instead of a superior alien race warning us we get a destructive one that is no better—and arguably worse—than humanity. There may be some interesting points to be made about how our environmental troubles are possibly beyond our ability to cope, but *The Day the Earth Stood Still* wasn't the vehicle to deliver it.

In spite of the failure of *Day*, we shouldn't give up on the potential for a remake to be as good as or better than the original film. For those still not convinced, the clinching argument falls outside of SF. The 1941 film version of Dashiell Hammett's hard-boiled detective novel *The Maltese Falcon* marked John Huston's directorial debut and helped make Humphrey Bogart a star. For many, it is one of the essential examples of *film noir*. Not as well known is that the movie was actually the third film version of the book. When Huston announced it as his chosen project, the executives at Warner Bros. thought him foolish, since it had failed twice before. Why remake it? Huston told them it was because he was going to do it the right way. The result was a classic film that totally eclipsed its predecessors.

Are good remakes the stuff that dreams are made of? No, they can be quite real. The secret is this: it has to be put in the hands of filmmakers like Huston or Kaufman or Carpenter or Cronenberg, who know why they're doing the remake in the first place.

GILLIGAN'S ISLAND EARTH

The 1950s were truly the Golden Age for science fiction movies, ushering in an impressive array of films, but now let's focus on a film often thought to be a classic... until you actually sit down and watch it.

This Island Earth (1955) was one of the biggest budget SF films up to that time and is fondly remembered. It was one of the few films of the era done in color and which took its characters to another world. It has a beautifully poetic title, and some of its special effects were outstanding achievements for its era. So much for its virtues.

When the folks at *Mystery Science Theater 3000* did their feature version in 1996, they knew that they would need to spoof a film that would look good on the big screen. *Manos, Hands of Fate* might work on TV (where most of us saw it, if at all), but they wanted something that would be visually engaging in a movie theater. There was some surprise when they chose *This Island Earth*. Wasn't that a "good" film? As Roger Ebert put it, "The odd thing about *MST3K: The Movie* is that its target is not that bad—or at least, not all that bad. On second thought, maybe it is. Let's put it this way: I liked it a lot more when I was 12 than I do now."

Presumably the reason it was chosen was that the parent studio for the *MST3K* movie, Universal, already owned *This Island Earth*, so the legal problems in chopping up and mocking the film would be minimal. Also, it was in color and had all those nifty effects. However, if you watch the film on your own, you may find yourself channeling Tom Servo and Crow T. Robot yourself. Special effects aside, this proves to be a very silly movie.

Let's start with the cast. The highest profile SF films of the era had stars who were either on their way up (Gene Barry in *The War of the Worlds*, Kevin McCarthy in *Invasion of the Body Snatchers*), stars whose glory days were behind them but still had prestige (Walter Pidgeon in *Forbidden Planet*), or even actors who were right in the middle of productive careers (Patricia Neal and Michael Rennie in *The Day the Earth Stood Still*). The leads of *This Island Earth* are Rex Reason, Faith Domergue, and Jeff Morrow. Looking through their credits, one is struck by the fact that a) they worked steadily in film and TV, no small accomplishment in Hollywood, and b) *This Island Earth* is probably the most prominent movie any of them ever did. Reason and Morrow would be teamed again for *The Creature Walks Among Us*, which isn't necessarily a plus. Clearly, Universal didn't think this was a movie worth spending money on when it came to the actors. Modern viewers are more likely to notice the appearance of Russell Johnson in a supporting role as another scientist, but only because of Johnson's lasting fame as The Professor on *Gilligan's Island*.

The same can be said for the choice of director. *The Day the Earth Stood Still* and *Invasion of the Body Snatchers* had up-and-coming directors Robert Wise and Don Siegel. *The Thing* had unknown Christian Nyby, a protégé of the film's producer, legendary director Howard Hawks. *War of the Worlds* had Byron Haskin, whose success led to a string of SF films, including *Conquest of Space*, *From the Earth to the Moon*, *Robinson Crusoe on Mars*, *The Power*, and several episodes of the '60s TV series *The Outer Limits*. Only *Forbidden Planet* and *This Island Earth* went with relative non-entities, and MGM was spending money on the cast and the effects to make up for it on *Planet*. *This Island Earth* had journeyman director Joseph M. Newman and, if reports are to believed, his work may have been supplemented by an uncredited Jack Arnold, whose filmography includes *Creature from the Black Lagoon*, *It Came from Outer Space*, and *The Incredible Shrinking Man*.

Then there's the plot. Based on a series of stories (later combined into novel form) by Raymond F. Jones, the movie seems in many ways to be a serial. Cal Meacham (Rex Reason) is intrigued when his scientific supply house not only sends him some equipment that shouldn't exist, but also provides a weird catalog that tells him what he'll need to build an Interociter. When it's completed, it turns out to be a communication device that connects him with Exeter (Jeff Morrow), a high-domed, white haired fellow who tells Cal he proved his worth by constructing the Interociter. Exeter invites him to join a secret science project. The Interociter then sends out beams to destroy the catalog. Cal unplugs the Interociter, which causes it to self-destruct.

This is mildly engaging stuff, until you start asking the obvious questions: The Interociter has to be *plugged in*? What sort of outlets do they have on Exeter's home planet, AC or DC? Even assuming this was a special version adapted for Earth, Cal seems too willing to go along with things. Does he not notice Exeter's alien-like appearance?

This is all set-up, however. Once he's at the country estate where Exeter and other odd looking folks play host to a group of scientists, all experts in atomic energy, Cal learns there's plenty of reason to be suspicious. For one thing, his old girlfriend Dr. Ruth Adams (Faith Domergue) is there, and she's decidedly cool. Finally we learn the truth. This whole research project is actually being conducted for the benefit of the planet Metaluna, where a terrible war is raging. Cal and Ruth decide to escape, rather than work for Exeter.

All right, we have some intrigue here, some '50s paranoia about authority and who's really pulling the strings, and if the characters weren't so wooden we might actually care about their fates. What happens next, though, is what some of the film's defenders claim redeems the proceedings but, in fact, exposes the movie as not having much to say at all.

Cal and Ruth escape in a plane, but the plane is then seized by a Metalunan space ship. On board, they are greeted by the ever-genial Exeter, who apologizes for the way they've been treated, and explains the dire straits his planet is in. The surface of his world has been destroyed by bombardment by the Zahgons, another alien race. The Metalunans are hoping to move to Earth. Instead, in short order, Cal and Ruth escape, Metaluna is destroyed, and Exeter dies. There are some nifty special effects, including a menacing mutant, but the whole trip to Metaluna has been a sideshow. Cal and Ruth get there, are menaced, and return to Earth.

The image of the mutant creature immediately entered SF film lore, but what was the point of the trip in the first place? It's largely an excuse to showcase the bombardment of Metaluna which, according to Kenneth von Gunden and Stuart H. Stock, in their *Twenty All-Time Great Science Fiction Films*, took twenty-six days to shoot and used up $100,000 of the film's estimated $800,000 budget. The special effects take up sixteen of the film's eighty-seven minutes. The problem is that, with characters who are little more than stick figures and a plot barely worthy of the name, the special effects are simply a fireworks show. Universal's publicity machine boasted about the fact that the mutant monster costume cost twenty to twenty-five thousand dollars, making it the most expensive monster created for a movie at that time. But who are they? Mutant Metalunans? Experimental creatures gone wrong? Captured Zahgons? As with everything else in the film, it simply is, with no time for further explanation.

It's not surprising to learn that *This Island Earth* was not a box office smash, and didn't lead to imitators or even, years later, to a remake. It fails, in spite of the science fictional trappings and the potentially complex alien Exeter, because in the end it's simply a shaggy dog story. When one looks at *The Day the Earth Stood Still* or *Forbidden Planet*, it's not hard to discern the message of the film. But what is the message of *This Island Earth*? Von Gunden and Stock argue that it is that human creativity cannot be forced, which is why enslaving the Earth scientists is doomed to failure. It's a valid point, but it's just as clearly not the focus of the film. Others say it's a reflection of '50s paranoia about the atomic bomb and nuclear war, but Metaluna is being destroyed by meteor bombardment, an interplanetary update on the catapult.

For fans of '50s SF, *This Island Earth* may be fun to watch, but it's no classic, lacking both the substance and the influence on the genre that we expect from the truly great films.

GUILTY PLEASURES

Critics and film buffs will sometimes talk about their "guilty pleasures," the way other people talk about their favorite "junk food." We know it's not good for us and it doesn't have any nutritional value, but we love these bad movies all the same. To qualify as a "guilty pleasure," it has to be a film that you can't justify artistically and which, in fact, might be filled with examples of what *not* to do in a movie. One of my guilty pleasures is the 1967 *Casino Royale*, a James Bond spoof that credits six (!) directors and which stars David Niven, Ursula Andress, Peter Sellers, Woody Allen, Orson Welles, Deborah Kerr, and so many other people popping in for cameos and featured parts that you lose track. The movie is a train wreck. Yet it's one I've watched many times (as opposed to Allen, who claims *never* to have seen it) with great enjoyment. I can't defend it, but I like it.

People who have fun with *Plan 9 from Outer Space* or *Robot Monster* or are part of the more recent cult for *Troll 2*, are responding to these movies with laughter and pleasure and not a small amount of affection. You don't see this kind of support for the big Hollywood bombs. There aren't cults built around disastrous star vehicles like *Ishtar* or *Gigli*. When Hollywood turns out their blockbuster science fiction disasters, whether it's *The Adventures of Pluto Nash* or *Battlefield Earth*, few people step up to defend those films, either. So what is it that separates the guilty pleasures from the just plain bad movies?

Part of it is the sense that the people making the movie were doing it because they wanted to make the movie, not because they thought if they opened it up on 2000 screens with no press screenings they could clean up on opening weekend before word got out about it. Often these people are struggling with small budgets or with a lack of talent in front of and/or behind the camera. Tim Burton's movie *Ed Wood* takes liberties with the story of the real life director, but it captures that earnest desire to tell stories like *Bride of the Monster* or *Glen or Glenda*, and Wood trying to do it as best as he knew how, oblivious to his own shortcomings as a filmmaker.

When you watch a movie like *Citizen Kane* or *2001* you can just sit in awe of the genius of an Orson Welles or a Stanley Kubrick, knowing that that's something you're unlikely to ever achieve. Watching beloved clunkers like *Message from Space* or *Frankenstein vs. the Space Monster* you find yourself thinking: I could do that. In fact, I could probably do that *better* than the people who made it. Yet there's no contempt for the filmmakers. I've seen audiences warmly cheer and applaud the makers of some truly awful films. They sense that whatever the problems with the actual movie, the people who made it really were hoping to please audiences, not just take the money and run.

Which brings us to one of my oldest guilty pleasures, which I have seen many times on television but have yet to see on the big screen. I'm told that there may not be theatrical print to be had. The film is an obscure 1962 opus entitled *Creation of the Humanoids*. Michael Weldon, in his invaluable *Psychotronic Encyclopedia of Film* claims it was artist Andy Warhol's favorite movie. One can see how Warhol might have responded to the minimalist style of director Wesley Barry, who apparently was able to get several stage sets built and ended up shooting the film as if it were a play, with one long talky scene on a single set after another.

The story is set in a society where much labor is done by robots, and the robots have become increasingly more like humans. Craigis (Don Megowan) is an official in the "Society of Flesh and Blood," an organization that is fearful of the robots, arguing that they are making humans obsolete. They strive to keep the robots—sneeringly referred to as "clickers"—in their place, which is already a giveaway of what's really on the minds of Barry and screenwriter Jay Simms. When Craigis goes to visit his sister (Frances McCann), he discovers that she has taken on a robot servant. It is implied that Pax (David Cross) is doing much more than just her cooking and laundry. They have undergone a process in which the robot has been programmed to be in perfect sync with her needs and desires, leading Craigis to deliver this shocked declaration: "My sister is in *rapport*... with a clicker!?" It doesn't quite resonate the way "Guess who's coming to dinner?" would a few years later, but the meaning is clear. The prejudice against the "clickers" is symbolic of the battle for civil rights in the '60s, which would make the Society for Flesh and Blood the film's version of the Ku Klux Klan or the White Citizens Council.

Craigis doesn't see himself as prejudiced. He feels he's defending the human race. When he leaves his sister's apartment, Pax starts to laugh. She asks why, and he explains that since he has been programmed with a sense of humor, the irony of the situation is making him laugh. What irony? Well, when Craigis and his female companion Maxine (Erica Elliott) confront Dr. Raven (Don Doolittle), they're in for a rude awakening. Raven is the chief robotics scientist, and when we first meet him he is an old man. However his own clickers (one of whom is played by Dudley Manlove, one of the aliens from *Plan 9 from Outer Space*) have transferred Raven's brain to a young robot body. Craigis is appalled that the robots have become indistinguishable from humans, and that's when we get to the big reveal: Craigis and Maxine are robots themselves. They were among the first of the new generation of identical-to-human robots to be created, and they are so human that they didn't even suspect their own artificiality.

However the irony isn't over yet. The heavy-handed message for tolerance and equality makes the film more interesting than it might have been. It's covering ground that *Blade Runner* would pick up on twenty years later in a far more sophisticated way. Now, at film's end, Craigis and Maxine are ready to face the reality of who they really are, and now the question remains whether Craigis's early fears will come true. Would these humanoid robots come to inherit the Earth? At this point, Dr. Raven turns to us in the audience and assures us that they did in fact succeed. After all, if they hadn't, he chuckles, *we* wouldn't be here.

Oh no! We're the humanoid robots! We thought this was a story set in the far future, and it was actually in our past! No doubt Pax, Craigis's robot-in-law, got full use of his irony circuits once Craigis learned the truth.

Creation of the Humanoids fascinates because it takes its message of tolerance absolutely seriously, and the actors play it straight. Don Megowan, who had a long career playing parts on TV (although he apparently had a small bit in Mel Brooks's *Blazing Saddles*), portrays Craigis as a tragic hero. This is Oedipus Rex as a cyborg, not realizing until the climax the cruel twist fate has had in store for him all along.

Sadly, it's not a very good film. It's visually static. The narrative is about as subtle as being hit over the head with a mallet. As for the acting... Well, calling some of the performances "robotic" would be going for an easy laugh, but it wouldn't be far off the mark. Yet in spite of all that, the movie is well meaning. You can tell that the people involved really were trying to do the best they could with the material that was at hand.

Creation of the Humanoids won't make anyone's list of the hundred greatest movies of all time. You won't see any clips from it in a tribute to the best science fiction movies. No, it's a guilty pleasure, and I have to admit it's one of mine.

MARS CONCEDES!

Christmas movies that intersect with our genre have never quite resonated with me. Being Jewish, I didn't grow up with Santa or holiday trees, and while I certainly enjoy seasonal classics like *Miracle on 34th Street* and *It's a Wonderful Life*, it was never personal. So when, in my early days as a film critic, people were up in arms over *Silent Night, Deadly Night*, with its serial killer in a Santa outfit, I wondered what the fuss was about—it was just another one of the slasher films of the era. Even a modern classic I truly like, *The Nightmare Before Christmas*, means more to me because of Halloween rather than Christmas. Indeed, when Jack Skellington finds the trees in the woods that lead to the domains of the different holidays, my reaction was that he was lucky he didn't end up in "Yom Kippur Land," where everyone spends the day fasting and atoning.

Part of it may simply be the sheer number of Christmas movies. For every film as delightful as *Elf*, there's dozens of examples of holiday treacle. There's the saccharine *Santa Clause* series. There are the numerous versions of *A Christmas Carol*, which hit its nadir with *Scrooged*. I can't imagine who enjoys the bizarre *One Magic Christmas*, whose message seems to be "believe in Santa or you'll never see your family again." Then there's the truly nightmarish *The Polar Express*, where the pseudo-realistic animation makes it seem as if the film is populated by soulless homunculi. As for the dysfunctional family "comedies" like the odious *Christmas with the Kranks*, which takes place in an alternate universe where people are punished for not decorating their houses for the holiday, don't get me started.

In terms of pure science fiction, the pickings are especially slim. This brings us to the beloved 1964 turkey, *Santa Claus Conquers the Martians*. From its warlike title, to the casting of a young Pia Zadora as a Martian child, this is a movie that has long been celebrated as one of the worst films ever made. It was savaged by the folks at *Mystery Science Theater 3000*, and was nominated for a Golden Turkey Award as "the Most Insufferable Kiddie Movie Ever Made." (The authors of *Son of Golden Turkey Awards* opted to give the award to *Pinocchio in Outer Space*, a painful bit of 1965 animation.)

Now, it would be easy to pile on this low budget film, which is in the pantheon of bad movies along with *Plan 9 from Outer Space* and *Robot Monster*. However, as I prepared to do so with glee, I thought of my friend and colleague Mark R. Leeper, who has been reviewing films on the Internet since 1984, and whose fanzine has put out more than 1500 *weekly* issues. Mark refuses to sneer at and mock bad movies, no matter how excruciating they are, believing they should be judged as attempts by people working within the constraints of their limited budgets and limited talent to do the best they can. If they fail, they fail, but they're entitled to be treated on their own terms. So let's take *Santa Claus Conquers the Martians* at face value and see what we find.

Since the film has fallen into public domain, it is readily available not only on video but on the Internet. (Unlike, say *2001: A Space Odyssey* or *Lawrence of Arabia*, this loses nothing when seen on a small screen.) The story begins on Mars, which seems like a truly dreary place. Their meals, with a surprisingly American menu, reduce everything to pill form. Everyone dresses almost identically, complete with helmets with antenna and odd tubing that seems to run between their ears and their cerebrums.

Kimar (Leonard Hicks), who is King of the Martians, notices that his children Bomar (Chris Month) and Girmar (Pia Zadora) have lost their appetite and seem to spend all their time watching Earth television. It seems beyond the ability of Kimar and his wife Momar (Leila Martin) to question their bland diet, but their concern over their offspring's obsession with Earth broadcasts has an easy solution: take the TV set out of their room. Instead, Kimar and the other Martian leaders go to consult with Chochem (Carl Don). Chochem is a wise old sage—which is exactly what his name means when pronounced in Yiddish!—and he declares that the problem is that the children are miniature adults. They are force fed enrichment education from infancy so that, by the time they can walk, they no longer know how to have fun. Here, in essence, is the theme of the movie, spoken by the only Martian not dressed up in the uniform everyone else wears.

Soon Kimar and his crew are off to Earth to kidnap Santa Claus (John Call), the jolly old elf who will bring joy and laughter, not to mention toys, to the children of Mars. Along on the trip is the evil Voldar (Vincent Beck), who thinks Kimar has gotten soft, and Dropo (Bill McCutcheon), a buffoon who not only provides the supposed comic relief, but also seems to refute everything we've been told about how the Martians are so serious and driven. How oafish is he? If a remake was being planned, the casting director would be shouting, "Get me Rob Schneider!"

When they get to Earth, they find a Santa on every street corner, and end up asking two Earth children—Billy (Victor Stiles) and Betty (Donna Conforti)—for directions. However, now that the children know the Martian plot, they are taken along as well. Once back on Mars, Santa sets up an automated workshop to churn out toys, all of which are culturally biased. There are baseball bats, though there's no indication Bomar plays the game, and the dolls all look like little versions of Betty, not Girmar. Santa apparently assumes everyone wants to be American. Yet when the dour Martian children meet Santa, they are soon laughing and enjoying themselves. Their parents realize that Chochem was right. Children need to be children. All astrophysics and no play make Bomar a dull boy. There's still the evil plot by the villainous Voldar to contend with, and then Santa will have to get back to Earth. That leaves funny old Dropo to be the Santa of Mars. This leads to a rousing sing-a-long version of the film's theme song, "Hooray for Santy Claus," written by Milton DeLugg, who would go on to become musical director of *The Gong Show*. (You can't make this stuff up.)

The film is as absurd and poorly executed as even this somewhat sympathetic summary indicates, so why has it continued to hold a place in the public imagination for nearly fifty years? The idea that parents may be putting too much pressure on their kids still resonates today. We may not yet be pumping information into infant brains, but there are expectant couples already selecting the proper *in utero* music for their forthcoming offspring, and stocking up on "educational" toys and videos for infants not even at the toddler stage. As for older kids, ask your children or grandchildren or nieces and nephews how much homework they're getting these days. Better yet, ask them how much unstructured, free playtime they have. Time spent at dance classes, little league teams, etc., doesn't count.

As for Santa, he doesn't really "conquer" the Martians so much as jolly them along into letting their children relax and be kids. Except for an odd moment when he rattles off the names of his reindeer and wonders if "Nixon" is one of them, Santa's attempts at humor are largely in character, so that youngsters will not be disillusioned or frightened by the goings-on as they might be if they stumble across a rerun of *Silent Night, Deadly Night*. Uncritical youngsters may find it silly, but they'll look beyond the cheapjack special effects to enjoy the adventure of going to Mars with Santa and teaching Martian kids to have fun.

Does that redeem the film? Not in the slightest. Anyone over the age of 7 or 8 will quickly realize we're in the presence of a great holiday turkey here, certainly no later than Dropo's first appearance. That's why the *Mystery Science Theater 3000* version, readily available on DVD, provides a context for the rest of us. With all due respect to those who wince at such mocking, the film may have a worthy theme, but it is so badly thought out and so cheaply produced that it invites such treatment. In the end, *Santa Claus Conquers the Martians* proves that the road to Mars, as well as Hell, may be paved with good intentions.

E.T. GO HOME

The first time I saw *E.T.* was the summer of 1982. Steven Spielberg's blockbuster was the hit of the summer, and would go on to become the one of the most popular movies of all time. The *wunderkind* director who had skyrocketed to fame with *Jaws* and *Close Encounters of the Third Kind* had stumbled badly with the bloated and awkward World War II comedy *1941*. Thanks to his friend George Lucas, he bounced back with *Raiders of the Lost Ark*, and now, a year later, on his own, he was back on top. I remember going to see it on a big screen with a date on a Saturday night, in a packed theater, oohing and aahing along with everyone else. It was a phenomenon. Three years later, I was now a film critic, and *E.T.* was being re-released. At last I would be able to weigh in on the movie. I showed up at the appointed time to a private screening room in Boston and discovered that I was the only one there. My colleagues had written about it back in 1982, and saw no reason to sit through it again. I turned to the projectionist and said I assumed that meant the screening was canceled. He replied that he was being paid to be there and would have to stay regardless, so if I wanted to see it, we could go ahead. I took my seat and the movie began.

Two hours later, I had completely changed my mind about the film and about Steven Spielberg. While I find him to be an undeniable craftsman, it was from this time forward that I came to see that there was little depth to this fable. It was just Spielberg pushing our buttons to get the desired reaction. Since then, I have liked an occasional film by him (*Minority Report*, *Catch Me If You Can*, the opening reel of *Saving Private Ryan*), but have come to see him as a showman rather than an artist, the modern equivalent of Cecil B. DeMille who, but for the spectacle of *The Ten Commandments*, would be forgotten today by everyone except the film buffs and historians. My prediction is that, in spite of his superstar status today, that will ultimately be Spielberg's fate as well.

What's wrong with *E.T.*? It works fine as a children's film, about how a young boy and a childlike alien who is lost become friends, and how the boy helps E.T. get home. Yet all of the great emotional moments that had worked so well three years before now left me feeling like Dorothy at the end of *The Wizard of Oz* when she sees the old humbug behind the screen. The problem begins right from the start with John Williams' bombastic score, telling us that *everything* is dramatic. Elliot (Henry Thomas) riding a bicycle early in the film is treated like the coming of the Messiah or Arthur pulling the sword from the stone. There's no subtlety and no balance. Film music should be used to heighten feelings already evoked by the scene, not to make up for their lack.

A scene where the score works is when Elliot is riding his bike with E.T. in the basket and they suddenly take off into the air. *That* is a dramatic moment, and the music, the most famous theme from the film, works perfectly. Elsewhere, Williams' music is like having Spielberg sitting in the seat behind you acting like an obnoxious seven-year-old, screaming and nudging, "Isn't that cool? What about *that*? Ooh, now get a load of *this* part!"

Then there are the bad guys. What's that? You don't remember the bad guys in *E.T.*? That's because Spielberg pulls every trick in the book to make the scientists tracking E.T. seem sinister and dangerous before revealing that they're not any such thing at all. The main strategy he uses is at least as old as *Battleship Potemkin*, Sergei Eisenstein's classic 1927 film about a ship's mutiny against the Tsar's officers. The most famous scene in that movie is the Odessa steps sequence, where Eisenstein's editing continues to inspire filmmakers. (Brian DePalma did a notable homage to it in his version of *The Untouchables*.) What Spielberg seems to have noticed is that, where Eisenstein gives us numerous closeups of the faces of the people who come to support the sailors, the Tsar's troops are shown in murderous lockstep without their faces ever being seen. Thus, Spielberg makes the scientists seem sinister and possibly deadly by giving us closeups of keys ominously dangling from a key ring, backlit trackers moving across a field, or faceless attackers in hazmat suits menacing Elliot, his family, and E.T. (He does the same thing with the science teacher passing out the chloroformed cotton balls to kill the frogs in Elliot's class, ensuring that adult authority remains mysterious and frightening.)

While it's possible to be charmed by a precocious Drew Barrymore as Elliot's younger sister—especially in the scene where she first discovers E.T., and she and the alien both scream at each other—the only idea that Spielberg seems to be interested in is how difficult it is to be a young boy in an affluent suburb, which may have been something that he was able to identify with, but isn't much to hang a story on. References to an absent father who is off in Mexico with his new girl friend gives Dee Wallace the opportunity to emote in a scene or two, but don't really amount to anything. To get us to care about these bland suburban kids, Spielberg does everything he can think of, from winking at the audience with references to his pal George Lucas's *Star Wars* movies (as when E.T. thinks a kid in a Yoda costume is a fellow alien) to Elliot's anguish over E.T.'s death and resurrection.

The scientists arrive to quarantine the house in the most obtrusive and menacing way possible. We see that E.T. has turned ashen and weak, and Elliot tightens the screws with a tearful, "I think he's dying." The lead scientist (Peter Coyote) is now revealed to be an overgrown boy, who tells Elliot he's been dreaming of meeting space aliens since he was a kid himself, and that he is envious of Elliot's friendship with E.T. So E.T. dies, Elliot cries, and the scientist gives the boy a moment alone with the corpse to say good-bye. Remember that they were so worried about alien pathogens that they had invaded the house in hazmat suits, but now the boy will have a tender moment with a supposed corpse of an extra-terrestrial because, after all, what could possibly happen now? It's not like E.T. might be filled with alien parasites looking for a new host, right? (The normal suburban household invaded by terrifying forces was in the other movie Spielberg produced that summer, *Poltergeist*.)

Instead, E.T. is resurrected, and manages to escape with Elliot and his friends. They elude the scientific and military authorities, as well as the police, so the gentle alien can meet the spaceship that has come back for him. It's a thrilling sequence with more flying bicycles, but in more recent video versions it no longer has any guns. Spielberg had them all digitally replaced with walkie-talkies for the 2002 re-release. Spielberg, the filmmaker who supposedly reveres Hollywood history and had learned so much from the giants of the past, has no problem revising his own films, even if it distorts the original. Asked about the criticism he received for such politically correct revisions, he brushed them aside noting that the deluxe DVD set also included the original version for "the purists."

E.T. and Elliot have a touching good-bye, and then with John Williams again dealing us musical body blows, E.T. finally goes home. When the houselights came up in the screening room, I was appalled. This was a movie that lacked any depth or subtlety whatsoever. It's a stretch, but one could try to argue that Elliot—a middle child—has finally learned to stand up for himself, but really he's only been manipulated by E.T. as the viewer has by Spielberg. He's not likely to be any different than he was at the beginning, in spite of a gratuitous scene where he kisses a girl in his science class. It happens when he is mentally linked to E.T., who was watching John Wayne kissing Maureen O'Hara in a TV broadcast of *The Quiet Man*. If the girl had been a significant character in the story, it might have some meaning, but she is not referred to again.

In writing about my disappointment with Spielberg, I could at least take solace that this was a children's film at heart, and surely Spielberg would grow and deepen as an artist. A quarter of a century later, it's clear that he has not. His movies are still filled with children in peril, favor special effects over character, and ultimately amount to little more than clever button pushing. This is not the place to discuss his "serious" non-genre films like *Schindler's List* and *Saving Private Ryan*, especially since I got yelled at by my own mother for not liking *Schindler*. However, much of Spielberg's career has been in the field of fantasy and science fiction, and while he's made a lot of money with only a few duds along the way, one is hard pressed to argue that this body of work is *about* anything. *Jurassic Park* is notable for its CGI dinosaurs, and *War of the Worlds* has an impressive alien attack scene early in the film, while *A.I.* only proved that Stanley Kubrick had been right to abandon the project as having unsolvable script problems. *Minority Report* is the notable exception in at least raising the interesting question of whether a person can be "guilty" of a crime not yet committed.

What stands out in his science fiction films (and, I'd argue, in his "serious" films as well), is that he seems to assume his audience consists of twelve-year-old boys who require sensational effects and who need to be told what to feel. They never, ever want to have to actually think about what's going on in the movie. Compare his films with the works of such contemporaries as David Cronenberg and, perhaps more to the point, Ridley Scott. In their science fiction films, they see no need to condescend to their audiences or to assume that, because it's SF, it needn't be taken seriously.

Scott's *Blade Runner* came out the same summer as *E.T.* It not only didn't succeed as *E.T.* did, but was considered a box office failure. It took a while for people to come around to *Blade Runner*, although it did best *E.T.* for the Hugo Award for best dramatic presentation at the next year's World Science Fiction Convention. Today, it is the adult *Blade Runner*, not the childish *E.T.*, which is considered one of the most influential science fiction films of the 1980s.

E.T. is like cotton candy. It's fun and satisfying for a while, but on closer examination, it's little more than sugar and air. In movies like *Jurassic Park* and *War of the Worlds*, Spielberg went more for the thrill ride than the heartstrings, as he continues to prefer bypassing the brain.

Call me a curmudgeon if you must, but that's why I continue to feel that in any serious study of science fiction films, *E.T.* should just go home.

JAR JAR BINKS MUST DIE

I remember it as one of my "pod people" moments. I was out of step with the people around me. If only they could leave one of the alien seed pods by my bed that night, I would wake up wondering how I could ever have thought differently. It was a panel on *Star Wars Episode 1: The Phantom Menace* at the January 2000 Arisia.

My views were pretty much what most critics had said: the film was a disappointment, overlong, lacking drama or suspense, and the character of Jar Jar Binks may be the single most annoying character in the history of science fiction film. I had not realized I was in a roomful of true believers, who could not accept that anything *Star Wars* could be flawed in any way. (The issue of the notorious *Star Wars Holiday Special* was not raised.) One of the people there, clearly disagreeing with my assessment, asked me how many times I had watched the film, which had been released the previous summer.

Only once, I noted. Ahh, came the reply, if I watched it several more times I would come to a different conclusion. All around me, people sagely nodded in agreement. The fault, it seemed, lay not with *Star Wars*, but with me.

Ten years after its release, I was finally prepared to take a fresh look at the film. Perhaps I had been too harsh. After all, I had seen the original *Star Wars* in 1977, before it became *Episode IV: A New Hope*. I had waited the three years for *The Empire Strikes Back*, generally regarded as the best of the whole series. I then waited another three years for *Revenge of the Jedi...* er, *Return of the Jedi*, as it was hastily retitled when it was pointed out that the Jedi don't take revenge. Then—for sixteen years—nothing. Well, nothing but TV specials with the Ewoks, re-releases of the films to theaters, home video, and cable, and finally the 1997 "special editions." It was with those special editions that I finally got to write about *Star Wars*, since I hadn't become a film critic until months after the last film came out.

Now, finally, along with whole generations, I eagerly anticipated the long-awaited "prequels," since we had long been told that the original trilogy were conceived as the middle three of a *nine*-film series, with only the two droids, R2D2 and C3PO, appearing as characters in all of them. The night of the sneak preview for the press was the most intense I had experienced since the 1989 release of *Batman*. Security was tight. Guests needed to be approved. Once we made it through the security gauntlet, we were given a disposable bracelet to wear, identifying us as "approved." If it was removed, we would not be permitted in the theater.

Finally, the movie began. The introductory text scrawled into space, and we learned this exciting space adventure was to be about... taxation of trade routes. Huh? Had they slipped in an episode of *Wall Street Week* instead of the movie? Nope. This was going to be a *Star Wars* movie where the war was about a commercial federation taking over the planet of Naboo after it refused to pay stiff tariffs. We see that the Republic's Senate is too busy dithering in debate to take any action. This anti-democratic attitude is jarring. Way back in 1977, I recalled critics comparing the finale of *Star Wars* to Leni Riefenstahl's Nazi tribute *Triumph of the Will*. Not that Lucas is a fascist, but representative government is presented in *Phantom Menace* as little more than a bad joke. Instead, the day is saved by the Chancellor sending private mercenaries (i.e., the Jedi) and, later, by armed resistance from the local population, which has been abandoned to its fate.

So the two Jedi, Qui-Gon Jinn (Liam Neeson) and his young apprentice Obi-Wan Kenobi (Ewan McGregor) arrive on Naboo after an ugly encounter with representatives of the Trade Federation. Here is where they encounter Jar Jar Binks, a computer animated character voiced in high-pitched Pidgin English by Ahmed Best. Two things are readily apparent. First, McGregor may be the best actor since Robert DeNiro in *The Godfather, Part II* to step into the younger version of a role created by a distinctive actor in an earlier film. McGregor's task was not simply to bring young Obi-Wan to life, but to make us believe he would later become the character portrayed by Alec Guinness. It was a difficult job, and that he accomplished it without turning it into a parody is to his credit.

The second thing is that, since the earlier *Star Wars* films George Lucas had apparently taken leave of his senses. The role of the comic sidekick has a long history in movies, science fiction and elsewhere, and it wasn't surprising that Lucas would want to utilize it in his space opera. However, having already created the two droids, what possessed him to add this horse-faced character whose every appearance would make audience members claw at their eyes? He's like Joe Besser in the later Three Stooges shorts, or Rob Schneider in any Adam Sandler movie: a character that *nobody* wants to see.

Lucas apparently put him in "for the kids," but subsequently learned his lesson, as the character virtually disappears from Episodes II and III. Jar Jar is introduced as someone so stupid that he was actually exiled by his own people for clumsiness. He nearly gets Qui-Gon killed in their first encounter, and ultimately helps fight the war against the robot soldiers through strategic klutziness. Usually such characters are lovable or amusing, but Jar Jar Binks is neither. Indeed, I might have ended up liking the movie better if it was Jar Jar rather than Qui-Gon who ended up making the ultimate sacrifice.

Meanwhile, back at the trade negotiations, Queen Amidala is living proof of Lucas's juvenile attitude toward his female characters. As if to show the people who criticized Princess Leia's hairstyle, which made it look as if she had attached baked goods to her head, Lucas takes the lovely and talented Natalie Portman and turns her into a grotesque caricature. And this is the heroine of the movie! Her contributions to the plot are to be a big sister (or more?) to young Anakin, to be manipulated into doing the wrong thing politically by turning on the current chancellor, who is her biggest ally in the Senate, and then to take an utterly absurd risk to resolve the crisis by going into battle herself in a fight she's likely to lose. That she makes Jar Jar a key component in her strategy only compounds her lack of judgment.

However, before we can get to the climactic battle, we have to have a long, *long* sequence on Tatooine where Qui-Gon and Obi-Wan first meet Anakin Skywalker (Jake Lloyd). It's hard to say which is more annoying. Is it that this slave boy they stumble upon by chance has a high level of "midichlorians" in his blood, making Qui-Gon think he is the "chosen one" who is prophesied to "bring balance to the Force?" Or is it that they risk everything, including their own freedom, on a nine-year-old winning a high speed race against adults? Perhaps it's simply the fact that the race seems to go on forever, even though the end result is never in doubt, despite the fact that it is utterly preposterous.

That may be the real problem here. Lucas has fallen into the trap of most Hollywood sequel/prequel makers of simply retelling the story he has already told, only louder. Instead of Obi-Wan and Yoda instructing young Luke in the ways of the Force, we have Qui-Gon and Yoda doing the same to young Obi-Wan. Instead of the battle to blow up the Death Star, we have the battle to blow up the ship controlling the warrior droids. Instead of the big celebration of Princess Leia's rescue and return, we have the bigger celebration of Queen Amidala's rescue and return.

Not only have we seen this already, but those things that are new—like the introduction of Darth Maul (Ray Park) and his double-sided light saber—fail to provide any real suspense. The big moment in the showdown between Darth Maul and the two Jedis has Qui-Gon mortally wounded and a disarmed Obi-Wan clinging for his life from a tenuous handhold on the side of a deep shaft. Can Obi-Wan possibly survive this encounter, or is he doomed? Wait a moment. Doesn't he appear in *Episode IV*, played by Alec Guinness? Isn't *that* the movie where he dies? And in that film, he doesn't seem to be any worse for the wear, except he's much older. So we know, beyond question, that no matter how bad it looks for Obi-Wan, he's perfectly safe.

Some may argue that future generations, watching the films in "episode order" rather than by year of release, won't necessarily have that knowledge in advance. Maybe so, but the big assumption being made there is not that people will want to watch *Episode I* first, but that after they watch it they will have any interest in continuing. Indeed, watched in that order, the story of the series is how Anakin grows up, becomes angry and disillusioned and turns into evil Darth Vader, and then is finally redeemed in death. Is that really the story that inspired George Lucas way back when he made the original *Star Wars*? Is that a story that moves and inspires us in the audience? The original trilogy was about how Luke (Mark Hamill) discovers his destiny, goes through ordeals and eventually triumphs, defeating evil and saving the galaxy. If the six *Star Wars* film are really about Annakin/Darth Vader, Luke's adventure is little more than an overextended subplot.

By the time he was giving interviews promoting *Episode I*, Lucas denied any intent of doing nine films and said that when he was finished, the six films would be the whole of it (notwithstanding the animated *Clone Wars* stories). That's too bad. Perhaps the only thing that could redeem the series at this point is continuing the story to where Luke is the old, wise Jedi teaching his own apprentice and showing that while Darth Vader and Emperor Palpatine are gone, the battle against evil evolves and is ongoing. The problem with that is that Lucas would have to think about the story he wanted to tell, rather than simply the merchandising possibilities of new characters and spaceships, and how many different times he can release the same films in new or tweaked formats.

There's no question that the original trilogy has a special place in the history of SF cinema, and that George Lucas has had a tremendous impact on the genre and the film industry. At the 2009 World Science Fiction Convention in Montreal, I was on a panel assessing Lucas's career (which was filmed for the documentary, *The People vs. George Lucas* about the love/hate relationship fans have with him and his films). However you weight the scales on the plus side (*Star Wars*, *The Empire Strikes Back*, *Raiders of the Lost Ark*, Industrial Light and Magic) there's little doubt that *Episode I* in general, and Jar Jar Binks in particular, fall with resounding thuds as minuses.

POST SCRIPT
The Modern Classics: A First Draft

In lecturing to groups ranging from college students to retirement communities, I find myself making the case for movies in two different directions. I have to convince the teens and twenty-somethings that movies made long before they were born—some without color and some without even sound—are not only worth watching, but are great entertainment. I usually win this argument, because I then proceed to show them such films in my various courses, and most of them find themselves enjoying at least some of what they see.

"You don't go into a museum and say, 'I'm not interested in the Renoirs and Picassos, just show me the new stuff,'" I tell them. "Why would you do that with movies?" Of course, most of them aren't going to museums either, but the point is taken.

Meanwhile, some of the senior citizens I speak to are convinced there are no good movies being made any more. Too much violence and sex, and who knows the names of these actors, anyway. (The latter is, ironically, the same problem I have convincing the students to watch old movies. It's just a different group of actors involved.) I tell them that, in any era, there are good movies and bad movies, and it's a matter of finding out what's out there, and then seeing the stuff that looks appealing. Simply watching whatever happens to pop up on cable or is scheduled for the communal theater space or opened that weekend at the local multiplex is no way to seek out good films.

Applying all this to the discussion of science fiction films in this book, it becomes obvious that there's been an emphasis here on older movies. This was by design, since many of the essays here were originally written for publications where my brief was spotlighting just such classic movies. I hope I've convinced the reader to seek out those older films they haven't seen, or to revisit the ones they haven't watched in a long while. However, including *Metropolis* and *The Day the Earth Stood Still* and *2001: A Space Odyssey* in the "canon" of classic SF films is easy. What are the modern films that ought to join them in the pantheon? Which are the ones that ought to be considered essential viewing for any serious fan of the genre?

Some choices provoke little debate. Would anyone seriously dispute *Blade Runner*? Others films are more open for discussion. Part of it is a matter of taste, and part of it is that not enough time has passed. What films from 2009, for example, will be considered enduring classics fifty years from now? *Avatar? Star Trek? Moon?* I'm hoping *District 9* holds up, but there's no way of knowing. So consider this a first draft, not the final word, as if any listing of the best of anything could be considered definitive. This is the start of the discussion, one that will be continuing for many years to come.

Starting with *Star Wars* in 1977, let's go through the following 25 years, up to 2002, and see what might be deemed "essential." It's not enough to be historic (i.e., a landmark in some way at the time) or merely entertaining. In the 1950s, *Forbidden Planet* is clearly an essential SF film in terms of production values and story, while *Them!* is well worth seeing, but is not the sort of movie that represents a serious gap in one's knowledge if one hasn't caught up with it yet. Or, to offer a literary example, someone reading the works of Isaac Asimov would have to put *I, Robot* on the "must read" list, while *Fantastic Voyage II*, though a good story, is not a book that defines Asimov's career.

These appear in roughly the order of release, at least for the initial film being cited, with minimal discussion for films already covered elsewhere in the book.

Star Wars: We start here, as opposed to earlier in the '70s, because this is the science fiction film that was the defining moment for a generation of SF fans. Even for older fans, it was a turning point both in terms of putting "space opera" on the big screen in a way that hadn't been seen before, and for the sheer inventiveness of the *Star Wars* universe. One of the ways it was influential becomes a major problem in sorting through contemporary SF cinema: it's part of a series. Are all six films "essential"? No, no more than declaring *The Godfather* and *The Godfather, Part II* as pivotal entries in the gangster movie genre means that *The Godfather, Part III* must be automatically included as well. Unfortunately, with all the tweaks and changes over the years, we can't really experience *Star Wars* the way audiences did in 1977, including without the declaration that it was *Episode IV: A New Hope*, but it is an important film that is just as entertaining and thought-provoking today as it was back then. Likewise its immediate sequel, *The Empire Strikes Back*, is also a likely candidate. Darth Vader and Yoda are iconic figures of science fiction movies that the serious fan is required to know. After that, though, none of the other *Star Wars* films necessarily reward repeat viewing. The turning point may well have been *Return of the Jedi*, where the introduction of the Ewoks demonstrated that merchandising was beginning to trump imagination.

Close Encounters of the Third Kind: Undoubtedly an important movie of its time, it might have launched the new age of SF films if *Star Wars* hadn't already done so six months before, but *Close Encounters* in retrospect has the problem that most of Steven Spielberg's SF offerings have: shallowness. Yes, there's some great "gee whiz" special effects, and some nice performances from Richard Dreyfuss and French director Francois Truffaut, but in the end, isn't it really a movie about abandoning your responsibilities to others in order to go off and see the magic space aliens? As a metaphor for Spielberg's subsequent career, it has a certain resonance, but it's really an example of the sort of narcissism and disengagement with life that seems the antithesis of serious SF. I've argued elsewhere in this volume about my disenchantment with Spielberg's SF films, and personally I would not include any of them as "essential" viewing, except to the viewer looking at the genre from a historical perspective. Still, Spielberg remains an important figure in the genre, and movies like *Close Encounters*, *E.T.*, and *Jurassic Park* were all immensely successful at the time of their releases. As time goes on, their influence seems to have faded away, but the case can be made that at least one of them is required viewing. I'd give the nod to *Close Encounters*.

Star Trek: If one was making a list of the essential SF television programs, then *Star Trek* and at least two of its sequel series (*The Next Generation* and *Deep Space Nine*) would qualify for the pantheon without question. However, on the big screen, *Star Trek: The Motion Picture* was notable more as a reunion of the original characters than for the achievement of the film itself. (It remains to be seen if that turns out to be the ultimate verdict for the 2009 reboot.) However *Star Trek II: The Wrath of Khan* and *Star Trek IV: The Voyage Home* ought to be must-sees for the serious fan. *Khan* took a villain from one episode of the original series and fashioned a sequel that makes Ricardo Montalban's Khan one of the great tragic villains of SF cinema: a super-advanced human who wants revenge for the awful, if unintentional, punishment he and his kind have suffered. Add to that, the film gives us the dramatic death of Mr. Spock, and an ending which signaled that it couldn't possibly be so. Finally we had a *Star Trek* movie worthy of the name. *Voyage* brings the crew to the present day of 1986 for a story that had both whimsical humor and social commentary, as we see the Vulcan nerve pinch used to silence a noisy bus passenger, and Dr. McCoy aghast at the savagery of what audiences would have seen as "modern" medical technology. Other entries in the series were hit or miss, but these two are the standouts.

Alien: Yet another series where two of the films are set apart from the rest. In some ways, all four movies are telling the same story of humans against morphing monsters, yet each tells it in a somewhat different way. Ignoring the utterly forgettable *Alien vs. Predator* hybrids, the four *Alien* films each offer their pleasures. However, it is the first two that best show how two very different directors were able to make the material their own. Ridley Scott's original film was a haunted house story, with the crew being picked off one by one by an alien that just kept getting scarier and scarier. The sequel, *Aliens*, was turned by James Cameron into a take-no-prisoners action movie that was a cinematic adrenaline rush. Key to the success of both films, besides H.R. Giger's original creature designs, was Sigourney Weaver as Ripley, a heroine for the modern age. She didn't scream when she saw the monster, she kicked butt.

Mad Max: As post-apocalyptic action films go, it's hard to beat *Mad Max* and the first of its two sequels, *The Road Warrior*. It's not clear what events led up to the present state of affairs, but it's now a Darwinian world of survival of the fittest, and Mel Gibson's Max, a former cop, will do what he has to in order to see justice done. Action-packed and violent, the films question just how much the human animal has been changed by civilization, and how quickly we might revert if that civilization fell apart.

Blade Runner: Although not a success on initial release, it's clear that this is the single most influential SF film of the last thirty years, not so much in terms of its impact on the film industry, but in how its "future noir" has irrevocably altered how we in the audience see the future. The story of Rick Deckard having to decide who is human and who is an artificial replicant grows more complex across the film and, indeed, on repeated viewings. By the climax it's not at all clear whom we should be sympathizing with as the real representatives of humanity. Indeed, Roy Batty's death scene may be the most moving end of an artificial life form since the shut down of HAL in *2001*. The film also marked the beginning of what would prove to be the surprising and surprisingly long-lasting love affair between Hollywood and SF writer Philip K. Dick, who died a few months before the film was released. At least ten of his stories and novels have been turned into movies, and more are in the pipeline.

The Terminator: It's hard to say just how important the original would be if not for the success of *Terminator 2: Judgment Day*. The original was a solid action adventure with a killer cyborg from the future, memorably played by future California Governor Arnold Schwarzenegger, relentlessly pursuing the woman whose son would prove to be the cyborg's greatest enemy. Alone, one might say the movies is worth seeing, but it falls short of greatness. However, by the time James Cameron returned to the story for the sequel, he had done *Aliens* and *The Abyss* and was a much more accomplished filmmaker. The CGI morphing effects were absolutely astounding at the time, and can still impress, even if they're no longer the cutting edge novelties they were once were. *Terminator 2* is definitely in. The earlier film is open to further discussion, and the later ones simply don't make the grade.

Back to the Future: The sequels were so-so, but the first film was a time travel comedy adventure that actually had fun with all of the paradoxes inherent in traveling into one's own past. The movie even moved into Oedipal territory when Marty McFly's future mom, then a teenager, ends up developing a crush on him rather than his future dad. For viewers of a certain age, *this* is the great time travel movie, not *The Time Machine.*

Brazil: Arguably Terry Gilliam's most successful film, *Brazil* is a mad comic dystopia that can send you from laughter to despair in moments. Its studio, Universal, had no idea what to do with it, so Gilliam managed to sneak out a print, which he then showed to the Los Angeles film critics, who promptly named it their choice for the best film of year. Backed into a corner, the studio had no choice, and quickly rushed it into release. A new film version of *1984* came out around the same time, but where that film was depressingly literal, *Brazil* was filled with the ironic touches that were more in tune with a new era. Now Big Brother wanted to get a few laughs before crushing you beneath his boot.

The Fly: Although David Cronenberg's films have drifted away from science fiction of late, he is without question one of the most important directors in the field, with *The Brood, Scanners,* and *Videodrome* in his filmography. *The Fly* is a masterpiece, mixing elements of unsettling horror with complex human characters, none of whom is completely a hero or villain. It says something about the force of the performances and characterization that when Seth Brundle is replaced by a puppet representing "Brundlefly," the genetic mutation of scientist and fly, you still feel the presence of actor Jeff Goldblum in a way the human actors are forgotten when the special effect outfits take over in movies like *Spider-Man* and *Iron Man.*

Robocop: Ignore the sequels. The original is a dark dystopian satire about corporate culture run amok, while also providing us with the viewpoint of the half-man/half-machine cyborg. Is he a robot? Are his human memories simple vestiges of a past existence, or does that make Robocop human? This is a film that has stood up surprisingly well after 25 years.

Total Recall: Philip K. Dick's Nebula Award-winning story "We Can Remember it for You Wholesale" was as brilliant as it was unfilmable, taking place mostly in the mind of its central character. The move took the concepts and plot elements and turned it into an Arnold Schwarzenegger action film that still had some of the "is it real or not" playfulness of Dick's story. Indeed, where some felt it had been dumbed down—the hero of the story has false memories implanted because he's a loser, not because he's built like Schwarzenegger—but paying close attention to the details of the story makes it clear that even what seemed obvious at first glance wasn't necessarily so. Was the climactic terraforming of Mars the triumph of the character or simply another wish fulfillment fantasy? You'll have to decide for yourself.

Independence Day: This is more fun than it is good, and probably doesn't warrant admission into the "must see" category, except that director Roland Emmerich does represent a strand of contemporary SF filmmaking. If one were to insist on the inclusion of a Spielberg film like *Close Encounters* or *E.T.*, then there should probably be one by Emmerich as well. This alien invasion story owes much to movies like *War of the Worlds* and *Earth vs. the Flying Saucers*, especially with its destructions of landmarks by the spaceships. It's not clear how that might play after 9/11, but it wowed audiences in the summer of 1996. A mixture of wit, absurd plotting (Earth software works on alien computers?), and bravura special effects, this certainly is one of the most entertaining examples of a real, if unfortunate, trend in Hollywood SF filmmaking.

Gattaca: Andrew Niccol's film about a genetically stratified society looks better with each passing year. It's a cleverly conceived future where the ramifications of the elites being designed at conception is thoroughly worked out. Arguably the best science fiction film of the 1990s, it's just as clearly the most intelligent.

The Matrix: The sequels are problematic, but the first film was a game changer in SF film, both in terms of action and in upping the ante in the "breakdown of reality" subgenre. All right, so the world around us is an illusion, so what? *The Matrix* asked the question most viewers might have ignored: if you had a choice, would you continue living the good life in the illusion, or would you be willing to face harsh reality instead? On a first viewing, Neo has a real choice to make. Does it make a difference? Our reaction is that of course it does, we want reality. The film makes us ask why that's the right choice, and whether it might not be more rational to take comfort in the illusion.

Galaxy Quest: No apologies necessary. This is a comedy that perfectly captures fandom and the lives of the actors of a *Star Trek*-like series with hilarious precision. It actually beat out *The Matrix* for the Hugo Award that year, which says something about how SF fans responded to it. This was a satire done with deep affection. A decade later, it still demonstrates heart and an unmistakable fondness for the genre.

28 Days Later: With the popularity of horror films in general and zombie films in particular, there are some that cross the line into SF as well. This British thriller from Danny Boyle creates its zombie menace from an infectious disease that is let loose from a laboratory. It is a relentless adventure of survival where we really can't be sure whether it will end on a note of hope or doom. (In fact, neither could the filmmakers, and two different endings were prepared for the film.) It's a zombie film with a strong "what if" element, and one that stays with you long afterward.

As with any such list, this is an opportunity to compare views and to get suggestions for movies you might have missed that are worth seeing. The omission of animated films, from the U.S. or Japan, does not mean there haven't been some marvelous offerings there, only that the author's focus was elsewhere. Likewise, movies that others might have included, say *Dark City* or *X-Men* or *Donnie Darko*, are titles you're free to put on your own list of candidates for modern classics. Nor do I consider all my choices to be the ultimate word. You might prefer *Stargate* to *Independence Day* or *Men in Black* to *Back to the Future*. Or perhaps your list would have all of those and drop movies I think are beyond question, like *The Fly* or *Gattaca*. There's also an admitted bias toward mainstream releases with no independent films like *Brother from Another Planet* or *Primer* that someone with different tastes might prefer.

That's why this billed as a "first draft." I plan on writing on some of the titles I have yet to tackle, and may come to change my mind or revise my opinion. This is a snapshot in time of one person's thoughts about contemporary SF film, no more. What seems beyond argument by anyone who has watched these and the other films discussed in this book is that science fiction is a vibrant genre, where some of the most entertaining and interesting films have been and are continuing to be made. Those who try to deny it or who insist that some film they like isn't "really" science fiction are revealing how little they know. Take pity on them. The debate is over.

We won.

Publication History

"Introduction—Science Fiction: The Forbidden Genre," "Atomic Ants" "My Bloody Valentine," "Guilty Pleasures," "E.T. Go Home," and "Post Script—The Modern Classics: A First Draft," appear here for the first time.

"Days of Futures Passed" appeared in *Space and Time* magazine.

"Future Tense," "Science Fiction or Not?" "Sleep No More," "Real Aliens Don't Ask Directions," "Keeping Watch," "Red Alert," "Nerds in Love," "Blue Genes," "Don't Call Me Shirley," "The Bare Necessities," "Being and Nothingness: The Movie," "Ironic, Isn't It?" "Love in the Time of Paradox," "Retro Robo," "The Future is Now," "We're Scientists, Trust Us," "A Funny Thing Happened on the Way to the Future," "Watching Me, Watching You," "Gilligan's Island Earth," "Mars Concedes!" and "Jar Jar Binks Must Die" appeared in the Internet Review of Science Fiction.

"*2001: A Space Odyssey* in 2001," "...But Somebody's Got to Do It," "*Destination Moon* in the 21st Century," and "The Mystery of *The Woman in the Moon*" appeared in *Artemis Magazine*.

"We Come in Pieces: The Alien as Metaphor" and "Remake Love, Not War" appeared in *Clarkesworld*.

Parts of "2009: A Miracle Year?" appeared in different form in the *Worcester Telegram and Gazette* and at NorthShoreMovies.net.

"SF, My Parents, and Me" appeared in *Emerald City*.

"Our Batman" appeared as "The Batman We Deserve" in *Batman Unauthorized* (BenBella Books).

"The Ultimate Book Movie" appeared in the QPBC Book of Days desk calendar.

"1953" appeared in PR4 for Noreascon 4, the 2004 World Science Fiction Convention.

"The Cranky Person's Guide to the 2009 'Best Dramatic Presentation, Long Form' Hugo Nominees" appeared in *The Drink Tank*.

"Not Coming to a Theater Near You" appeared in *Argentus*.

"The Time Traveler's Movie" appeared in the *New York Review of Science Fiction*.

Daniel M. Kimmel is a past president of the Boston Society of Film Critics. When it was discovered he is also a science fiction fan he started getting invitations to participate at a number of SF Conventions, which he continues to do. He reviewed for the *Worcester Telegram and Gazette* and now writes for Northshoremovies.net. He is a correspondent for *Variety*, the "Movie Maven" for the *Jewish Advocate* and teaches film—including a course on SF and horror—at Suffolk University. His essays on classic science fiction films have appeared in several publications including *Clarkesworld, Space and Time,* and the Internet Review of Science

Author photo by Carsten Turner

Fiction. He is the author of a history of FOX TV, *The Fourth Network* (2004) which received the Cable Center Book Award. His other books include a history of DreamWorks, *The Dream Team* (2006) and *I'll Have What She's Having: Behind the Scenes of the Great Romantic Comedies* (2008).

CPSIA information can be obtained at www.ICGtesting.com
Printed in the USA
270391BV00001B/55/P